Diagnostic
Teaching of Reading

TECHNIQUES FOR
INSTRUCTION AND
ASSESSMENT

Diagnostic Teaching of Reading

TECHNIQUES FOR INSTRUCTION AND ASSESSMENT

Barbara J. Walker

EASTERN MONTANA COLLEGE

Merrill Publishing Company
A Bell & Howell Information Company
Columbus • Toronto • London • Melbourne

Published by Merrill Publishing Company
A Bell & Howell Information Company
Columbus, Ohio 43216

This book was set in Garamond Light.

Administrative Editor: Jeff Johnston
Production Coordinator: Linda Bayma
Art Coordinator: Mark D. Garrett
Cover Designer: Jolie Muren

Library of Congress Catalog Card Number: 87-62717
International Standard Book Number: 0-675-20615-4
Printed in the United States of America
1 2 3 4 5 6 7 8 9—92 91 90 89 88

To Lorrin, Sharon and Chris

Preface

As our national diversity grows, teachers must increasingly celebrate our likenesses, empathetically discuss our differences, and resolve that there is not one best way to teach all children to read. The great debate has continued but the conclusions have been the same. "No one approach is so distinctly better in all situations and respects than the others that it should be considered the one best method and the one to be used exclusively" (Bond & Dykstra, 1967, p. 123). However, we have increasingly expanded our concepts of the instructional process. At the core of this knowledge has been the continued assertion that effective instruction is executed by effective teachers. This book provides a tool for teachers to understand the various instructional frameworks underlying diagnostic teaching techniques.

Embodied within this book is that strong belief that as a nation of readers our strengths lie in our individual differences. These individual differences need to be nurtured within our instructional programs, building upon the unique strengths that each student possesses. Furthermore, effective teachers use these strengths to expand students' conceptual knowledge, creating intelligent citizens.

Teachers are often keen observers and reflective thinkers. This book promotes the idea that teachers can make sophisticated diagnostic judgments and identify appropriate instructional techniques. This text delineates the process of diagnostic teaching so that teachers can make informed instructional decisions towards a renewal of teachers' decision-making power.

How the Text Developed

When I began writing diagnostic evaluations, I used the traditional battery of tests, and from these tests I made an educated guess about how a particular problem reader would respond to instruction. I sent my report (based on both normative test data and criterion-referenced tests) to the parents, who in turn took the report to the school. BUT NOTHING CHANGED. I was not really communicating with my clients because I had not told them how to *teach* the problem reader. They did not know how to translate the test data into effective instruction.

Then I began using teaching lessons during the diagnostic evaluations. Working with graduate interns in the reading clinic, I would suggest a certain technique to use during assessment, but they would be unable to implement the suggestion until I had personally explained the steps. Missing in the reading field was a simple, straightforward, written explanation of how to implement specific teaching techniques. So I began to write down step-by-step procedures to guide them. Chapter 6 was born.

Then one astute graduate student asked, "How do you know what will work?" What I had learned to do as a clinician was intuitively to measure the sparkles in the clients' eyes. When I analyzed why specific techniques had worked with certain students, the decision-making cycle of diagnostic teaching moved from intuitive to instructable. This book is the outcome of that transformation.

Who Will Use the Book

This book can be used in a reading practicum and in reading clinic experiences. It also supplements coursework in diagnosis and remediation of reading difficulties. Furthermore, school psychologists, learning specialists, and remedial reading teachers will find it a useful reference. The instructional techniques were written in a step-by-step fashion so that classroom teachers and practicum students can readily follow the prescribed procedures. My goal is to increase communication between the practitioner and diagnostic specialists as well as the practicum student and the college professor.

How the Book Is Organized

Chapter 1 presents the decision-making process of diagnostic teaching. It presents some common initial diagnostic decisions and lays the groundwork for the rest of the text. Chapter 2 describes the influences on diagnostic decisions. Factors impacting the student's reading performance are the reader, the text, the task, the technique, and the context. Chapter 3 presents strategies for effective diagnostic teaching, while Chapter 4 develops a framework for a diagnostic teaching session.

Chapter 5 classifies the diagnostic teaching techniques using several methods: the targeted skill taught, the strategy taught, the instructional framework implemented, the type of text used, the response mode used, the structure of instruction selected, and the cognitive processing emphasized.

Chapter 6 presents a simple description and procedures for 50 techniques. Following each description is an explanation of when that approach is most effective in teaching reading. It describes the view of reading underlying the technique and provides a checklist for the diagnostic teacher to assess its effectiveness with a particular student.

Chapter 7 explains how to gather diagnostic data, while Chapter 8 shows how to formulate hypotheses using the collected data. Chapter 9 provides the procedures for using teaching (rather than testing) as a method of reading evaluation.

Acknowledgments

This text represents a point of view developed over years of clinical experience. There are several people whom I would like to acknowledge as inspiration to me. First, I want to thank Darrell D. Ray, Oklahoma State University, who has been my mentor and advisor. At the cornerstone of this text is his strong belief that children who experience reading difficulty need instruction that uses their strengths and is continually adjusted to meet their changing needs. I thank him for initiating my quest to understand individual differences in learning to read. Also, I want to thank my knowledgeable friends who read parts of the text and offered suggestions, criticisms, and support for my efforts. I am especially grateful for the ideas and comments of Claudia Dybdahl, University of Alaska, regarding qualitative assessment and William Powell, University of Florida, regarding quantitative assessment and classifying techniques. Their professional critique of my initial ideas set the course for the view of assessment in the text.

Equally important have been the number of undergraduate and graduate students in the Reading Clinic at Eastern Montana College who enthusiastically implemented the techniques in this book. Several students contributed in unique ways to the development of this text. I am especially indebted to Laurie Markle for working on the diagnostic teaching format, to Jean Muir for collecting the initial references, and to Vance Dols and Rilla Hardgrove for editing the first draft of the text.

Special thanks are extended to Merrill's reviewers for their thorough critiques of various drafts of the manuscript: Tim Blair, Texas A&M University; Jill Fitzgerald, University of North Carolina; Jean Dreher, University of Maryland; Ann Marshall Huston, Lynchburg College; Donald O'Brien, SUNY at Buffalo; Robert Panchyshyn, Western Kentucky University; William R. Powell, University of Florida; Robert Rude, Rhode Island College; and Amy J. Thorleifson, Seattle University. I have also appreciated the astute judgment of the staff at Merrill Publishing Company, especially Jeff Johnston, administrative editor, for his encouragement and perspective as I labored with the initial drafts and Linda Bayma for her untiring efforts to keep the project moving at all times. I am especially thankful for the editorial work of Jeanne Zingale who shared my thoughts about children, adding an extra dimension to the text.

I owe a great deal to each of the eager students who willingly let me test my ideas about instruction. I am especially indebted to my own two children, Chris and Sharon, who let me teach them in different ways. They were very patient children as they shared their mother with the reading profession. Last, I would like to thank my husband, Lorrin, and my good friend, Marleen Moulden. They have listened to my ideas about instruction, offered counsel, and shared my belief in children throughout the writing of this text.

Adjusting instruction to meet the changing needs of students in our classrooms and clinics is a challenging and rewarding task. This text is designed to facilitate that decision-making process.

Contents

What Is Diagnostic Teaching?

Instruction that fits the needs of the problem reader improves reading performance and promotes fluent reading with comprehension. This book explains the process of identifying instructional alternatives that fit the problem reader. Diagnostic teaching uses instruction to understand how a student solves the reading problem. While teaching, the instructor assesses how the problem reader approaches the reading event. Using this information, she establishes the instructional conditions necessary for the problem reader to learn. Diagnostic teaching, then, is the process of using assessment and instruction at the same time to establish the instructional conditions that produce optimal learning.

In *Becoming a Nation of Readers,* Jeanne Chall states:

> The underlying causes of the reading difficulties of individuals are not always easy to detect . . . [But research and clinical practice] indicate that the best treatment is *excellent instruction,* which in turn seems to heighten interest and hope as well as improve reading skills and uses of reading. Thus *concern for individual needs,* as well as improved instruction . . . will be needed if we are truly to become a nation of readers. (pp. 124–125, emphasis added)

The diagnostic teacher identifies specific instructional alternatives for problem readers that result in improved reading performance. As a reader begins to experience successful reading, he attributes his reading improvement to effective reading strategies. This attribution, in turn, increases his use of these strategies. The diagnostic teacher's task is to monitor this improvement and identify the instructional modifications that produced it. Therefore, she formulates her diagnostic hypotheses by observing those instructional conditions that improve reading. This process is outlined in Figure 1–1.

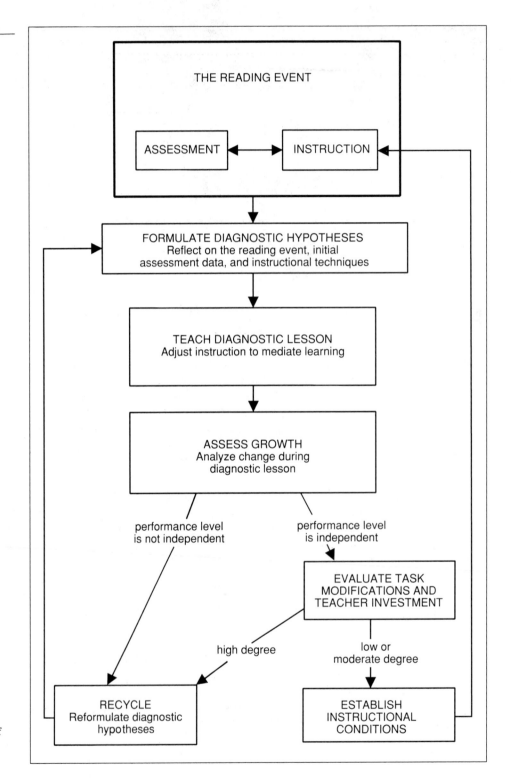

Figure 1–1
The Decision-
Making Cycle of
Diagnostic
Teaching

Diagnostic teaching is the process of using assessment and instruction at the same time *to identify the instructional modifications that enable problem readers to become independent learners.*

According to Harris, "diagnosis is nothing more than the application of a straightforward, common sense, problem-solving approach to the study of children who have difficulties in reading" (1984, p. 416). The diagnostic teacher is thus an active problem solver. She is much more than a test giver. She is first and foremost a teacher. As she teaches, she explores how a particular student solves the reading problem. She knows that his reading is affected not only by the skills he knows but also by the strategies he uses. Thinking about what the student already knows and does when he learns, the diagnostic teacher selects techniques that will teach the needed skills and strategies in the most efficient way. Rather than looking for the causes of reading disabilities, "the focus of diagnostic teaching is . . . on the here and now of what the child can and cannot do . . . and on matching this information with appropriate opportunities for learning" (Harris, 1977, p. 25).

INTERACTIVE READING PROCESS

The diagnostic teacher makes decisions based on her understanding of how reading occurs. In this book, the theory of reading acquisition is based on an interactive view of reading. This view holds that reading involves using both information from the letters and words in the text and information that the reader already knows to construct meaning. Efficient reading "requires readers—real live readers with ideas and attitudes of their own—to interpret what the author is saying" (Langer, 1982, p. 41). The reader is an active learner who interprets what he reads using what the text says (text-based information) and what he knows (reader-based information). In other words, the reader uses these two sources of information at the same time to interpret text. These information sources are strategically combined as the student reads. Effective readers use the following strategies:

1. Effective readers coordinate the reading process using both the text and personal knowledge. While reading, such readers construct a tentative model of meaning based on inferences about the author's intended meaning. They shift between using what they know (reader-based inferencing) and what the text says (text-based inferencing) to construct their model of meaning (Pearson & Johnson, 1978).
2. Effective readers elaborate what they read (McNeil, 1987). They think about how the text they are reading relates to what they know. Thus they make connections that help them remember and interpret what

they read. These new connections become part of what readers know.

3. Effective readers check their understanding to see if it makes sense (Baker & Brown, 1984). If it does not make sense, effective readers check their purposes for reading to see if they were on the right track, check their own knowledge and compare it to what they are reading, and vary their strategies to remove difficulties in interpreting text.

4. Effective readers use the context of the situation to focus understanding. This focus, or perspective, influences the construction of a "successful text." Such readers ask, "What's the right text for this context?" (Harste, Woodward, & Burke, 1984, p. 201). The readers' perceptions and presuppositions about the context of the reading event affect their comprehension.

Readers vary in their use of these strategies. The point of view of this text is that problem readers often experience a deficit in either a skill or strategy that causes them to shift away from one information source. They compensate by using their strength and thus eliminate a need to use their deficient knowledge source (Stanovich, 1980). This overreliance on their strength often results in inefficient reading. It is the diagnostic teacher's role to use these strengths to show students how to use their weaker information source when text interpretation breaks down.

Reading is viewed as an interactive process where readers shift between sources of information (what they know and what the text says) to construct meaning. Problem readers, however, shift away from their weaker information source and rely on their strength to construct meaning. This results in problems in text interpretation.

INSTRUCTIONAL PROCESS

The goal of diagnostic teaching is to establish appropriate learning opportunities for problem readers. If the students use effective strategies and make adjustments for themselves, a simple lesson framework of readiness, active reading, and reacting is sufficient. Problem readers, however, have difficulty making adjustments and employing effective strategies. Inefficient readers often need to be shown exactly how to use effective reading strategies. They need instruction modified during the lesson framework. The diagnostic teacher, as a result, continually assesses what and how problem readers are learning and makes instructional adjustments to ensure successful reading. The process of adjusting instruction to ensure learning is called *mediating learning*.

*The diagnostic teacher mediates learning, which means she adjusts
instruction to ensure successful text interpretation.*

The diagnostic teacher specifically selects activities that will directly mediate
learning for each problem reader. She establishes what the student already knows
and adjusts instruction to overlap his present knowledge with new information.
Furthermore, she evaluates how the student learned what he knows to establish
strategy strengths. The diagnostic teacher mediates learning by "starting with adjustments that permit students to demonstrate strengths" (Wilson & Cleland, 1985,
p. 112). Then the diagnostic teacher shows the student how to incorporate non-
preferred strategies into how he solves the reading problem. A problem reader
often relies heavily on his strengths. Initially, the diagnostic teacher selects a technique that allows him to demonstrate these strengths. As the student experiences
success with the new reading task, the diagnostic teacher selects a second technique that has a more integrative instructional approach. This allows the diagnostic
teacher to use learner strengths (what he already knows and does) to show him
how to use his weaker information source when reading.

Diagnostic teaching techniques were developed from different views of reading and learning. The three major views are these:

- **Bottom-Up View**   Simply stated, the bottom-up view of reading focuses on text-based processing as the major instructional concern of
  teachers. Learning to read is viewed as a series of associations or sub-
  skills that are reinforced until they become automatic. Letters are
  linked to form words, words are linked to form sentences, and sentences are linked to form ideas; that is, the parts of reading are put together to form the whole. This is viewed as bottom-up processing, in
  which processing text shapes the learner's response.
- **Top-Down View**   The top-down view of reading focuses on the
  reader-based processing as the major instructional concern of teachers.
  The reader is viewed as an active problem solver who guesses what
  the author is saying. Then he samples textual information to check his
  guesses. Ideas about what the author is saying are verified through a
  minimal amount of textual cues; that is, reading is viewed as negotiat-
  ing meaning between an author and a reader. This is viewed as a top-
  down process, in which the reader's ideas create his response.
- **Interactive View**   The interactive view of reading focuses on the
  active-constructive nature of reading as the major instructional concern
  of teachers. The reader is viewed as using both reader-based (top-
  down) processing and text-based (bottom-up) processing to form a
  model of meaning. Although he is active, his guesses are formed on
  the basis of what the text says and what he already knows about this

information; that is, reading is viewed as constructing meaning. This is viewed as an interactive process where the reader strategically shifts between the text and what he already knows to construct his response.

The techniques from differing points of view can be matched to the learner strengths. The diagnostic teacher selects instructional techniques that allow students to use their strengths. Then she uses these strengths to show the students how to solve their reading problems. Finally, the diagnostic teacher leads problem readers to more integrated reading by selecting techniques that have a more interactive approach to reading. This sequence allows the diagnostic teacher to use learner strengths to show problem readers how to use their weaker information source.

ASSESSMENT PROCESS

In diagnostic teaching, assessment is continuous. As the student learns, diagnostic information is immediately incorporated into the lesson. The teacher thus attacks the problem as she teaches, not after she has gathered the facts.

During a diagnostic teaching lesson, for example, the teacher discovered at midpoint in the story that a student could not sequence the events. Rather than continue trying to teach using the instructional format of predict, read to find out, and summarize, she introduced a story map (see "Story Map" in Chapter 6), a visual arrangement of the sequence of events that are related to the problem. The information from the beginning of the story was reviewed and placed on the map. The instructional format was changed to summarize what was on the map, make a prediction, and read to find out what happened next. The final step became to add to the story map, tell how the new information fits into the story, and how it fits with the previous prediction. The lesson format changed because the teacher assessed the difficulty during the lesson and changed the instructional conditions or format. This modification increased student learning.

To lead students to more efficient reading, the diagnostic teacher looks for recurring patterns among the variables of the reading event (see Chapter 2 for further discussion) and uses this information when she establishes the optimal instructional conditions. As she teaches, the diagnostic teacher assesses student performance and changes her instruction in order to mediate learning, thus showing students how to use what they already know to solve new reading problems. This leads readers to more efficient strategy use.

Diagnostic teaching means that assessment is continuous as the student is learning. The diagnostic teacher adjusts instruction as she teaches, not after she has gathered the facts.

As materials and activities are adjusted to the needs of the problem reader, the diagnostic teacher maintains a close match between the text and the student's reading level. Although this attitude permeates all instruction, the degree that the diagnostic teacher uses continuous assessment is not practical for the classroom teacher. The classroom teacher cannot continuously assess and modify her instruction in 25 different directions at once. The classroom teacher makes some adjustments in the instruction, but the majority of the time she teaches to an instructional group as a whole. At every instructional point, however, the diagnostic teacher assesses how the problem reader is learning from her instruction and adjusts her instruction. Assessment becomes an integral part of diagnostic teaching.

✦ DIAGNOSTIC TEACHING PROCESS

Diagnostic teaching is a process of using assessment and instruction at the same time to identify the instructional conditions that enable problem readers to become independent learners. In other words, the diagnostic teacher shifts between instruction and assessment during a lesson. Diagnostic decision making becomes increasingly more reflective as additional information is gathered. Before beginning instruction, the diagnostic teacher makes some initial diagnostic decisions. She decides on the presenting problem and the instructional placement. These decisions remain tentative throughout diagnostic data collecting.

Initial Diagnostic Data

1. ***Identifying the Presenting Problem.*** Problems in two general areas may inhibit reading performance: deficiencies in print processing and deficiencies in meaning processing. These two processes are combined to form fluent reading with comprehension. As the diagnostic teacher works with a student, she asks herself, "What is inhibiting fluent reading with comprehension? Is the student having difficulty recognizing the words (print processing), or understanding the content (meaning processing), or both?"

To read fluently with comprehension, some students need assistance with what the printed words look like (print processing). Once these students can recognize the words, they will be able to understand what they read. If fluent reading with comprehension is impaired by print processing, the diagnostic teacher listens to the child read orally and asks him questions to check comprehension. This is known as *oral reading analysis* (see Chapter 7 for further discussion). Other students call words fluently but need assistance in how to derive meaning from the words that they recognize (meaning processing). To process meaning while reading, the student combines several sources of information. If fluent reading with comprehension is impaired by meaning processing, the diagnostic teacher has the child do one of two procedures. She can have him read paragraphs silently and ask him questions, or she can break a story into segments and discuss the story after each segment. These procedures are known as *silent reading analysis* (see Chapter 7 for further discussion). For the diagnostic teacher, this initial decision merely begins her analysis of how the student is approaching the reading task.

Q.3
1.

Initially, the diagnostic teacher establishes the major presenting problem. She thinks about how print processing and meaning processing affect the student's reading.

---

2. ***Deciding on Instructional Placement.*** To establish placement, a sampling of reading performance on a series of graded passages is used to predict the reading level at which a student will profit from instruction. This procedure is known as *informal reading assessment*. Reader responses in easy, moderate, and difficult texts establish a level where the student will experience success in classroom instruction. Three estimates of reading performance are derived.

- *The student's independent reading level* provides an estimate of the level where the student can read fluently with a high level of comprehension. The student reads and understands enough of the text to monitor his own reading performance. He applies appropriate correction strategies when reading breaks down, using both reader-based and text-based processing; therefore, teacher-directed instruction is not necessary.
- *The student's instructional reading level* provides an estimate of the level where the student experiences a mild level of stress between the text and his present reading strategies. It is assumed that classroom instruction would increase the student's understanding of new textual information.
- *The student's frustration reading level* provides an estimate of the level where the reader is not fluent and has little recall of textual information. It is projected that at this level, guided instruction would be extremely demanding and time consuming because the reader does not know enough about what he is reading to make adequate connections between the new information and prior knowledge.

Informal reading assessment provides an estimate of reading performance in selected texts based on oral reading errors and percentage of comprehension. The instructional reading level is an estimate of the level where the student "might experience some difficulties when reading classroom materials at sight, but most of these difficulties should be overcome after the student has had an opportunity to read the same material silently" (Johns, 1981, p. 7). Therefore, the guidelines for regular classroom instruction are more in line with traditional scoring criteria in informal assessment (Betts, 1946). These criteria use 95% word identification and 75% comprehension as an estimate of instructional reading level.

Although the diagnostic teacher uses the same constructs of informal assessment, she interprets the information in a different fashion. She uses the informal reading inventory as a measure of what the student can do when he independently (without instruction) solves the reading problem. However, she also establishes how the student solves the reading problem as she is teaching. Therefore, she continues her assessment and establishes a level where the student profits from her instruction.

The student's mediated reading level determines the level where the student can efficiently be taught. This level is determined by evaluating the "distance between the actual developmental level as determined by independent problem solving and the level of potential development as determined through problem solving under adult guidance or in collaboration with more capable peers" (Vygotsky, 1978, p. 86). First, the diagnostic teacher identifies at what level the student can incorporate the targeted reading strategies as a result of specified instruction. This is determined by calculating the "difference between the level of unaided performance a child can achieve, and the level he could achieve with aid" (Powell, 1984, p. 248). Therefore, the diagnostic teacher establishes the highest difficulty level where the student profits from instruction.

Rather than estimating an instructional placement from informal reading assessment, the diagnostic teacher actually establishes the level where the student learns from her instruction. She uses the constructs of informal reading assessment to identify a level where the student will experience a moderate amount of difficulty when reading but is not frustrated. When analyzing oral reading, an error rate greater than 10% (1 error every 10 words) is considered frustration level reading. "If there is more than 10 percent of error in the record rate this is a 'hard' text for this child" (Clay, 1979, p. 14). When evaluating comprehension, less than 50% recall is considered frustration level reading. According to Barr and Sadow (1985),

> When individual students are missing more than half the questions posed or having difficulty with more than 1 word in every 10, the materials are inappropriate, representing frustration-level work. . . . By contrast, students who perform in the borderline region between frustration level and acceptable instructional level may be helped by instruction that has been developed with their particular problem in mind. This borderline region is characterized by an accuracy of 90–94% on oral reading and 50–74% on comprehension questions. (p. 177)

Since the goal is to determine how instruction improves reading performance, a text that is moderately difficult (90% oral accuracy and 60% comprehension) provides a more appropriate measuring tool. Using a moderately difficult text allows the teacher to assess the student's growth in reading performance as a result of instruction. She wants to observe how the student learns from her instruction. After instruction, the selected text should be read at the independent level (98% accuracy and 90% comprehension). If this happens, the diagnostic teacher selects a more difficult text and teaches another lesson. She continues until the student does not achieve an independent reading level after instruction. Placement is thus determined by identifying the highest difficulty level where the student profits from instruction.

For example, a teacher took two short segments from a story in a text that was designated as moderately difficult for a student. Using the passages, she developed two assessments according to the constructs of informal reading assessment. Without teacher instruction, the student read the first segment with an error rate of 1/11 words and 60% comprehension. After the targeted vocabulary words were introduced and a discussion about how these words related to the selection was conducted, the second segment was read with an error rate of 1/50 and 90% comprehension. For this student, a text that was read near frustration without teacher direction could be read at independent reading level with instruction by the teacher.

The diagnostic teacher continued this procedure with a more difficult text. The highest level of text that the student read fluently after instruction was designated as the text to use during instruction. The level was then called the *mediated performance level*—the highest level of text that can be read fluently after instruction (Powell, 1986).

The diagnostic teacher establishes the mediated performance level, the highest level of text that can be read fluently after instruction.

For the diagnostician, decisions about placement involve more than just establishing at what level the student will profit from instruction. Since she is actually teaching during her assessment, she also evaluates the amount of task modification necessary to create the desired reading change (Feuerstein, 1979). Prior to instruction, the diagnostic teacher decides on certain task conditions that will enhance learning for a particular student. Some of these decisions include these questions: Will she segment the selection? If so, how will she do it—sentence by sentence, or paragraph by paragraph? Will the instruction be entirely silent reading? Or will oral rereading be necessary? How many new vocabulary words will be introduced before reading the selection and how will instruction occur? Should part of the discussion be written down so it can be referred to later? These decisions involve how she will modify the task so that learning will occur.

Considering such questions, a teacher decided to model silent reading comprehension alternately with the student. She read the first paragraph and thought out loud about what it said. On the second paragraph, the student was to read and think out loud. At the end of the second paragraph, the teacher realized that she was asking questions and that the student could not talk about what had been read. So she broke the next paragraph into sentences and modeled every other sentence alternately with the student. As she modeled her self-talk, she recorded the information on a story map (see ''Story Map'' in Chapter 6), a visual representation of the sequence of the events. At the end of the selection, the teacher decided that there had been a high degree of task modification to ensure the desired reading change.

Because there had been a high degree of task modification, the diagnostic teacher needed to select either a less difficult text or a different teaching technique. Therefore, placement can be determined by the amount of task modification needed to ensure fluent reading comprehension. If there is a high degree of task modification during the lesson, a less difficult text or different technique is more appropriate. However, if there is a low degree of task modification during the lesson, a more difficult text can be selected.

The diagnostic teacher evaluates the amount of task modification (changes in the reading task) that she makes during instruction—like changing from oral to silent reading, or from one technique to another.

A third consideration is the amount of teacher investment necessary to engage the student in an active interpretation of text (Feuerstein, 1979). As she teaches, the diagnostic teacher adjusts her instruction to the needs of the student. She asks herself, "How can I phrase these questions so that the student will understand the main idea? What does he already know that will help him understand the story? How much time do I need to wait before I assist? What kind of assistance, questioning, or modeling will be most helpful?" These questions focus her involvement during instruction.

After reading a selection, for example, a teacher asked the question, "Why was Seth more irritated than frightened?" Such a question requires evaluating detailed information in the selection and relating this information with previous experiences (a nonliteral response). Since the student could not answer the question, the teacher rephrased the question and asked the following series: "What had Seth forgotten? Have you ever gone camping and forgotten something? How did you feel? Do you think Seth was feeling that way too? What was the author trying to tell you about Seth?" This series of questions resulted in the same kind of comprehension, but the teacher's investment (time, energy, and assistance) was extremely high; she took a sequence of literal responses supplied by the student and had to weave them together with leading questions to form the nonliteral response that the original question demanded.

During instruction, the diagnostic teacher evaluates the amount of her investment. If the time investment is extremely high, changes in placement are needed that decrease the complexity of the task (an easier text or different teaching technique). If the investment is low, changes in placement are needed that increase the complexity of the task (a more difficult text or higher level questioning).

The diagnostic teacher evaluates the amount of teacher investment or the changes she makes regarding her interaction with the student, which includes prompting, rephrasing, and feedback.

The diagnostic teacher uses three criteria to determine the mediated reading level, the highest level where the student can profit from her instruction. She finds a reading level that is moderately difficult and teaches a lesson at this level. Then she evaluates the amount of reading growth due to instruction as well as the amount of teacher investment and task modification needed to ensure successful text interpretation.

The Diagnostic Teaching Cycle

Diagnostic teaching is a dynamic process in which decisions about what the reader needs change as the student learns. The decision-making cycle becomes increasingly more reflective as diagnostic information is gathered. Initial diagnostic information can be gathered through screening or from classroom instruction. This initial information is then expanded through informal assessment. The informal assessment allows the diagnostic teacher to identify the major presenting problem and a placement level that is moderately difficult for the student. From this information the diagnostic teacher makes tentative decisions about placement and instruction. She selects instructional techniques and considers her various roles during instruction (see Chapter 3).

As she teaches, the diagnostic teacher also analyzes the effects of the variables of the reading event (see Chapter 2) to help her formulate her hypotheses. She gathers further data about the strategies that the student uses to understand the text (see Chapter 7). After the lesson, she reflects on the information she has gathered, the reading event where instruction occurred, and her roles during instruction to formulate and refine her diagnostic hypotheses. Reflecting on this information, the diagnostic teacher selects techniques to adjust instruction in order to mediate learning for the problem reader.

The diagnostic teacher again instructs a lesson, using her new plan. At this point the diagnostic teacher may choose to cycle back through the process and instruct a new lesson; or she can continue to the next step, which assesses the reader's growth during instruction. To establish the amount of the reader's change, the diagnostic teacher assesses the reader's growth that resulted from the instructional adjustment or implementation of a different instructional technique (see Chapter 9 for the format to assess growth).

Several conclusions can result. If no independent level was obtained or there was a high degree of task modification and teacher investment to achieve an independent reading level, the diagnostic teacher reformulates her hypotheses based

on the additional information gathered as she taught the lesson. If the reader has obtained an independent reading level with a moderate degree of task modification and teacher investment, however, the diagnostic teacher establishes the instructional conditions that produced the optimal reading and returns to gather further diagnostic data as she teaches. The decision-making cycle of the diagnostic teacher illustrated in Figure 1–1 is thus complete.

SUMMARY

The process of diagnostic teaching uses instruction to understand how the problem reader approaches the reading event. The goal of diagnostic teaching is to identify instructional alternatives that create improved reading performance for the problem reader. Instruction is viewed as mediating learning, where the teacher focuses on how the learner solves the reading problem by gathering data as she teaches. Furthermore, she views reading as an interactive process where the reader uses what he knows to interpret what the text says. Therefore, the diagnostic teacher uses the student's strengths (knowledge and strategies) to lead the student to integrate new information as well as new strategies into his reading repertoire. She then assesses reading growth due to her instruction.

The diagnostic teacher makes several initial diagnostic decisions. First she decides on the major presenting problem that is inhibiting fluent reading with comprehension. Next she designates a reading level at which the student can profit from her instruction. Finally she selects an instructional technique that allows the problem reader to demonstrate strengths. These initial decisions become increasingly more refined as the diagnostic teacher considers the reading event, evaluates the strategies of the problem reader, and matches those with appropriate techniques.

The Reading Event

2

Diagnostic teaching establishes those instructional conditions that will result in improved reading of more difficult text. The diagnostic teacher (unlike the regular classroom teacher, who focuses on a progression of skill development in graded text) bases his decision making on the patterns of interactions during the reading event (see Figure 2–1). Those patterns that recur are considered the most representative of the student's reading behavior. From these patterns, the diagnostic teacher predicts what instructional circumstances will positively affect a student's reading behavior; the ultimate goal of assessment, therefore, is to identify optimum instructional conditions for the individual reader.

During instruction, the diagnostic teacher analyzes five variables of the reading event—reader, text, task, technique, and context—and evaluates their effect on the reader's performance. The variables do not act in isolation but affect one another during the course of instruction. Rather than limiting the effects of the variables, the diagnostic teacher evaluates how changing any one of them affects a reader's response.

Through repeated instructional opportunities, the teacher evaluates the interactions of these five variables. During the lesson he evaluates the diagnostic task (*what* he asks the *reader* to do) and the technique (*how* he asks her to complete the task). He evaluates *what is read* and how it affects reading performance. In this way he assesses how the text affects reading performance. The diagnostic teacher evaluates the reader's performance to assess her approach to the instructional event. Equally important, he evaluates the *context* where instruction occurs. The context of the instructional event affects the student's perception of the task as well as her use of prior knowledge related to the text content. As shown in Figure 2–2, these five variables influence reading performance during any given reading event and continuously interact as instruction occurs. This chapter elaborates on each variable.

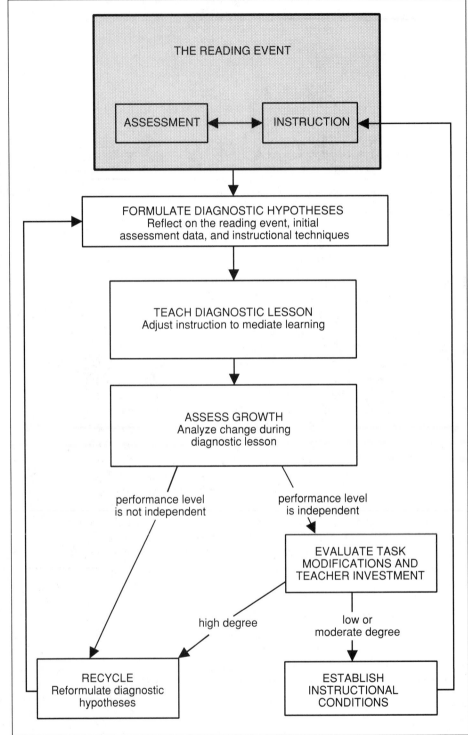

THE READING EVENT

ASSESSMENT ⟷ INSTRUCTION

FORMULATE DIAGNOSTIC HYPOTHESES
Reflect on the reading event, initial
assessment data, and instructional techniques

TEACH DIAGNOSTIC LESSON
Adjust instruction to mediate learning

ASSESS GROWTH
Analyze change during
diagnostic lesson

performance level
is not independent

performance level
is independent

**EVALUATE TASK
MODIFICATIONS AND
TEACHER INVESTMENT**

high degree

low or
moderate degree

RECYCLE
Reformulate diagnostic
hypotheses

**ESTABLISH
INSTRUCTIONAL
CONDITIONS**

Figure 2–1
The Decision-
Making Cycle of
Diagnostic
Teaching

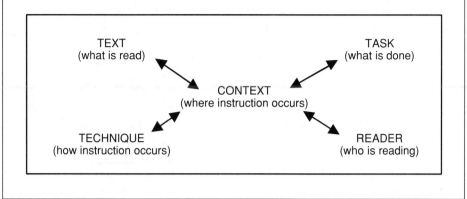

Figure 2–2
The Reading Event

TASK

Students are often mystified when trying to figure out what task they are to complete during an instructional lesson. In fact, many teachers evaluate precisely that: the rapidity with which students can figure out the task. It is not unusual that after reading a paragraph and being asked literal questions, students ask for a second chance, now that they know what the teacher wants for an answer.

The kind of task students are asked to do affects their reading performance. For instance, students who are repeatedly asked one type of question pay more attention to that type of information (Reynolds, 1980). In other words, the type of questions asked narrows a reader's purpose for reading and therefore limits comprehension. For example, a description of a room was read by two groups; one group pretended to be potential home buyers and the other pretended to be burglars. The two groups remembered different information because their purpose or task perception was different (Pichert, 1979). The reader's purpose or task perception influences responses to teacher-generated questions.

As the diagnostic teacher varies the task demands and questioning strategies, students' performances also change. Reading comprehension can be assessed using two formats. The teacher can use direct questions: "How did Johnny solve his problem?" Or he can ask students to retell the story: "Tell me this story in your own words." However, the kind of information required and the organization of the response make these tasks quite different. Direct questioning asks for information from the text that relates specifically to the stem of the question. An oral retelling, however, asks students to organize a response according to what they think is important.

The types of questions asked also change the task. Sometimes the diagnostic teacher uses a series of direct, literal questions: "Who were the characters? What did they do? What was the outcome?" Answering these questions is different from answering questions about the overall theme: "What was the author trying to tell you in this story? Do you think the author has a reason for including this character?"

These questions require different kinds of reasoning (Johnston & Pearson, 1982). The first group of questions requires a factual recall of stated information. The second group requires that readers use inferential thinking about the author's intended meaning. The readers have to use several parts of the text to construct a rationale for their answers. Still other questions ask students to respond personally to information in the text: "Have you had similar experiences to Jack's? Did you feel the same?"

Besides the reasoning requirements, the order in which the teacher asks the questions can also change the task. Questions can probe a logical sequence of story development, or they can require nothing more than a random recall of unrelated facts. These two tasks are different. Questions that probe a logical sequence of story events cause students to think about story development and, therefore, increase the comprehension of the story (Beck, Omanson, & McKeown, 1982). Unrelated literal questions, however, are harder to answer because there is no relationship among the answers. Furthermore, asking students to relate story comprehension to their own experiences can prompt them to associate what was read with what they already know and thereby increase comprehension (Johnston, 1983).

The questions that the diagnostic teacher asks change the task, making it harder or easier to understand stories. If the teacher probes to clarify a response, he influences comprehension and changes the original task demands. This change often increases comprehension. When incomplete responses are unprobed, valuable information about comprehension is lost. When possible, the diagnostic teacher probes the students' responses and records the task modifications that increase reader performance.

In addition to the task demands placed on the reader during story discussion, the diagnostic teacher uses either silent or oral reading during the diagnostic lesson. Sometimes oral reading is performed to prove a prediction; thus students are reading material that has been previously read. Therefore, they use meaning to facilitate their oral reading. At other times, however, the oral reading occurs on an initial reading of the passage. This places an additional demand on the processing of information (Allington, 1984b). In this instance, readers must attend not only to meaning but also to oral production of the text.

Finally, the task changes if the readers can refer to the text for answers. The difference in the responses when the text is available and when it is not becomes a task condition. Consequently, different task conditions result in various instructional conditions that can be modified by the diagnostic teacher.

In summary, the task can vary during reading instruction. It can be the oral or silent reading of sentences, paragraphs, or stories. After students read the story, the task can vary from answering direct questions to elaborate, unaided recall of textual information. Sometimes these responses require students to locate the answer in the text, while at other times the text is not used to answer questions. Questioning can also vary from literal teacher-generated questions to nonliteral student-generated questions. Furthermore, responses to these questions can require different kinds of reasoning; they vary from factual recall to personal application. As these tasks change, an equally important variation is the perceived purpose of the task by the reader. Altering any of these conditions changes the

Does the student understand the task?

What the teacher asks students to do affects the kind of information he has about them. Many a beginning teacher evaluates only oral reading and believes that his students have no reading problem. If he had asked questions after silent reading, he would have found that the students did not comprehend what they read silently. They did not know how to think about what they were reading. The diagnostic teacher thinks about what he asks students to do when they read. Then he formulates tentative decisions about the students' reading performances.

nature of the information obtained during a diagnostic lesson. It is the diagnostic teacher's responsibility to analyze the major task features of the diagnostic lesson and vary them (when necessary) to enhance reading performance. The following list provides task considerations that establish what the child is asked to do and can be used to focus reflective thinking about the reading event.

- Purpose for the task
- Task segment
  Sentences, paragraphs, stories, etc.
- Question type - *that probe a logical sequence of story events causes the student to think about story development and therefore increase*
  Literal, nonliteral, main idea, vocabulary *comprehension*
- Production requirements
  One-word response, retelling, finding answer in text
- Reasoning requirements of task
  Factual recall, inference, application
- Oral or silent reading
- Availability of text

TEXT

Traditionally, variation in student performance is attributed to the readability level of the text. However, the influence that the text has on reading performance is much more complex. The diagnostic teacher, therefore, systematically evaluates what he asks the student to read. He thinks about the possible textual characteristics that affect reading performance (Graves, 1986). He thinks about the content, length, and complexity of the passage, as well as its coherence, words, and structure. The length of the passage, for example, can affect both error rate and comprehension performance. Many short passages have an extremely heavy information load, requiring an extraordinary amount of comprehension in a short span. Longer passages, on the other hand, often contain examples, diagrams, and explanations that aid comprehension. Reading a long passage orally, however, often reduces comprehension and accuracy because of the attention demanded by oral production over a long period of time. The diagnostic teacher thinks about how passage length, amount of information, and use of examples affect reading performance.

Reading performance also changes when reading narrative or expository text. Each of these textual formats requires a different kind of reading strategy. Narrative text is organized using characters who have problems that are solved. The story line is developed through the actions, consequences, and events that occur in solving the problem. Expository texts are organized around main ideas, key vocabulary used to relate those ideas, and the supporting details that explain the main idea. Since each of these formats is organized differently, readers are not the same in their experience with them, which increases the variability of their performance (Garner, Alexander, Slater, Hare, Smith, & Reis, 1986).

The way the text is written, moreover, influences what is remembered. Authors who logically organize the text using the formats for narrative or expository text facilitate reader performance. If a text follows a logical organization, it is easier to comprehend and remember (Stein & Trabasso, 1982). Thus the style the author uses will affect reader performance. When expository text is written in a more engaging style (more like a novel), it is more easily remembered (Slater, 1986). Logical organization and engaging style affect reading performance.

The content likewise affects reading performance. Students differ in what they already know about the topic they are reading. The more students use what they already know about a particular content, the more they will remember when they read the text (Pearson, Hansen, & Gordon, 1979). The diagnostic teacher analyzes the content of the text and how much prior knowledge students need to know before they read the text. For example, the sentence "She wore a parka" requires more prior knowledge on the part of the reader than "She wore a parka to protect her from the cold wind." The diagnostic teacher evaluates the effect that text content and required prior knowledge have on reader performance.

Sentence structure also affects reading performance. Some texts are constructed of simple sentences that require the reader to infer causality. For example, "The dog ran. The chair fell" requires that the reader infer that the dog ran when the chair fell. Other texts are constructed with more complex sentences that reveal causality and facilitate comprehension. The wording "The dog ran because the chair fell" describes the relationship between the dog running and the chair falling (Beck, McKeown, Omanson, & Pople, 1984). Sometimes the simple sentences do not tell a story. If the sentences are combined to form a well-structured story, they are easier to understand (Brennan, Bridge, & Winograd, 1986).

The predictability of the sentences also affects reading performance. If the text contains repeated language patterns, the child can predict a word by using the pattern of the language. For example, the language pattern in the following paragraph allows readers to use a minimal amount of visual cues to guess the words: "There was an old fisherman who swallowed a shark. He swallowed the shark to catch the piranha. He swallowed the piranha to catch the crayfish. He swallowed the crayfish to catch the gnat. He swallowed the gnat as he yawned on the shore."

In addition to predictable patterns, other word choices affect recognition and comprehension of text. Some texts have words that are easy to read but do not convey the exact meaning (Graves, 1986). For example, "This boy had that" uses easy words, but it does not describe the exact meaning of the story. In another text, the words may be harder to read but more precise in conveying the intended meaning of the text: "The tall boy had the ice cream cone." This sentence uses harder words, but the meaning is clearer because the words are more precise.

During initial reading instruction, word choices are highly related to reading performance. For children who have profited from instruction in synthetic phonics, a text that is decodable is easier to read ("The pig went to dig a hole") than a text that consists primarily of sight words ("The children have gone to the house") (Barr, 1974–1975). As children apply the rules of the phonetic system to a text that has a high percentage of sight words, the error pattern will reveal a different set of problems than might appear if the text contained decodable words that followed the rules they had been taught (Juel, 1984) (see Chapter 7).

The diagnostic teacher thinks about the words in the text. He evaluates whether the words can be easily decoded using phonic rules. If the students were taught to read using a sight word approach (see "Sight Word Approach" in Chapter 6), the diagnostic teacher evaluates whether the words are the words that they have been taught in the program. If so, students can use this knowledge to read the unfamiliar text. They figure out a word by thinking, "What word do I already know that starts with a *b*?" If the words are unknown, the diagnostic teacher checks to see if the new words have similar letter patterns to the words that the students already know. If the new words have the same pattern as the known words, students can figure out a word by thinking, "What word do I already know that looks like this word?" However, if the word has not been taught and does not have a similar pattern, students will stumble over words, substituting words that make sense but do not look like the words in the story. Therefore, the diagnostic teacher evaluates the words in the text to assess their influence on student performance.

The text can help or hinder reading performance. The kind of text that is read will affect the information the teacher gathers about students' reading. For example, an informal reading inventory placed a student at the sixth-grade reading level; however, this same student had difficulty when she read the 10-page story in the sixth-grade reader. Three text characteristics had changed. The content had changed from information about sunflowers to a story about a boy who was cleaning his room. The text length had changed from short paragraphs to a long story. The text format had changed from expository to narrative.

A reflective teacher looks closely at the kind of text he has asked students to read. He asks himself, "Are there features of the text that affect students' reading?" Then he asks, "Have these same features affected the reading before?" In other words, "Is this a consistent problem?"

In conclusion, a variety of textual characteristics affect student reading performance. Passage length, content, and complexity affect student performance. Equally important is the density of information and the elaboration of information by the use of examples, pictures, diagrams, and headings. Through their word choices, authors can require an extensive background knowledge or coherently organize the text to develop word meanings. Furthermore, an engaging style (whether the text is expository or narrative) facilitates comprehension of the text. In other words, the diagnostic teacher examines the text to evaluate these features that affect student reading performance:

- Passage length
- Passage type
  Informational or narrative
- Type of content
- Organizational structure
  Headings, diagrams, etc.
- Background knowledge required of reader
- Grammatical complexity
- Word choices
  Decodability, distinctive meanings
- Density of information
- Elaboration or use of examples
- Coherence or unity of text
- Engaging style

READER

Bringing to the task and the text their own knowledge and strategies, learners perform in distinctively different ways; therefore, the diagnostic teacher observes students' interactions within the reading event to assess learner differences. Readers differ not only on *what* they already know (knowledge-based differences) but also on *how* they integrate new information into what they already know (strategy-based differences). Initially, the diagnostic teacher evaluates knowledge-based differences. He establishes reading levels for instruction. He matches the readability of the text with the level of reading performance for the students. Concurrently, he finds out what the readers already know about the task of reading and the content that he is to teach. As the instruction begins, the diagnostic teacher looks for patterns within the reading event to analyze skill knowledge. Word identification skills (e.g., sight word knowledge, phonic knowledge, and context use), vocabulary knowledge, and fluency are evaluated in relation to overall reading. Comprehension skills (e.g., identifying the main idea or problem, the key details or events, and the theme or the resolution) are also evaluated during instruction.

Equally important to skill knowledge is the general knowledge the students possess. Some students have a rich variety of experiences and are able to talk about their experiences. Talking about experiences indicates that students are organizing and classifying their worlds of experience. When they read, they use their prior experiences and the words they know to express them. Other students have limited experiences or limited word knowledge, which provides difficulty when reading (Harris & Sipay, 1985). Therefore, students' knowledge of the world and the words they use to describe their experiences influence comprehension and word identification (Barr & Sadow, 1985).

These knowledge-based differences are accentuated by differences in problem-solving strategies. Students differ in the strategies they use for solving the reading problem. Some students select meaning cues, while others select graphic cues. Some students rely heavily on their background knowledge, while others use only the text to form hypotheses while they are reading. Some students revise and monitor their model of meaning readily, while others need concrete facts before they revise their models (Spiro & Myers, 1984). These problem-solving strategies are observed by evaluating the pattern of verbal responses and word identification errors as the students read and answer questions. Looking for these consistent patterns, the diagnostic teacher notices students' selection strategies (the way they find cues and use sources of information), monitoring strategies (the way they check their understanding), and organizational strategies (the way they relate new information to what they already know). Initially, the diagnostic teacher notices whether or not the readers explore a range of clues to enhance comprehension and remedy word identification errors. To repair mistakes, students can use the overall meaning ("Oops, that doesn't make sense") or the way the word fits into the sentence ("That doesn't sound like a sentence"). Sometimes students use what the word looks like or sounds like ("Oops, I didn't say what those letters say") to restore comprehension. Efficient readers select appropriate cues and flexibly use sources of information; however, inefficent readers often use only a single source of information to remedy errors when reading.

Readers also differ in their monitoring strategies, or when and how they check their understanding. Students' strategies for monitoring word identification and comprehension are evaluated through oral reading and story discussions. Young and less skilled readers monitor their reading less frequently (August, Flavell, & Clift, 1984; Paris & Myers, 1981). They tend to read a string of words without checking to see if they make sense. When their understanding breaks down, students differ in their persistence to regain meaning. Many poor readers tend to give up when encountering repeated mistakes, while good readers persist in employing a variety of strategies to solve problems.

Finally, readers differ in the way they organize responses. During a discussion, some students answer literal-level questions with exact, text-based responses, while others answer questions by relying heavily on the overall theme of the story and inferring facts about the story rather than recalling specific information (Pearson & Spiro, 1980). Retellings can also indicate students' ability to organize and elaborate verbal responses. In an oral retelling, the brevity or elaboration of the story theme is noted to indicate a preference for generalizing or using specific facts.

Through instructional interactions, the teacher notes students' affective responses to instruction. Students respond differently to the type of feedback and prompting that the teacher uses. Some students need specific feedback that tells them what they did wrong and how to do the problem the "right" (expected) way. In other words, they prefer a high degree of teacher guidance. Other students prefer a simple acknowledgment that they are on the right track. They prefer to work out their mistakes on their own. Therefore, students also differ in the number of exact examples they need to incorporate a skill or a strategy. Some students rapidly understand a single example and transfer the new strategy to other situations, while other students need a series of examples and teacher guidance over a period of time before they understand how to apply the new strategies.

The teacher also notes the students' need for "sense making." Some students like to work practice examples and actually love workbook exercises, despite their lack of a substantial purpose in the instructional program. Such students believe the teacher is right. There are other students, however, who have a high need for activities to be purposeful. They use sense making to check their reading. They need reasons for doing the work they are asked to complete.

Finally, the diagnostic teacher evaluates how the students respond to their own successes and failures. Some readers persist when confronted with a difficult task, while others give up easily and are more likely to attribute failure to a lack of ability (an attribute not subject to control). When these readers are successful, they attribute success to luck or an easy task (Bristow, 1985).

How readers approach the reading event affects the kind of information a teacher has about them. A teacher makes many diagnostic decisions about differences among the learners in his classroom based on what his students know, how they learn, and their affective needs. Although this is appropriate, a teacher should evaluate how the other variables of the reading event affect the reading patterns that the readers use. He asks, "Is what I am observing an attribute that I always see in these readers, or has something in the reading event affected their performance?" Therefore, to assess the readers, he looks for a consistent pattern of responses over different reading events.

In conclusion, readers differ not only on what they already know as evaluated by level of performance, skill knowledge, and content knowledge, but also on the strategies they possess. These strategy-based differences include patterns of organizing knowledge, cue and strategy selection, and monitoring and shifting of these strategies. Students also have different affective needs during instruction. Some need a high degree of structure, teacher direction, and frequent feedback; others prefer little structure, self-directed learning with minimal feedback, and tasks that make sense. By evaluating the following patterns of reading performance, the diagnostic teacher detects the strategies readers use when reading.

- Knowledge-based patterns
  Level of performance
  Skill proficiencies and deficiencies
    Print and meaning processing
  Language proficiencies and deficiencies
    Word and world knowledge
- Strategy-based patterns
  Strategies used and needed
    Selection—source of information
      Text or prior knowledge
    Monitoring—active or passive
    Elaboration and level of response
      One word or embellished
      Literal or nonliteral
- Affective needs
  Need for structure and feedback
  Need for human sense
  Attribution of success or failure

TECHNIQUE

A key to effective instructional decision making is an analysis of the intervention, or the techniques, that the diagnostic teacher employs. During the lesson, the diagnostic teacher thinks about how the readers will best profit from instruction. Subsequently, he analyzes how various techniques approach instruction so that he can match readers' strategies with the most efficient instructional techniques. There are several considerations when analyzing instructional techniques.

Initially, the diagnostic teacher must decide whether a technique is to introduce a skill/strategy in isolation or to help the student learn more about reading stories (Pearson & Johnson, 1978). Some techniques incorporate strategy instruction as they teach skills, while other techniques focus only on the skills (Samuels, 1980). Question-answer relationships (see Chapter 6) is a technique developed to teach the skill of answering comprehension questions. Students learn to analyze questions as to the source of information needed to answer the question. The sources are explained as "right there," "think and search," and "on my own." Students are not only taught the skill of answering comprehension questions that are both literal and nonliteral, but they are also shown when it is most efficient to use the various skills. They are given strategies for using the skill. On the other hand, a typical synthetic phonics lesson (see Chapter 6) is different. It teaches the skill of blending sounds together to form words. However, students are not taught how that skill is used as a flexible strategy when errors occur as they read.

Techniques also differ in their function within the instructional framework and the texts appropriate for the instructional format. Some techniques develop prerequisite knowledge in order to understand the content of the story. Techniques that introduce vocabulary and develop background knowledge are used prior to reading, while other techniques focus on developing active reading during the actual reading of the text. Techniques like the directed reading-thinking activity, reciprocal questioning procedure, and reciprocal teaching (see Chapters 5 and 6) are used during the reading of the story to promote active comprehension. Furthermore, after a story is read, techniques can extend the comprehension of the story (see "Story Map" in Chapter 6) or reinforce word identification and fluency (see "Repeated Readings" in Chapter 6).

Techniques also differ in the mode of response that readers are asked to use. Some techniques ask students to discuss verbally what they learn when reading. By sharing their thoughts through a discussion, students select what is important to reconstruct the story. They actually construct an answer rather than merely recall events. Other techniques ask students to write about what they have read, which facilitates meaning construction. Again students must decide what is important, as well as how they will communicate what they learned. Readers vary in their ability and preference for response modes. Some students like to discuss what they have learned and share ideas and thoughts. Other students, however, prefer to write what they are thinking so that they can revise their understanding before communicating what they think. The diagnostic teacher selects a response mode that will mediate learning for a particular student.

Techniques also differ in the nature of the structure that is provided by the diagnostic teacher during implementation. Some techniques require that the teacher present the information in a rather nondirective format and simply provide thoughtful questions and support for reading. These techniques rely on students to construct their own rules for the consistency of language. When using these techniques, the diagnostic teacher immerses students in contextual reading and then facilitates their inquiry. It is assumed that students will be able to discover the consistency and meaning of the text on their own. The language experience approach (see Chapter 6), where students read stories that they have dictated to the teacher, is based on an implicit, nondirective approach to learning. This technique allows students to learn to read by using their own language structures.

Other techniques require that the teacher direct learning by modeling how the skill/strategy is to be used when reading text. Furthermore, students are directed in how to incorporate this skill/strategy into their reading. Reciprocal teaching (see Chapter 6) is a technique that uses explicit instruction. Students are shown how to summarize, ask good questions, clarify difficult parts, and predict what will be discussed. First the teacher models the strategy; then the students lead the discussion with the teacher offering encouragement and talking about when it is best to use the strategies.

Not only do techniques differ in their function as exemplified by their instructional frameworks, they also differ in the cognitive demands placed on learners by the instructional sequence. Some techniques present reading tasks as a whole and show students how the parts are organized within the whole. They often use visualization rather than words to develop understanding. The predictable language approach (see Chapter 6) is an example of a technique that introduces the story as a whole. Children read along with the teacher to develop the predictable pattern. After the story has been read as a whole several times, students are asked to identify individual words.

Other techniques present the parts of the reading task in a sequential, step-by-step progression that leads to the formation of the whole. These techniques emphasize verbalizing the separate parts, logically structuring these parts into a whole, and explicitly stating rules for organizing the parts into a whole. Synthetic phonics is an example of a technique that is sequential in nature. The synthetic phonics approach begins by teaching the sounds of letters. These sounds are then blended to form words, and finally rules for the different sound combinations are given.

How the teacher directs the reading event affects the information he gathers. Techniques vary in the demands placed on learners. For example, a teacher explicitly tells a student to look at the sounds of letters and blend the sounds together to form words; however, the student prefers to create her own rules, and thinking about sounds is her weakness. The ineffective teacher continues to teach the letter sounds, providing a high degree of feedback about her errors and finally concluding that she is passive and a nonreader.

However, the effective diagnostic teacher probes further. He changes the technique to include predictable stories that have phonetically consistent words. When the student self-corrects, the teacher asks, "How did you figure that out?" The student then tells him her reasons for phonics: "I thought about other words that looked like this word and then I substituted the sounds. You see hopping *looks like* popping. *Words that look alike at the end usually sound alike." The diagnostic teacher changed the technique from explicit instruction in letter sounds to implicit instruction in a text that requires students to create their own rules for phonics. The reflective teacher thinks about how he is directing instruction. He asks himself, "Are there other ways to present this task so that this student can learn more efficiently?"*

Although there seems to be an either/or situation in evaluating techniques, in reality the techniques can be placed upon a continuum of instructional features. For example, a technique is neither an explicit nor an implicit technique; rather, each technique falls along a continuum with a tendency to approach instruction from a more or less explicit or implicit structure. The relative significance of its approach depends on the learner's task knowledge and task independence as well as the teacher's execution.

In conclusion, teaching techniques vary in the way the diagnostic teacher presents instruction. Techniques are designed to teach skills or strategies or both. The techniques can be more appropriately placed either before, during, or after instruction. Some techniques are more appropriate for narrative text while others are better for expository material. Techniques also vary in the amount of teacher direction necessary for their implementation. Some techniques present information as a whole (simultaneously) and then show the parts (sequentially), while other techniques present information in separate parts (sequentially) and then show how the parts fit into the whole (simultaneously). The diagnostic teacher evaluates the instructional features of each technique as well as the students' responses to the techniques. These features include the following:

- Skill instruction
  Word identification, fluency,
  vocabulary, comprehension, or study skills
- Strategy instruction
  Predict, monitor, elaborate
- Instructional framework
  Before, during, or after reading
- Type of text
  Narrative or expository
- Mode of response
  Discussion or writing
- Instructional structure
  Implicit or explicit
- Instructional sequence
  Simultaneous or successive (sequential)

He then selects the most efficient technique to mediate learning for his students.

CONTEXT

Context plays a key role in influencing the learning that occurs during the instructional event. How teachers and students exchange information about what they are reading affects reading performance. In one study, for example, children's story retellings were more complete when conveyed to a peer who had not read the story than when told to a teacher who had read the story (Harste, Burke, & Woodward, 1982). Likewise, when inner-city children were interviewed in a testing situation, they were unable to draw logical relationships in conversation. But when these same children were interviewed in a social situation, they were expressive and logical (Labov, 1972). Students' perception of the context, whether it is assessment or discussion, affects their responses. A fifth grader explained this very simply: "It is like school has a big circle around it. Once I walk into this circle, I don't talk. Outside this circle, I talk a lot. I talk with my friends about the ideas I have. But in school, I don't talk about the ideas that I have" (S. R. Walker, personal communication, February 17, 1982).

This negative perception develops through classroom interaction. Much of the time teachers ask questions to assess learning rather than discuss ideas (Durkin,

1978–1979). Continual random assessment after reading a story can inhibit an exchange of relevant information. By focusing on irrelevant facts without connecting them to the reader's knowledge, the teacher inhibits reading comprehension and reinforces a context of interrogation rather than discussion (Beck et al., 1984). The above examples emphasize not only the influence of context on reading performance but also the influence of students' perception of their role in the instructional situation. Previous experiences with instructional contexts will influence reading performance.

Children's perception of the reading group can also influence their oral reading errors. For many children reading orally in front of a group elicits extreme anxiety, and this alone is the cause of oral reading errors. Asking these children to practice before they read or having them read to just the teacher eases the anxiety and results in more effective reading strategies. Therefore, the instructional situation (in terms of small group, total class, or one-on-one instruction) affects reading performance.

The prompting that teachers use during oral reading also influences how children think when they are reading. Readers who are prompted with "Does that make sense?" increasingly think about the meaning of the text as they read. They become fluent oral readers who correct their own mistakes. However, those students who are given the word or told to sound it out do not develop a meaning base for reading. They continue to focus on the words in the text without thinking about their meaning. This leads to less fluent reading and narrow strategies for correcting oral reading errors.

Teachers differ not only on how they prompt but also on when they prompt students. Sometimes teachers interrupt at the point of error and prompt with a word-level prompt. At other times teachers wait until the end of the sentence and then say, "Try that again; that didn't make sense" (Allington, 1980). Allowing students to read to the end of the sentence rather than interrupting at the point of error facilitates more active reading strategies and communicates to readers that they can think through problems when they read (Cazden, 1981). When teachers interrupt students at the point of error and focus on accuracy rather than meaning, they encourage a helpless approach to problems. Many times this focus is projected in teachers' expectations for students. If teachers expect failure and little effort, then their language, wait time, and prompting can convey this expectation to the readers. Consequently, the readers respond according to the teachers' expectations (Bloome & Green, 1984).

The diagnostic teacher analyzes his own dialogue as well as the students' responses. He is aware of the silent time between responses and how he prompts students when they do not understand (Bloome & Green, 1984). He thinks about how he formed his questions and how they influence the response. If students are unable to respond to literal questions, the diagnostic teacher rephrases his question. For example, he can suggest they look together for the page in the text where it talks about the topic. Then he can ask students to read the page orally. And finally, he can rephrase the quesion using words directly from the text and show students how to find the answer. This type of prompting engages students in a meaning search to find information that was forgotten.

At other times the diagnostic teacher can ask students if they have had similar experiences. This can prompt an elaboration of information from the text with background knowledge. When students are reading orally, the teacher waits until the end of the sentence and then asks them to think about the meaning and to reread the text. If meaning cannot be regained, he thinks about how he can help students correct their errors. He asks himself, "Do I need to explain what the word means or do I need to reread the text with expression?" These on-the-spot analyses allow the teacher to rephrase questions and segment the task to ensure successful task-completion (Cioffi & Carney, 1983).

Another contextual constraint of reading performance is the point during the instructional lesson that the teacher assists learning. The teacher decides at what strategic points during the lesson framework he needs to provide direct instruction to increase comprehension. If he provides assistance before the lesson, students might read the story with ease; however, they might profit more from talking about reading strategies as they read the story. If he intervenes at the appropriate instructional points during the reading event, he is able to increase story comprehension and build more appropriate student-teacher discussion. In this situation, the diagnostic teacher evaluates his presentation as well as students' responses.

The context of the reading event is a powerful influence on readers' performances. The situational context affects the information the teacher gathers about students' reading. For example, an informal assessment that used only factual questions after silent reading placed a student at the third-grade level; however, this same student was able to answer inferential questions at the eighth-grade level. When she discussed the same story with her peers, she recalled 80% of the facts as she needed them to support her interpretation. In this case, the context had changed from silent reading and answering factual questions in a relatively sterile context to silent reading and discussing the story in an interactive instructional group.

As the teacher becomes a sympathetic partner in understanding text rather than an assessor of students' deficits, he increases reading behavior through an instructional context that focuses on meaning. As an active listener responding creatively and consistently within the reading event, he carefully analyzes his own behavior and its effect on reading performance.

In conclusion, the context (or where instruction takes place) influences diagnostic decision making. The context can vary by who is a member of the instructional group and the students' perception of that group. Teacher expectations and prompting also influence the context. The time allowed on the task, the wait time during instruction, and the timing of teacher assistance are influential factors in reading performance. The diagnostic teacher evaluates all these factors in the following list in order to make diagnostic decisions.

- Learning situation
  One-to-one, small or large group
- Previous learning situations
- Teacher expectation
- Teacher dialogue
- Wait time
- Time allowed on task
- Point of intervention during lesson

SUMMARY

In summary, five interrelated variables establish the parameters of diagnostic teaching, which occurs in an interactive learning situation rather than a static, product-oriented situation. By evaluating these five variables, the diagnostic teacher identifies the instructional conditions for optimal learning. Reading instruction and assessment are redirected to the interrelationship of the variables rather than just student deficits.

Roles of Diagnostic Teaching

3

Effective diagnostic teaching involves making instructional decisions before, during, and after the reading event. At the core of decision making is the effective teacher who reflects on her instruction. As she teaches, the diagnostic teacher continually identifies those instructional modifications that enable problem readers to become independent learners (see Figure 3–1). This chapter delineates five roles of effective diagnostic teaching: reflecting, planning, mediating, enabling, and responding. These roles are supported by eight instructional guidelines that focus diagnostic teaching and encourage students to realize their individual potential as learners. As the effective teacher assumes these roles, she views problem readers from different perspectives. As she reflects on her decision making, therefore, she considers each of these roles and its influence on her instruction.

The first role of effective diagnostic teaching is reflecting. Central to diagnostic teaching is the teacher who reflects on the interactions during the reading event. She checks the instructional decisions she makes with her personal assumptions about reading and cross-checks her lesson plans with students' learning. As she is teaching, she analyzes how she modifies instruction and the language she uses to mediate learning. Teaching as reflecting means that every interaction is analyzed so that appropriate instructional adjustments can be made.

The second role of diagnostic teaching is planning. As the diagnostic teacher plans her lesson, she thinks about the *whole act of reading* and decides on a sequence of reading experiences that allow her to teach not only reading skills but also how those skills fit together when reading. As she plans her lessons, she selects activities that will not only stimulate learning, but *ensure success*. Once reading activities have been successfully completed, the diagnostic teacher attributes the success to the students' abilities and efforts. Teaching as planning means that the diagnostic teacher focuses on the whole act of reading, ensuring success for each child.

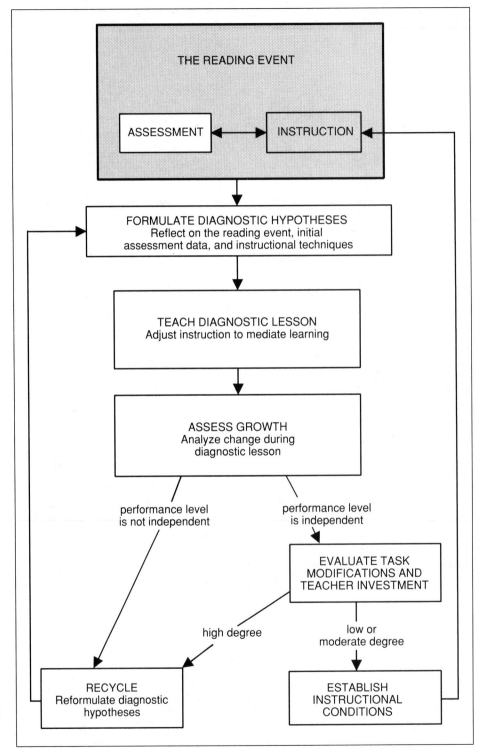

Figure 3–1
The Decision-
Making Cycle of
Diagnostic
Teaching

The third role of diagnostic teaching is mediating. The effective diagnostic teacher *encourages active reading* by asking questions that not only lead students through the story but relate the events and key ideas to what students already know. As she teaches, the diagnostic teacher becomes an active participant in the reading event. She shares her interpretations and her active thought processes by thinking out loud as she solves the reading problem. During the lesson, the diagnostic teacher *assesses while she instructs* so she can modify her instruction to meet students' changing instructional needs. Teaching as mediating means that the diagnostic teacher uses students' present strategies to lead them to more active reading strategies.

The fourth role of effective diagnostic teaching is enabling. She helps her students develop a *concept of themselves as readers.* Immersing her students in relevant and successful reading experiences, she attributes their success to the effective strategies they use. As she plans lessons, she thinks about how to *build students' control* over their learning. She plans lessons where she models her own internal thinking, asks students to share in thinking through the problem, and actively listens and encourages students to tell her how they solve the reading problem. Teaching as enabling means that the diagnostic teacher provides students with the resources to understand themselves as readers, thinkers, and problem solvers.

In the fifth role, the diagnostic teacher views teaching as responding to individual human needs. An effective diagnostic teacher *accepts the individual differences* among her students. She knows that the experiences of her students vary widely and plans her instruction to account for the differences in what her students already know. She thinks about the different ways her students solve problems and plans lessons that use their problem-solving strengths. In accepting their individual differences, the effective teacher *fosters a reality-oriented environment* by accepting individuality but expecting all students to read. She uses laughter to develop a relaxed atmosphere where students learn to cope with their mistakes and produce intelligent ideas. Teaching as a human response means that the diagnostic teacher discusses individuality and making mistakes as human conditions.

These roles and the instructional guidelines they represent work together to create an instructional environment where all students learn. This model fosters instructional interactions that focus on the whole reading event, giving students self-control of their own learning and creating a coherent learning experience for them. Figure 3–2 suggests the interrelation between the roles and guidelines discussed in this chapter.

REFLECTING

The reflective diagnostic teacher uses what she already knows about the child, the text, and the task to make instructional decisions. When the reflective teacher encounters difficult teaching situations, she uses her strengths in teaching to systematically introduce new activities to meet the individual needs of the hard-to-teach child. As she teaches, she extends her teaching by a reflective analysis of the situational variables that interact as the lesson is being taught. She is con-

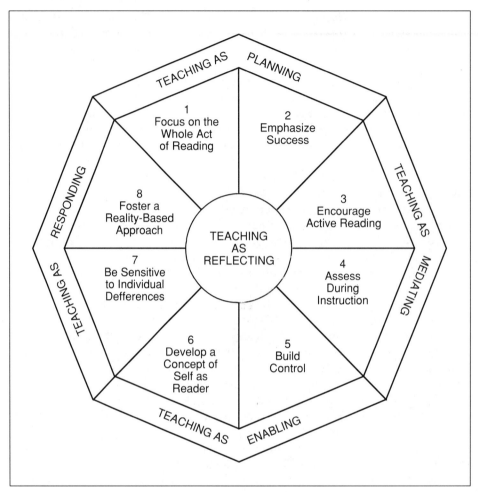

Figure 3–2
Roles of Diagnostic
Teaching

stantly evaluating the assignments made, the teacher-student interaction, and the resulting student gain as these changes are made. Inherent in this principle is the necessity for reflective analysis of the instructional decisions that are made.

Before she introduces a lesson, she analyzes how she reads the story she is going to teach. As she reads, she checks skills and strategies by using an introspective analysis (Meichenbaum, 1983). She reads the story, therefore, asking herself the following questions:

- What do I need to know in order to understand the text?
- What sources of information am I using?
- How often do I need to reread?
- Do I reread because I don't have enough background knowledge or because the text is unclear?
- Does my background knowledge distort the author's message?
- What would make this more understandable?
- Am I using the skills that I plan to teach the student?

Thus, the reflective teacher examines examples, questions, and practice exercises before she teaches. Then she chooses only those activities that are appropriate for learning and applying the designated skill or strategies. She double-checks her personal response to the planned lesson with her goals for student learning.

During instruction, the diagnostic teacher reflects on how she interacts with different students in her classroom. She thinks about her behavior in the different instructional groups in her classroom. Teachers treat students in low reading groups differently from those in their high reading groups. This indicates that they view the reading needs of poor readers as different from the reading needs of good readers (Cazden, 1981).

Teachers allow more interruptions in low groups and are more engaged as teachers when instructing high groups. They interrupt poor readers at the point of error, while they let good readers continue reading to see if they are going to recover meaning. They use more word-level prompting to poor readers, while they use meaning-level prompting to readers in their high groups (Allington, 1980). These teaching behaviors affect reading performance. The reflective teacher uses a mental checklist to analyze her interactions while she is teaching to provide the most effective reading instruction for *all* of her students.

The reflective teacher analyzes her own preferences for learning and how these preferences affect her teaching. She focuses on how she learns and how she teaches, not only on what she is teaching. She watches herself to cross-check strategies for teaching with personal beliefs about reading. Andrews (1976/1977) found that teachers who believe that word recognition and accuracy are important in reading introduce isolated vocabulary words and practice them through flashcard drill, pointing to each word as they read it and using such phrases as "perfect," "that's exactly right," and "go back and read that again." Furthermore, using the Theoretical Orientation to Reading Profile (TORP), Deford (1985) found a significant match between teacher behavior as rated by three observers and the TORP score.

Teachers make instructional decisions that reflect their assumptions about reading and learning. The diagnostic teacher is aware of her orientation to reading and reflects on how her orientation is influencing her instructional decision making. Reflective teaching means primarily that the teacher reflects on herself—that she looks at what she says, how she says it, what she assigns, and how she assigns it—in order to analyze how she affects learning to read.

PLANNING

Prior to the reading event, the teacher thinks about how instruction will occur. She thinks about the variables of the reading event: task, text, reader, and context. Then she selects teaching techniques that focus on reading stories that ensure success. As teachers focus on the broad aspects of reading, they talk with students about why and how the parts of reading will improve their reading performance. In doing this, they create activities that are both challenging and successful.

This planning creates an expectation that the reading event will produce independent readers. Effective teachers expect the students in their classrooms to read and interpret stories. Furthermore, this prior planning allows the effective teacher to think about the strategies needed to complete the assigned reading task; therefore, she can attribute students' success to both their abilities and efforts. Teaching as planning means that the teacher preplans her lessons to focus on the whole act of reading and to ensure success. These two guidelines are delineated below.

Guideline #1: Focus on the Whole Act of Reading

As the diagnostic teacher plans her instruction, she creates a literate environment by focusing on the whole act rather than the parts of reading. Furthermore, she realizes that children learn what teachers teach (Berliner, 1981). If teachers instruct children to recognize vowel sounds, they will learn vowel sounds. If teachers emphasize literal comprehension, they will, in fact, become excellent fact finders and comprehend the literal information of a story. However, if teachers instruct students to react to whole stories using important textual information and their own prior knowledge, they will actually become comprehenders who flexibly shift between reader-based and text-based knowledge. As a result, focusing instruction on the whole act of reading is extremely important.

Effective teachers focus on reading whole stories and relating them to relevant personal experiences. They encourage sustained silent reading of stories as well as mastering specific skills. Furthermore, classrooms with high reading achievement are characterized by silent reading of selections followed by small group discussions where students exchange ideas about the meaning of the story (Rupley & Blair, 1978). Through the small group discussions, students justify their interpretations by relating the text to what they already know. This focuses instruction on meaning rather than decoding.

There is, however, a different focus of instruction for readers in low reading groups. Good readers were observed to be engaged in contextual reading 57% of the time; poor readers, only 33% of the time. Poor readers, in fact, had an extended amount of time practicing the skills of reading in short, isolated drills (Gambrell, Wilson, & Gantt, 1981). The results are even more astounding in remedial programs. In these programs the average number of words read a day was 43 (Allington, 1977). Even though research supports the premise that skill knowledge is best mastered during contextual reading (Anderson, Hiebert, Scott, & Wilkinson, 1985), it appears that remedial instruction in both classrooms and clinics continues to focus on the parts rather than the whole act of reading.

Focusing on reading stories does not preclude skill and strategy instruction. The diagnostic teacher does select appropriate skills and strategies to teach. Nevertheless, she teaches more than just the skill; she explains when and why the skill is used. The diagnostic teacher gives students reasons for learning the parts of reading and shows students how the parts affect the total reading process. As skills or strategies are presented, therefore, the teacher explains when it is most appropriate to use them. For example, when reading different types of text, the teacher explains the utility of using or not using the particular reading strategy she is teaching. When she teaches the rule for short *a,* she explains that this will

facilitate word identification when the student cannot guess the word from the context and the initial letter. If the teacher is instructing the use of formulating predictions based on prior knowledge, she explains that if the student does not know anything about the topic, he must read two or three paragraphs, summarize the information, and then create a prediction based on the new information and what he knows about it.

In summary, the effective diagnostic teacher explains how to use skills and strategies within the whole act of reading. She explains the process of shifting between reader-based knowledge and the text and how the skills of reading will influence reading efficiency when problems in text interpretation arise. This focus means that students are given rationales for the various reading activities and are shown how these activities relate to the whole act of reading.

Guideline #1: Focus on the Whole Act of Reading

- *Focus on reading whole stories*
- *Provide rationales for skill activities*
- *Show students how the parts (skills and strategies) of reading relate to the whole act of reading*

Guideline #2: Emphasize Success

As the diagnostic teacher focuses on the whole act of reading, she must at the same time ensure successful reading for students. Berliner (1981) stresses that reading achievement is directly related to the amount of time spent reading material where students have a high success rate. It is not only the amount of time engaged in reading that matters, but readers must experience a high level of success. Thus, in order to develop a notion of efficient reading, students must first experience numerous successful reading experiences. When students have success, they repeat the successful activity. Obviously, success is a powerful motivating factor.

On the other hand, if students experience numerous failures in an activity, they often give up and avoid subsequent opportunities to engage in this activity. Poor readers are often placed in material that is very difficult for them (Allington, 1984b; Clay, 1979). They have either a low rate of recognizing words or understanding the content, which discourages them from further reading. These unsuccessful reading experiences contribute to an unsystematic evaluation of reading performance. These students have a serendipitous notion about success. Success is attributed to external factors such as "baby reading material," "it was my lucky day," or "the teacher gave it away when she helped me."

To encourage a healthy attitude toward success, the diagnostic teacher creates a series of consistently succesful reading events. She keeps a close match between the students' abilities and the texts that she chooses for reading instruction. In addition, the teacher expects students to read the text once these instructional modifications have been made. She expects students to read lots of words and to express ideas based on what they have read. A major characteristic contributing to the success of all readers is the teacher's expectation that all students will read and learn (Berliner, 1981).

Maintaining appropriate expectations is extremely demanding for the diagnostic teacher. Because of the repeated failures of problem readers, they do not recognize the effective strategies that they do use. When asked how they got an answer, students often respond with "I don't know." Because of their continual failure, these students do not have enough experience with successful reading to recognize when and how their effective strategies work. It is extremely important, therefore, not only to maintain high expectations but also to share with students how those expectations are to be met. Realistic assessments of students' unique strategies and levels of reading performance can be effectively shared with them. As a result, adjustments in instruction can be viewed as steps toward reading improvement, rather than scapegoating assignments or attempts to make school "easy."

How the activities are expected to influence reading performance is explained to students. These rationales are shared so that changing reading behavior is a mutual responsibility that demands effort from both the teacher and the students. The teacher acknowledges students' successes by charting their reading progress. During the charting, the teacher discusses the students' performances and attributes their success to their own efforts and unique abilities. Students are assured that this successful reading performance can be repeated in future reading events. As they experience success, they will spend more time reading. This honest dialogue about unique strategies for problem solving, coupled with the expectations of the resulting success, creates not only a positive learning environment but higher reading achievement.

Guideline #2: Emphasize Success

- *Create a series of successful reading events*
- *Maintain high expectations*
- *Attribute student success to unique abilities and effort*

MEDIATING

The diagnostic teacher mediates learning by phasing in and out of the reading event as she guides student learning. She asks questions that promote an active interpretation of text. She listens to the students and uses what they understand about the story to elicit more elaborate interpretations and applications of the text. She gives them time to develop predictions and formulate answers. When students are unsure of a response, she asks them what they know so far about the story. Then she asks them to explain how they came to that conclusion. From this information the teacher develops leading questions or examples that will guide the students' interpretation. Using students' responses, the diagnostic teacher assesses their learning as a result of her instruction. Teaching as mediating means that the teacher phases in and out of the reading event in order to encourage active reading and assess learning as a result of her instruction.

Guideline #3: Encourage Active Reading

Reading is an active, problem-solving process that involves predicting (or guessing) what the author is going to say, based on expectations about story events. After making a guess, children select clues from the story to confirm their guesses and then check this knowledge with what they already know.

Interactic

The following scenario illustrates this active process when encountering an unknown word. A text has a picture of a baseball diamond with a figure running toward second base at the top of a page and the following sentence at the bottom of the page: "The girl hit the home run." From the picture of the baseball diamond, a child guesses that the story is about a boy. However, when the sentence about a girl is read, the graphic cue *g* instead of *b* cues the reader that the story is about a girl rather than a boy. The initial hypothesis, that the story is about a boy, is based on previous experience with similar situations and stories.

The reader selects cues from the text and measures them against his own background knowledge and important textual information. If the response is confirmed, or fits, reading continues. For example, when the expected response for the baseball story could not be confirmed because the word *girl* does not look like *boy,* the reader asked himself, "What word is like *boy* that begins with a *g*?" In other words, he wanted to know what word semantically and graphically fits.

Our experiences and the language used to describe them build our schema, or our personal world view. By watching television, playing in the neighborhood, and listening to storybooks, children develop a schema that the game of baseball is played by both males and females; however, when they read about baseball, the stars or characters are mostly boys. In the baseball story example, the expected response of *boy* was revised according to grapho-phonic information, and the resulting sentence was read, "The girl hit the home run." This information caused the reader to refine the schema that "stories about baseball usually have boys for heroes" to be more inclusive, namely that "stories about baseball usually have boys for heroes, but sometimes they have girls."

Efficient readers create expectations about what the text will say and, as they read, select important textual information to confirm or revise these expectations. However, remedial readers do not monitor their reading. Some remedial readers rely heavily on the text without developing an overall expectation for the meaning. This causes them to miscall words or ideas and continue reading without checking these words or ideas against an overall meaning to see if they fit.

Another group of remedial readers relies heavily on <u>prior knowledge</u> when reading. They read without using the text to check this overall expectation; therefore, they miscall words or ideas that do not match the text but fit the overall interpretation of the paragraph. Some of these readers forget to monitor their reading; as a result, they continue to read even when their interpretations do not make sense. Other children lack experiences necessary to create appropriate expectations; consequently, they cannot interpret the text.

asking question

The diagnostic teacher can encourage active reading by asking questions that require students to construct ideas rather than give right or wrong answers. In these lessons, the diagnostic teacher creates an expectation about the story before a story is read. She asks the children what they already know about the topic and to think about what the text might say. As the children read, the teacher asks questions that focus on comparing what they thought the text might say with what was written. This process encourages an active reading of text based on reader knowledge and textual information.

active comprehension

The line of questioning also influences <u>active comprehension</u> of text. If questions focus on the important organizational parts of the story (setting, problem, goal, events, and resolution), comprehension is enhanced (Beck, Omanson, & McKeown, 1982; Singer & Donlan, 1982). When developing her questions, the diagnostic teacher reads the text, selects the most important points of the passage, and constructs questions that will lead students to think about these important points (Pearson, 1985a). She also encourages active comprehension by directing students to formulate their own questions. Students who generate their own questions during reading perform better on interpretive comprehension tasks than students who answer only teacher-posed questions (Helfeldt & Lalik, 1979; Walker & Mohr, 1985).

Although teacher-originated questions are prevalent in the classroom, asking appropriate questions is a complex skill. Learning what to ask and how to ask questions is extremely demanding. The diagnostic teacher learns to monitor not only the kinds of questions she asks but also the way she asks them. Initially, she allows three to five seconds between the original question and her probes. Increasing the wait time from one second to three seconds positively affects the number of student responses as well as the organization of the response (Rowe, 1973). Furthermore, the amount of time between the students' responses and the teacher's response affects the elaboration of the answer. Thinking takes time. Silence may mean that students are constructing thoughtful answers to higher level questions. Therefore, the amount of time the teacher allows between responses during a discussion affects active reading behaviors.

Not only should the diagnostic teacher increase her wait time, but she must also deal effectively with inappropriate responses. Initially, the teacher uses part of the students' answers to probe reasoning. Sometimes she rephrases or reduces her question so that a response is more manageable. At other times she asks students to justify their answers by supplying information from the text. During the lesson, she remains flexible, phasing in and out as she shows students how to justify their answers using the text and what they already know. Finally, if the line of reasoning is justifiable, the diagnostic teacher accepts the response as a valid point of view. As the diagnostic teacher increases her wait time and deals creatively with inappropriate responses, she develops an atmosphere that promotes active interpretation of text.

In summary, the diagnostic teacher encourages active reading by asking logical questions that build a cohesive framework for text interpretation, encouraging students to generate and evaluate their own questions, and providing a questioning atmosphere that promotes thinking rather than interrogation.

Guideline #3: Encourage Active Reading

- *Ask questions that focus on key ideas*
- *Promote thinking by allowing time for reflection*
- *Deal effectively with miscomprehension*

Guideline #4: Assess During Instruction

As the diagnostic teacher implements the lessons that she planned, she keeps a mental log of the students' responses. Her instruction, therefore, not only creates active readers but also provides a means for assessment. As the diagnostic teacher mediates learning, she observes how she modifies the initial reading task to create learning. This record of students' responses to instructional modifications is called dynamic assessment.

During dynamic assessment the teacher probes responses when questions are missed or answers are not clear. For example, when a child read a story about two mountain climbers in Chile, South America, he miscalled the word *Chile* (actually he pronounced the *ch* sound and then mumbled). In the oral retelling, he referred to Chile as the location. When the diagnostic teacher probed how he got the answer, the student said, "Well, the author talked about the Andes Mountains, and I know the Andes Mountains are on the west coast of South America . . . so I decided that the country must have been Chile."

From this information, the teacher assessed that this student had a wide range of prior experiences and used them to interpret text. He was also able to mentally self-correct word recognition errors. This was a sign that he was an active rather than a passive reader. His reading problem stemmed from overrelying on his background knowledge when he encountered several words that he could not recognize. Probing the student about how he arrived at an answer during the instructional situation gave the diagnostic teacher a more accurate picture of the student's potential for learning new information.

As the diagnostic teacher assesses while she instructs, she evaluates children's present use of strategies in a specific context. Then she investigates their understanding of the reading process (i.e., how active they are). Do they use both text-based processing and reader-based processing when they are reading? If not, what can she do to help them understand the active nature of reading? When she has modified the task, do they gain more understanding and control of their reading processes? With this line of questioning, the diagnostic teacher thinks about what students already know that she can use to guide them to more integrated understanding of the reading process. Dynamic assessment evaluates students' performances as they are guided to use more effective reading strategies. This type of assessment reveals the students' acquisition of strategies during instruction rather than unaided levels of competence (Brown & Campione, 1986).

Finally, as the diagnostic teacher assesses learning while she teaches, she evaluates whether or not her instruction is appropriate for her learners. She evaluates the reading event and asks if there is another way to teach students the task. She asks herself:

1. Am I leading students through the task according to their present strategy use? If not, should I try another way?
2. Is this an appropriate text for these students? If not, should I try another text?
3. Am I using the students' strengths as I am teaching? If not, should I try another way?
4. Is this an appropriate technique for these students? If not, should I try another way?
5. Is this an appropriate learning context for these students? If not, should I try another situation?

As key variables of instruction are changed, assessment is based on the resulting changes in reading performance. The diagnostic teacher evaluates students' improvement due to her instruction. If students do not improve, the diagnostic teacher looks for another way to modify her instruction to produce improved reading performance.

Guideline #4: Assess During Instruction

- *Probe students' answers to evaluate how they arrive at answers*
- *Assess reading change due to mediated learning*
- *If reading performance does not change, try another way*

ENABLING

During the reading event, the diagnostic teacher enables students to control their own learning and, therefore, think of themselves as readers. To enable students, the diagnostic teacher helps them develop control by sharing how she thinks while she is reading. The students and teacher work together to figure out a story and then discuss how they reached their conclusions. As the teacher shares her thinking and works with the students to gain understanding, she enables them to control their own learning and talk with themselves about their own understanding of a story. As the diagnostic teacher builds control, she finds ways to show students that they can read and think. She chooses easy but relevant reading material so that students can engage in an active search for meaning. She acknowledges the effective strategies they use when they read efficiently. At times, she allows students to read for their own purposes without teacher questions and discussion.

Guideline #5: Build Control

The fifth guideline requires that the teacher not only instruct the strategies of reading but systematically plan how students will assume responsibility for their own learning. The diagnostic teacher not only directs the learning process by explaining the steps and guiding the practice; she also gives students ownership of their learning by encouraging them to think about their thinking. Efficient readers monitor their understanding. As they are reading, they monitor their comprehension by actively choosing alternate strategies when reading does not make sense. Remedial readers, on the other hand, are characterized by disorganized strategies and failing to spontaneously self-monitor (Bristow, 1985). Consequently, they continue to rely on the teacher to monitor reading performance.

To change this dependence, remedial readers need explicit instruction in effective monitoring behaviors so that they can progress from teacher-directed to self-directed learning. The initial step is to redirect assessment from the teacher to the child by thinking out loud about reading. To do so, the teacher purposely makes mistakes while reading so that she can model how she monitors an active meaning search. Too often remedial readers perceive proficient reading as error-free reading. By making mistakes, the teacher can model her own coping behaviors.

The teacher begins the modeling by saying, "Oops, did that make sense?" When the answer is negative, various alternative corrective strategies are modeled. She shows readers that they can ignore the mistake and read on to see if they can figure out the meaning. Or that they can reread the sentence to check the overall meaning to see what might fit.

As she continues to model this active meaning search, the teacher illustrates the self-questioning process that goes through the mind of an active reader:

> If I don't understand, I ask myself a series of questions, the first one being "What would make sense?" If I can't regain the meaning, I ask more questions. Most of

the time I need to figure out either a word I don't know or what the author was trying to say. I can use two different sequences.

First, to figure out a word, I ask myself, "Can I say it that way?" (syntactic fit) or "What word does it look like?" (graphic fit) or "What does it sound like?" (phonic fit).

Second, to figure out meaning, I ask myself, "What does the text say? What do I already know about what the text says? How does this information fit together?"

After modeling the self-questioning process, the teacher and students work through a couple of examples. The students follow the teacher's model and think aloud, asking themselves questions about their reading. The students actually talk about how they solve the reading task. The teacher, in turn, provides encouragement for their thinking about thinking. Pearson (1985a, p. 736) states that "teachers assume new and different roles: they become sharers of secrets, coconspirators, coaches and cheerleaders."

Guided practice involves an interaction between students and teacher that begins with talking about how to solve the reading problem. This thinking aloud allows the teacher to provide feedback about the appropriateness of strategies used. She comments, "Did you notice how you reread that sentence to see if it made sense? That was very effective." When necessary, she models appropriate trouble-shooting strategies. This is an intermediate step between teacher direction and student control of the reading process.

As the teacher builds control by modeling active reading and the flexible use of trouble-shooting strategies, she encourages internalization of these strategies. She assumes an active role by asking students to explain what they are going to do the next time they read a passage they cannot understand. This type of questioning focuses instruction on the inner speech that accompanies logical thought, heightening students' awareness of the problem-solving process.

The diagnostic teacher builds student control of the reading process by modeling the process of active reading and the corresponding trouble-shooting strategies that efficient readers use. In addition, the teacher thinks out loud, showing students how she knows what she knows. In turn, students think out loud using the steps of active reading, and the teacher reinforces the thinking process rather than focuses on right or wrong answers. Finally, control of the process is gradually released by the teacher, who encourages students to actively think about the strategies they are using.

Guideline #5: Build Control

- *Model your own thinking while reading to students*
- *Collaborate in thinking about how reading is occurring*
- *Release teacher control by encouraging self-talk about how students solve their reading problems*

Guideline #6: Develop a Concept of Self as Reader

Children come to school with well-developed problem-solving abilities; they have learned to walk, to talk, and so on. Through their everyday living, they have learned many of the principles of communicating their ideas through language. However, because disabled readers repeatedly fail when learning to read, they develop a concept of themselves as nonreaders. This self-assessment is very difficult to change. As inefficient readers learn to read, word identification is difficult, and the sympathetic teacher assists these students more readily, allowing them to depend on teacher assistance rather than using textual meaning to correct errors. This type of interaction inhibits an active search for meaning and encourages a passive view of reading, emphasizing word calling rather than meaning as the goal of reading.

While listening to such readers, one notices that they "read as if they do not expect what they read to make sense, as if getting every individual word right were the key" (Smith, 1978, p. 34). This passive attitude is also exhibited when comprehending text. Disabled readers seem to monitor their reading less frequently and accept whatever argument is presented in the text without applying their prior knowledge. They seldom reread text to check initial interpretations and try to maintain interpretations even in light of contradictory information (Palincsar & Brown, 1984). These ineffective strategies can be altered by the teacher who is sensitive to her influence on the students' concept of themselves as readers. This concept can be developed using three teaching strategies: immersing students in reading, attributing success to effective strategy use, and allowing time for personal reading.

To be engaged in the actual reading of text is the first important requisite for developing a concept of self as reader. Immersing students in relevant reading activities will increase their concept of themselves as readers. As they read material that is repetitive, relevant, and rythmic, they can feel themselves reading. Poor readers, however, have few opportunities to read connected text. In first-grade classrooms, Allington (1984a) found that children in high reading groups read 10 times as many words as children in low reading groups. In this study, children in low reading groups read silently a total of only 60 words during the five-day sample period. It is difficult to consider oneself a reader when one only reads 12 words a day. Therefore, increasing the amount of fluent contextual reading each day is the first step toward developing a concept of self as reader. Difficult reading material causes students to focus on the word level of reading, precluding an active search for meaning. Reading text fluently at an independent level allows students to read enough words correctly so that they can engage in an active search for meaning.

Inefficient readers, however, need more than easy reading material to change their concept of themselves as readers (Johnston & Winograd, 1985). Often the teacher needs to model the strategies of active reading by constructing minilessons and thinking aloud, using various trouble-shooting strategies when reading breaks down. Although inefficient readers have adequate knowledge to read the words, their repeated failures have encouraged a rather passive attitude toward reading instead of an active meaning-seeking stance. They have developed a view that reading is simply calling words correctly and waiting for teacher assistance when reading breaks down. They attribute their reading performance to forces outside their control rather than to effective use of strategies. Therefore, by being given feedback related to the strategies used rather than being told of right or wrong answers, the students' attention is refocused on those behaviors that they can control.

When effective strategies are reinforced, students can attribute success not only to the product but also to the process of active reading. They begin to see themselves as active readers who can construct meaning from text. As the children build their self-concepts as readers, a second major task of the teacher is to talk about the strategies used to derive meaning from text and reinforce those strategies as the students read.

The purpose for reading can also influence children's concepts of themselves as readers. When children read for their own purposes and enjoyment, their inter-actions with text are perceived as real and relevant reading; consequently, they perceive themselves as readers. Teachers need to set aside time in the classroom for children to read for their own enjoyment and then share their reading. In build-ing the students' concept of themselves as readers, the teacher allows time for them to share the knowledge they have gained from reading in a creative way with their peers. She creates a "read and tell" time that reinforces individual varia-tion in text interpretation. This allows students to have ownership of their own responses to text and builds the concept of themselves as readers.

When students think of themselves as readers, they identify questions to be answered, read to answer those questions, and actively engage in text interpreta-tion. They view themselves as in control of their reading. Teaching strategies can build children's concepts of themselves as readers. The sensitive teacher creates independent readers by having them read a lot of text, stressing the strategies of active reading, and having them read relevant materials for their own enjoyment.

Guideline #6: Develop the Concept of Self as Reader

- *Immerse students in reading*
- *Attribute active reading to effective strategy use*
- *Allow students to read for their own individual purposes*

RESPONDING

In all her interactions, the teacher responds as a person rather than a controller of activities. She responds to the different children she has in her classroom and challenges them according to their individual needs. She uses what they already know to present concepts in the way they learn best. Using the unique strengths

of the individual learners in her classroom, she reduces stress for each learner.
Furthermore, she acknowledges the realities of the educational situation.
Using personal statements about her own reading process and laughing about
her own mistakes increases students' awareness that reading is constructing a response rather than getting the answer right.

Guideline #7: Be Sensitive to Individual Differences

Students bring to the reading task their own sets of experiences and knowledge that affect their reading behavior. At the same time, they bring their own strategies for dealing with the world. Some children are impulsive, some are simultaneous, and some are quiet, while others are highly distractible. Even though each of them is different, seldom do these differences affect instruction in public schools. This is partly due to a limited exploration of how learners are alike and different. Understanding human similarities increases one's sensitivity to human differences. When learning something new, people are alike because new learning creates disequilibrium, or stress. As people solve the problem or learn the information, they reduce this stress (Elkind, 1983).

People learn this new information in two ways. First, they all use what they already know to formulate hypotheses about new information (Pearson & Johnson, 1978). Second, they use their strengths to reduce this stress (learn the information). Therefore, in this state of disequilibrium (new learning), people use what they already know to make sense of the new information. However, people differ not only on *what* they already know (knowledge-based differences) but also on *how* they integrate new information with what they already know (strategy-based differences).

Knowledge-based differences are evident in the scope of vocabulary knowledge and the variety of experiences that students have. Some children come to school with a rich variety of experiences and a well-developed oral language. Some children have had repeated experiences with books and have developed concepts about print. Other children come to school with limited experiences with reading events and require more exposure to a variety of experiences with both print and concepts.

These knowledge-based differences are accentuated by differences in problem-solving strategies. All remedial students do not learn the same way (Bond & Dykstra, 1967; Juel, 1984). Some students select meaning cues, while others select graphic cues. For example, Clay (1979) found that many young readers did not integrate cueing systems. Some of these students used a visual cueing system; they matched the missed word with the initial letters of other words they knew. Other students used the phonic cueing system; they matched the missed word to the sounds they knew.

Some students rely heavily on their background knowledge to form hypotheses while they are reading. These students check what they already know without thinking about the text. Other students rely heavily on the text to form their hypotheses while reading (Strange, 1980). Some students summarize stories, giving the overall gist of the text, while other students give explicitly stated information (Moore & Cunningham, 1984). Some students revise and monitor their model of meaning readily, while others need concrete facts before they revise their model of meaning (Collins, Brown, & Larkin, 1980). Some students organize information within broad, simultaneous categories, while others organize information in discrete, hierarchical categories (Kaufman & Kaufman, 1983).

Because the reading event is more stressful for remedial readers (Gentile, 1983), the demand for instruction using background knowledge and processing strengths is greater for them. By using appropriate instructional methods that utilize learning strengths, the diagnostic teacher can reduce the stress associated with the reading task and increase learning (Kogan, 1971). For example, teachers have differentiated prompting by using language that emphasizes the preferred cueing system and then encouraging the integration of word identification cueing systems (Clay, 1979). For instance, the child using the visual cueing system can be prompted with "what makes sense?" and "begins with. . . ." Teacher prompting can effectively differentiate instruction by using children's processing strengths and then encouraging them to incorporate more flexible strategies.

Being sensitive to individual differences requires that the diagnostic teacher evaluates two broad categories of learner differences. First, she evaluates what the students already know, because using what they already know will increase what is learned. Secondly, she assesses the way the students learned what they already know so that new information can be presented using the children's strengths. These two categories, knowledge-based differences and strategy-based differences, help the diagnostic teacher understand and identify individual differences among learners.

Guideline #7: Be Sensitive to Individual Differences

- *Adjust instruction to what children already know*
- *Tailor instruction to use students' strategies*
- *Reduce stress by using students' strengths*

Guideline #8: Foster a Reality-Based Approach to Instruction

Even though each child is different and some are harder to teach than others, the diagnostic teacher interacts with her students as a person. She is a participant in the learning process, sharing with them her reactions to reading events and student learning. Honest communication and sharing of the knowledge of the students' strategies for reading set the stage. In classrooms where real-life problem solving is stressed, the context makes sense. The teacher focuses on what is already known and builds relationships between new concepts and past experiences. In these classrooms, the key ideas become important and are evaluated from a "making-sense" perspective.

Individual sense making is encouraged through the use of *I* statements. The teacher models "I think . . .," talking about her own reading and thinking aloud about how she figured out a particular answer. Showing the *how* and modeling "I think . . ." release students from the necessity of having to do the process in the same way. "I do it this way" implies that others can do it a different way but that the question needs to be resolved. Furthermore, this attitude eases the need to conform and acknowledges that even though a particular process or strategy for solving problems is not a very effective strategy for reading, it may be effective in other situations. For the impulsive child, the teacher often remarks, "Someday your rapid-fire decision making may help you become a great artist, but when you are reading text, you need to think about what the author is trying to say."

Coupled with using *I* statements, another characteristic of reality instruction is to incorporate laughter into the remedial program. Laughter relaxes students and helps them develop a realistic assessment of their own reading behavior, as opposed to a tense, perfectionist view of their learning. The teacher becomes human as she talks about her own mistakes and coping behaviors, focusing on the process rather than the products of reading. As the teacher finds humor in her mistakes and proceeds to correct them, so too will remedial readers learn to reflect on their mistakes in a lighthearted manner, realizing that they can correct incongruencies as they read. Mistakes become a tool for learning rather than an indication of failure. Modeling self-correcting strategies in a relaxed atmosphere helps students develop a risk-taking attitude toward reading (Gentile, 1983) and increases their active reading behavior.

Neither using *I* statements that allow for individual variation in problem solving nor incorporating laughter during instruction precludes solving the reading problem. Effective teachers expect students to think, cope with their mistakes, and resolve problems as they read. Once the diagnostic teacher has made adjustments during instruction, she expects students to complete the necessary reading. She emphasizes that real life involves coping with limitations and using one's strengths to solve difficult problems.

In this way, she fosters reality-based instruction that gives the student more than a reading experience; it provides them with an experience to use what they already know to learn new information. She allows them to use their strengths to control the reading process, thus giving them a tool for further problem-solving situations. Solving the reading problem is associated with solving any problem. It involves taking risks by using what they already know, correcting mistakes as they try out new ideas, and resolving problems by using their strengths.

As the teacher learns to make sense in her classroom, creating meaning and modeling *I* statements (which release everyone from doing things in the same way), she encourages individual variation in problem solving. Furthermore, she interacts with her students in a relaxed and humorous atmosphere, where laughter is used to reduce stress and encourage a realistic assessment of reading behavior.

Finally, a reality approach to instruction is just that: it makes reading a real, personal event.

Guideline #8: Foster Reality-Based Instruction

- *Use I statements to acknowledge individual variation in problem solving*
- *Incorporate laughter to reduce stress*
- *Teach that real life requires coping with errors*

SUMMARY

Effective diagnostic teaching is coordinated by the reflective teacher, who bases her decision making on individual assessment of the readers' responses during instruction. Thus, at the core of diagnostic teaching is reflective teaching. The effective diagnostic teacher plans instruction, mediates learning, enables thinking, and responds honestly so that children experience success when reading interesting stories that require personal interpretation. Consequently, diagnostic teaching requires planning a whole reading event, the emphasis of which is success. Furthermore, the diagnostic teacher's goal is to create active, engaged readers who use what they already know to interpret text.

With this goal in mind, she encourages active reading by assessing reader response while she instructs. She is sensitive to the individual differences among her students and accepts the uniqueness of each reader in her classroom. She enables students to read with confidence, creating the expectation in students that they can read. Doing this, she reacts to the instructional event not only as the planner, mediator, and enabler, but also as a participant in the reading event. She acknowledges her own personal response to literature, modeling her control of the reading process and then fostering in her classroom real responses to reading, learning, and thinking.

The Diagnostic Teaching Session: An Overview

4

The diagnostic teaching session places a premium on tailoring programs that specifically fit problem readers. It provides a structure for lesson planning that uses both assessment and instruction to identify instructional alternatives and monitor their effectiveness. The session is composed of several lessons and may be spread out over several days or a week, depending on the amount of individual contact the teacher has with the student.

The session includes four elements that find expression in the various steps of the decision-making cycle (see Figure 4–1). *Guided contextual reading* focuses on meaningful interpretation of whole stories, while allowing students to demonstrate their strengths. *Skill and strategy instruction* explicitly remediates those skills and strategies that are inhibiting performance. *Continuous diagnostic assessment* uses the principles of dynamic assessment to monitor the effect of mediated instruction on students' learning. It is a way to assess growth by gathering data about students' unaided performance in the text that is used for guided contextual reading. During *personalized reading and writing,* both the students and the teacher engage in reading and writing for their own purposes and self-fulfillment. This chapter explains the instructional premises of the diagnostic teaching session as well as discusses its features, which are further elaborated in the chapters on instruction and assessment that follow.

Premises

The diagnostic teaching session is based on several premises:

1. Effective diagnostic teaching results from monitoring the effect instructional adjustments have on reading performance. Continuous

The diagnostic teaching session is based on a teaching procedure developed by Darrel D. Ray and used in the Oklahoma State University Reading Clinic. The author is grateful for the perceptive insights gleaned from her work in that clinic.

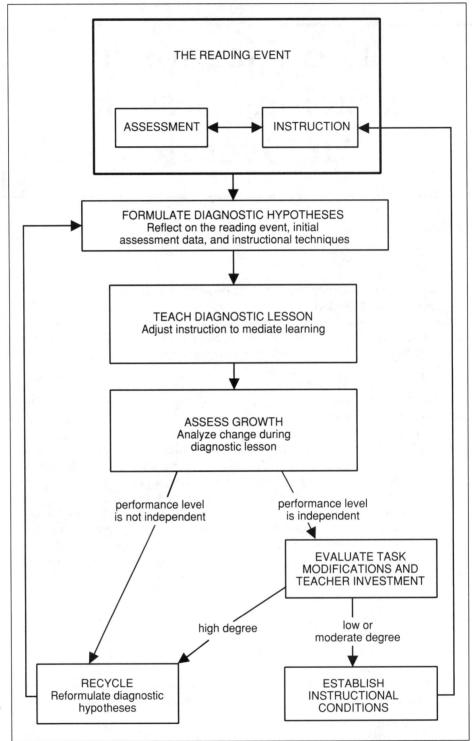

THE READING EVENT

ASSESSMENT ⟷ INSTRUCTION

FORMULATE DIAGNOSTIC HYPOTHESES
Reflect on the reading event, initial
assessment data, and instructional techniques

TEACH DIAGNOSTIC LESSON
Adjust instruction to mediate learning

ASSESS GROWTH
Analyze change during
diagnostic lesson

performance level
is not independent

performance level
is independent

EVALUATE TASK
MODIFICATIONS AND
TEACHER INVESTMENT

high degree

low or
moderate degree

RECYCLE
Reformulate diagnostic
hypotheses

ESTABLISH
INSTRUCTIONAL
CONDITIONS

Figure 4–1
The Decision-
Making Cycle of
Diagnostic
Teaching

diagnostic assessment provides baseline data about students' reading performance prior to instruction. During guided contextual reading, the reading lesson is adjusted to meet the students' needs. The difference between performance without aid and performance with aid is recorded using the data from these two elements.

2. Effective diagnostic teaching allows students to demonstrate their strengths (what they already know and do) by overlapping what is known and done with new information and new strategies. In other words, the diagnostic teacher uses the students' strengths to understand problem areas when reading a particular story. This enables problem readers to read with success.

3. Effective diagnostic teaching results in an interplay of contextual reading with skills and strategy instruction. Guided contextual reading uses whole stories to teach reading as interpreting and discussing text. Skill and strategy instruction provides minilessons in specific skills or strategies that are inhibiting reading performance.

4. Effective diagnostic teaching results from an interplay of implicit and explicit instruction. Guided contextual reading is characterized by implicit (guided) instruction during which the teacher acts as guide and participant in the learning process. The focus is on the meaningful interpretation of the text while practicing the whole skill of reading. Skill and strategy instruction, on the other hand, is characterized by explicit (direct) instruction in skills and strategies.

5. Effective diagnostic teaching results from an interplay of challenging and easy reading tasks (Beck, 1981). Schneider (1979) has found that a balance of high-success and medium-success reading tasks results in higher student achievement. Thus, reading materials are validated by the diagnostic teacher, and texts are chosen to maximize success on both independent and mediated reading levels. Guided contextual reading provides instruction in material that is moderately difficult, while personalized reading and writing are characterized by easy reading material. During skill and strategy instruction, the diagnostic teacher uses a combination of moderately difficult texts and easy texts, depending on the instructional needs of the learners.

These premises underlie the elements of the diagnostic teaching sessions. Taken together, the elements provide a vehicle for monitoring the effect of instructional adjustments and the interplay between instruction using strengths and instruction in areas of need, between contextual reading and skill lessons, between implicit and explicit instruction, and between challenging and easy reading tasks.

GUIDED CONTEXTUAL READING (GCR)

Each teaching session includes a guided contextual reading lesson (GCR) that focuses instruction on the communication of the ideas gleaned from reading whole stories. Guided contextual reading involves 60% of instruction in the diagnostic teaching session; therefore, students read contextual material for the majority of the time. The reading selection is of sufficient length to allow for comprehension of story line and character development; however, it is short enough to provide a sense of closure for the reader. During GCR, the diagnostic teacher differentiates instruction according to the strengths and reading levels of the students. Texts that maximize student performance are chosen. An instructional sequence is developed that uses the students' strengths; therefore, specialized techniques are selected that compensate for reading deficiencies so that the reading selection can be read fluently with comprehension. In other words, the diagnostic teacher asks, ''What can I do to make these stories more understandable for my students? Do I need specialized reading techniques to ensure fluent reading of these stories? At what point in the instructional sequence do I need to adjust my instruction?''

Students who have a limited ability to deal with oral language receive an extended vocabulary development program and direct experiences with the prerequisite concepts that are necessary to read a particular selection with understanding. For these students, GCR requires an extended amount of instruction before they read the story. Vocabulary maps (see ''Vocabulary Maps'' in Chapter 6), which require students and teacher to construct a visual diagram relating the vocabulary words to background knowledge, are used to introduce the story. Therefore, the instructional adjustment occurs prior to reading the story. This facilitates the students' understanding of the concepts in the story and increases their ability to read the story fluently with comprehension.

When students experience little difficulty with understanding what the words mean, however, the instructional adjustments are different. For students who show extreme difficulty with oral accuracy, the diagnostic teacher spends more time on word identification and fluency and less time on developing word meanings. Before a story is read, for example, a language experience story (see ''Language Experience'' in Chapter 6) might be written using the targeted vocabulary words. The teacher encourages rereading of this story to create an expectation for the vocabulary in the text. After the selected story is read, readers theatre scripts (see ''Readers Theatre'' in Chapter 6) could be constructed from the story so that increasing oral reading fluency becomes purposeful. The diagnostic teacher incorporates specialized techniques both before and after reading the story. For these students, the adjustments facilitate reading the story fluently with comprehension.

The guided contextual reading element can incorporate specialized methods, but the generic format of readiness, active reading, and reacting needs to be followed consistently in a text that is moderately difficult. *Readiness* means that the students' attention is focused on the key concepts of the story prior to reading. These concepts are then related to the students' own experiences. Predictions related to the story theme are developed by the teacher and students together, thus increasing students' active reading of the story. Open-ended questions need to focus on predictions that will engage the students in active reading through the entire length of the story (Pearson, 1982). Therefore, purposes or predictions that can be answered on the first page of the story hardly represent the main story theme.

During this brief discussion, the teacher anticipates problem vocabulary words and provides instruction in either word identification or word meaning. This instruction needs to be directly related to the story to be read, predictions that have been made, and the key concepts or story theme. Time is of the essence in diagnostic teaching. Consequently, only the important words, meanings, and concepts need to be stressed.

The second step of the guided contextual reading is silent reading to confirm the predictions. This is called *active reading.* Questioning is the key tool for the teacher as a dialogue about the story is maintained. Realizing the importance of questions, Beck and McKeown (1981) suggest that teachers develop story maps (see ''Story Maps'' in Chapter 6) to serve as a guide to logical questioning of story events. Rather than questions that are text-based, literal, and often unrelated to the story theme, questions developed from the story map should lead the students in developing an understanding of the purposeful actions of the characters to resolve the problems in the story. In other words, logical questions help summarize the main actions and events that occur in the story to resolve the problem.

The third step of guided contextual reading is *reacting* to the story as a whole. This requires an analysis of the story in terms of the characters' motivations, the author's purpose for writing the story, and other stories and experiences with similar themes. A key component of this phase is relating the story to similar personal experiences and analyzing the effect these experiences have on the comprehension of the story. Experiences may include other stories, movies, songs, and personal situations the students have encountered with similar plots and characters. Analysis should focus on the similarities and differences of these cases, using textual and nontextual information to support statements.

These steps form the framework for guided contextual reading, the major component of the diagnostic teaching session. During GCR, the diagnostic teacher differentiates instruction according to learner strengths in order to provide fluent reading with comprehension. The ultimate goal is to focus on the whole act of reading in connected text that will allow the students to integrate their prior knowledge with the text to develop personal interpretations.

FOCUS OF GUIDED CONTEXTUAL READING

- *Read whole stories*
- *Focus on meaningful interpretation of text*
- *Guide reading using the three-phase format of readiness, active reading, and reacting*
- *Differentiate instruction so that the text can be read fluently with comprehension*
- *Encourage personal interpretations*

SKILL AND STRATEGY INSTRUCTION (SAS)

Skill and strategy instruction (SAS) consists of a series of minilessons planned to develop and modify reading skills and reading strategies. As such, the diagnostic teacher selects texts that teach a designated skill or strategy. He carefully selects varying levels of text difficulty to provide for an interplay of easy and challenging reading. There are three requirements for the effective execution of skill and strategy instruction. First, prior to teaching a skill or strategy, a task analysis is conducted. Task analysis of reading performance pinpoints specific skills or strategies that, when directly taught, will increase students' reading performance (Wilson & Cleland, 1985). Second, after the task analysis has identified those skills and strategies inhibiting proficient reading, lessons that explicitly teach those strategies are developed. Explicit instruction is a minilesson that is constructed so that the teacher can easily explain and model how to use a particular skill or strategy. Finally, the targeted skill or strategy is monitored by the students and teacher using a graphic representation of progress.

Task Analysis

Task analysis identifies inhibiting behaviors and isolates the specific skill or strategy to be taught directly. Using the constructs of informal assessment, miscue analysis, and think aloud procedures (see Chapter 7), the diagnostic teacher identifies particular reading skills and strategies that if learned would easily increase student performance.

An initial informal assessment of Mary, for example, identifies fluency of word identification as inhibiting reading performance. Further analysis indicates that she can decode words in isolation. During the diagnostic lesson, however, it is evident that when miscues are made, Mary does not use what the word looks like or means in the story to correct the miscue. In other words, she does not ask herself, "What makes sense and starts with a . . . ?" This analysis indicates that she would benefit from explicit instruction in applying a making-sense framework, or using the overall context to self-correct errors. Therefore, the task analysis results in recommending strategy instruction in self-correction.

Explicit Teaching

After the task analysis has identified those skills and strategies inhibiting proficient reading, lessons that explicitly teach those strategies are selected. For most skills or strategies, the diagnostic teacher selects an easy text to introduce the new skill or strategy. This limits other possible problems in text interpretation. As the skill or strategy is learned, the diagnostic teacher increases the difficulty level of the text so as to lead students to use the new skill or strategy in reading situations that are moderately difficult. The activities need to be carefully chosen so that the teacher can model active reading. For Mary, therefore, an effective diagnostic technique would be an adapted repeated reading (see "Repeated Readings" in Chapter 6) that incorporates explicit teaching of the self-talk "What would make sense and starts with a . . ." as an intervention between the first and second readings.

Initially, students are informed of their inefficient strategies and shown the efficient counterpart, as modeled by the teacher (see "Explicit Teaching" in Chapter 6). After explicitly stating how the skill or strategy works, the teacher gives students a rationale for its inclusion in their program and tells them why doing these specific exercises will increase reading performance. Then students are led systematically through a series of short teacher-directed activities. In the first examples, the teacher models the desired reading behavior. Then students imitate the teacher's model.

In Mary's case, after the first reading of a selection, the teacher reviews miscues and suggests that reading would be more effective if she would check the miscue to see if it made sense. Then he explains how he would self-correct those errors using a making-sense framework and checking the initial letter. For example, before the second reading, the teacher explains that when reading breaks down, Mary should ask what would make sense and starts with a ". . . ." "If I had made this mistake," says the teacher, "I would have asked, 'What would Dad use that starts with a *sh*?' Then I would have corrected the sentence to read 'Dad shoveled the garden' and said, 'That's good! I can make sense of my reading by fixing up my mistakes.' Then I would continue to read. Now *you* try the next sentence with a miscue."

Finally, the diagnostic teacher reinforces active reading with task-specific comments. His comments are directed to the targeted tasks and students' improvement in those tasks. Furthermore, he encourages self-evaluation. For Mary, the teacher says, "I like the way you reread that sentence to correct your mistake. What do you say to yourself when you correct your mistakes?"

Graphing of Progress

Whatever skill or strategy targeted for explicit instruction needs to be monitored by some form of graphing. Graphing of reading progress provides an avenue for the students and teacher to discuss the strategies that the students are using and how this new skill or strategy will improve reading performance. The students, therefore, assume increasing responsibility for changing their reading behaviors. Progress charts can vary in complexity; however, the focus of charting should be the evaluation of progress toward the goal and how this progress fits into the whole skill of reading. Progress charts can be skill oriented, as in the sight-word card chart in Figure 4–2. Or they can be a self-evaluation chart like the chart of reading fluency in Figure 4–3. As progress toward the goal is made, the teacher allows students to assume the role of monitoring their own performances. He reinforces their trouble-shooting strategies and encourages self-evaluation.

Skill and strategy instruction is like many regular classroom lessons; however, it is different because it is specific to the readers' weaknesses. In diagnostic teaching,

Word	M	T	W	Th	F
GO	●	●	●	●	●
RUN		●	●	●	
COME	●		●		●
CANDY	●		●	●	●

Figure 4–2
Progress Chart for
Word Card Review

How I Read Today	M	T	W	Th	F
FLUENTLY IN PHRASES					
MOSTLY IN PHRASES				●	●
SOMETIMES WORD BY WORD		●	●		
MOSTLY WORD BY WORD	●				

Figure 4–3
Progress Chart for
Self-Evaluation of
Fluency

it is important to identify those skills and strategies that are limiting reading improvement. The diagnostic teacher asks, "What skills are limiting reading improvement? Will explicit instruction in these skills or strategies improve reading performance?" It is important to identify which skills will improve overall reading performance if they are taught directly. Therefore, SAS is different from regular classroom instruction's sequential introduction of reading skills because here the skill instruction is specific to students' reading development and identified through a task analysis.

In *Becoming a Nation of Readers*, Anderson, Hiebert, Scott, and Wilkinson report that "though children of all levels require direct instruction from teachers, low-ability children usually do less well than high-ability children when working alone or in small groups without a teacher" (1985, p. 91). Therefore, the key characteristic of SAS is the identification of specific skills and strategies that problem readers lack and that, when explicitly taught, will improve reading performance.

FOCUS OF SKILL AND STRATEGY INSTRUCTION

- *Task analysis of inhibiting skills and strategies*
- *Explicit instruction of those skills*
- *Graphing of student progress*

CONTINUOUS DIAGNOSTIC ASSESSMENT (CDA)

Continuous diagnostic assessment (CDA) contains an unaided, "at sight" assessment taken from the selected text used during guided contextual reading. This is the vehicle used to monitor reading performance. During the other elements, the diagnostic teacher adjusts instruction as the students read; therefore, the students' performance without instruction is not evaluated. Continuous diagnostic assessment allows the diagnostic teacher to collect a sample of reading behavior prior to instruction. Then the diagnostic teacher compares performance data without guided instruction (CDA) and reading performance data with instruction (GCR). This sample of reading behavior allows the diagnostic teacher to develop hypotheses about the changing reading needs of the students.

The assessment provides two kinds of information. First it provides information about the appropriateness of the text that is being used during the guided contextual reading element. If the material proves too difficult (at frustration level) or too easy (at independent level), an alternate text is selected and checked for an appropriate match (see Appendix for procedures to determine performance level). Basically the teacher asks himself, "Am I using an appropriate text (moderately difficult) in GCR?" Second, this assessment provides baseline data so that the teacher can analyze the difference between unaided reading performance and the students' reading performance with instruction. He asks himself, "Is the student profiting from my instruction? Is there a difference between the reading performance in GCR and CDA?"

To monitor progress, the teacher follows the procedures found in Chapter 7, "Gathering Diagnostic Data." First, a segment from the text used in guided contextual reading is read without prior instruction (at sight). A passage about 150–200 words long is selected and questions written that focus on the main idea or problem, key facts or events, key vocabulary words, and inferences. The selection is read orally or silently, depending on the reading concerns for the students (see Chapter 7). Error or miscue rates and percentage of comprehension are calculated. Decisions are made as to the appropriateness of the text. If the selection is at frustration reading level (oral accuracy below 1/10 running words and comprehension below 50%), the teacher immediately moves to easier reading material in the GCR segment. For example, Chris reads a selection from an end of second-grade text with an error rate of 1/7 and 60% comprehension on constructed questions. Since this indicates frustration-level reading, the clinician selects an easier text to use during guided contextual reading.

If the selection reflects the mediated reading level, the diagnostic teacher continues using the material and records errors to establish a pattern of reading performance. For example, Sally reads a selection from an end of second-grade text with an error rate of 1/15 and 80% comprehension. After three samplings in this text, the error pattern indicates that the substitution errors most prevalent are key vocabulary words that are limiting comprehension. The diagnostic teacher develops a program of word identification based on word meanings related to both the text to be read and the background knowledge. He adapts instruction during GCR by using a vocabulary map of key words to increase both word identification and word meanings of those words (see "Vocabulary Maps" in Chapter 6). After the story is read, he returns to the map and adds new understandings to reinforce word meaning with word identification.

If the selection is at an independent level, a more difficult text needs to be evaluated in the continuous diagnostic assessment phase. The diagnostic teacher selects a more difficult text and prepares a segment for evaluation. For example, Toni can read silently a segment from a third-grade text with 100% comprehension. There is no previous instruction before this segment is read. Therefore, a text at the fourth-grade level is selected. An on-level assessment is conducted and scored. This on-level evaluation is read silently with 70% comprehension on the constructed questions. As a result, the text used in GCR is changed to the fourth-grade text, which reflects a level that is challenging and has a moderate success rate.

In all the elements, the diagnostic teacher is assessing the response of the children to instruction. To monitor progress, however, a segment of a text is read without prior instruction (at sight). Continuous diagnostic assessment is an integral part of the diagnostic teaching session because it provides the framework for a dynamic assessment by providing baseline data about the students' performance in the selected text without instruction.

FOCUS OF CONTINUOUS DIAGNOSTIC ASSESSMENT

- *Monitoring of reading behavior*
- *Maintenance of baseline data*
- *Analysis of reading growth*

PERSONALIZED READING AND WRITING (PRW)

In personalized reading and writing (PRW), students are engaged in 10 to 15 minutes of personal reading and writing. This element offers students a time of quiet reflection to respond personally to the language arts. Writing and reading "positively influence each other and both develop as a natural extension of children's desire to communicate" (Gambrell, 1985, p. 512). In this phase, time is set aside for the students and teacher to read and write for their own purposes. Easing the structure of the teaching session is crucial. If the students do not experience "choosing to read and write," they may not choose to read and write for their own purposes later on as adults.

For the silent reading time (see "Sustained Silent Reading" in Chapter 6), children select books, magazines, newspapers, or their own writing to read during the designated time period. This is a time for students to read for their own individual purposes. As Berglund and Johns (1983, p. 534) suggest, "It frees their minds to enjoy reading on their own terms in materials they have selected." En-couraging students to read books for their own enjoyment rather than instruc-tional purposes develops the desire to read. They learn to ask themselves, "What do I want to read about? What kind of stories to do I find more interesting?" This facilitates habits of book selection and defining interests (Trelease, 1985).

Students are taught to match the book to their reading levels by using the rule of thumb (Glazer, 1984). This means that as they read a page from their selected book, they put a finger on each unknown word starting with the little finger. If they reach their thumb before the end of the page, the book is too difficult and another should be selected. Therefore, personalized reading and writing experience encourages children to select books they can successfully read and moves the con-trol of the selection of reading material from the teacher to the students. In fact, during this element, the students are in control; there is no have-to reading. If the students want to skip pages, look at pictures, laugh or cry, they can read and think whatever they want. The students control what they learn from books.

For the sustained silent writing (see "Dialogue Journals" in Chapter 6), the students and teacher communicate through writing. During each session, students write to the teacher about anything of interest or importance to them. Following the journal entry, the teacher comments with a brief, personal, and honest reac-tion to what was written. For example, a student wrote: "Today my cat died." The teacher responded: "I bet you are sad. My cat died last year and I cried." According to Glazer (1984), "comments concerning content should be empathetic, noncritical, and encouraging." In other words, the teacher responds during each session to what the children have written.

The teacher comments can be an empathetic response or can ask for more information. Such comments (e.g., "That sounds like fun, I would like to know more about . . ." or "Can you describe what it looked like?") allow the diagnostic teacher to encourage the fluent writing of ideas without evaluations. The focus is communication between students and teacher; therefore, the teacher should not correct any spelling or grammatical errors.

The teacher encourages the writing of ideas as he models correct writing forms in his responses to the student. This stream-of-consciousness communication is based on the students' personal, real-life experiences. The topics, length, and for-mat are self-selected. As children compose text, they think about ways to express ideas. This thinking about how ideas are expressed sensitizes students to the visual aspects of text (how words are spelled and the order of words in sentences); con-sequently, students become more aware of how words are used.

Personal reading and writing develop within students an interest in reading and writing for their own enjoyment. It releases students from the have-to assignments made during direct and guided instruction, thus placing them in con-trol of their interests, ideas, and emotions. Besides being an avenue of control, personal reading is a major source of knowledge about word meaning and sentence and text structure (Anderson et al., 1985). Personal writing is a major vehicle for self-reflection because the students have written their thoughts and can now reflect on them. Furthermore, during personal reading and writing, there are no wrong answers. In fact, there are *no* answers; thus students cannot fail.

FOCUS OF PERSONALIZED READING AND WRITING

- *Self-direction*
- *Personal response*
- *Time for quiet reflection*

SUMMARY

Reflecting on his roles as a diagnostic teacher and the variables of the reading event, the diagnostic teacher plans a teaching session which allows him to assess and instruct at the same time. During guided contextual reading, he guides students' learning; therefore, he is constantly asking what will make this a successful reading event for the students. As he teaches the planned lesson, he encourages active reading by focusing on deriving meaning from text. He probes with leading questions: "What did the author mean when she said? Does that (the answer) make sense in relation to the other ideas presented in the story?"

During skill and strategy instruction, the diagnostic teacher decides which skills and strategies would, if directly taught, result in higher reading achievement. Then he develops short demonstration activities to explicitly teach a specific skill or strategy. He uses progress charts to encourage self-evaluation of reading performance. Therefore, he builds responsibility within the students by gradually giving them the control to monitor their own reading behavior.

During continuous diagnostic assessment, the diagnostic teacher monitors the effects of his instruction by comparing unaided reading performance and mediated reading behavior.

During personalized reading and writing, the diagnostic teacher allows time for students to read and write for their own purposes. In these situations, the readers are in control of the meaning they derive from print.

The format of the diagnostic teaching session allows the diagnostic teacher to develop instructional alternatives that fit the strengths and needs of problem readers. By systematically planning instruction, the diagnostic teacher provides learning opportunities that enable problem readers to become independent learners.

Selecting
Techniques

5

Knowing *how* instruction occurs allows the teacher to modify her teaching effectively during the reading event. To mediate learning, she thinks about the techniques she uses and their influence on learning. A thorough analysis of each technique is necessary to provide the most efficient reading instruction. Therefore, this chapter classifies each teaching technique in the following ways:

1. the targeted reading skill
2. the targeted reasoning strategy
3. the point at which the technique is implemented during the lesson
4. the type of text
5. the mode of response
6. the type of structure embodied in implementing the technique
7. the cognitive process emphasized during implementation

This classification serves two functions: (a) to select techniques that fit the readers' patterns and (b) to focus instructional modifications during the reading event.

Initially, the diagnostic teacher selects a technique and analyzes its underlying characteristics. This analysis increases her effectiveness in implementing a particular technique as well as broadens her knowledge of instructional alternatives. According to Brophy, "most teachers seem to be reluctant to change their routines even if they are not working well, and when they do make changes, they tend to be minor adjustments rather than major revisions. This may occur mostly because teachers simply lack readily available alternatives, at least alternatives that they perceive to be preferable to the orginal plan" (1984, p. 83). Another reason teachers resist change is due to a lack of knowledge about why one technique may be more effective in certain situations. Chapters 5 and 6 provide reasons why one technique might be more effective under certain conditions than another. Knowledge about techniques allows teachers to make instructional changes that facilitate student learning and is a key factor in the decision-making cycle (see Figure 5–1).

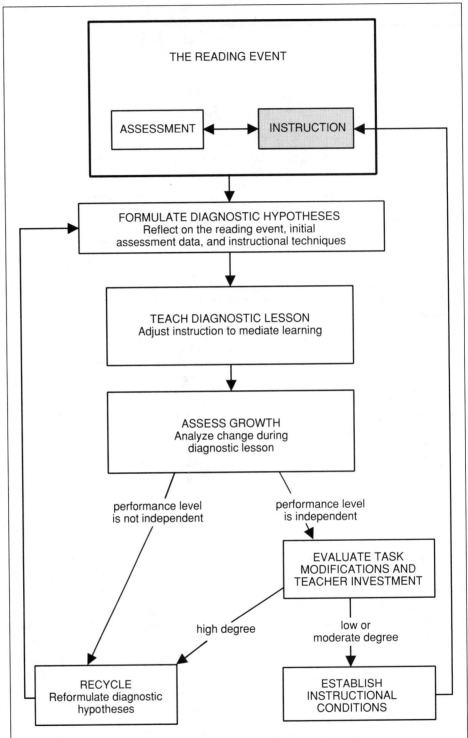

Figure 5–1
The Decision-
Making Cycle of
Diagnostic
Teaching

Knowledge of the underlying orientation of the techniques is important when considering an approach to instruction that mediates learning. Basically, reading is an interactive process where readers use various sources of information (reader-based and text-based) at the same time to interpret text. However, techniques differ in which information sources are emphasized during instruction. Some techniques emphasize reader-based sources of information, while others stress text-based sources of information. Furthermore, problem readers often experience a deficit in either a skill or strategy that causes them to shift away from one information source. They compensate by using their strength and thus eliminate a need to use their deficient knowledge source (Stanovich, 1980). Therefore, a variety of techniques that remediate major reading problems have been classified, enabling the diagnostic teacher to select techniques that match the students' strengths as she is teaching a new task. As the task is learned, she can select techniques that have a more integrative instructional approach. The diagnostic teacher can thus use learner strengths to show students how to use their weaker information sources when text interpretation breaks down.

As she selects techniques, the teacher chooses those techniques that approach reading using what students already know and how they learned what they already know. To select appropriate techniques, the diagnostic teacher asks herself questions about the students' reading:

- Is there a skill (the targeted skill) that my students are not using when they read? If so, how should I mediate learning so that they incorporate this skill using their strengths?
- Is there a strategy (the targeted strategy) that my students are not using? If so, how should I approach instruction so that they can use the new strategies in combination with the strategies they already use?
- At what point during the instructional framework can I implement a technique so that the students can read fluently with comprehension?
- What technique will best suit the type of text I am using?
- How much explicit instruction do these students need at this time?
- If my students are compensating for deficits by using a strength in cognitive processing, can I match this strength in order to show them how to use their weaker processing style in combination with their strength?

Diagnostic teaching techniques from different views of reading have been classified according to these key questions so that the diagnostic teacher can match the students' strengths and needs to design lessons that mediate learning for each child.

CLASSIFYING TECHNIQUES BY READING SKILLS

Although meaningful interpretation of the text is the ultimate goal of reading instruction, certain tasks consume a major portion of children's thinking capacity as they develop. The following explanation will provide a discussion first of the process of learning related to the targeted skills and then of the major skills in-volved at a given stage. Even though these skills have been associated with typical techniques, there are a variety of ways to develop each skill from various points of view. The diagnostic teacher selects the technique that mediates learning best for the particular child.

Stage One

For beginning readers, the major task is the association of oral language with its written equivalent. Young children have learned to communicate using oral language within a social context. To read, however, they must infer the com-municative intent of printed words. This new task places demands on learners. They must learn that printed words represent both a concept and spoken words. Therefore, the task of young readers is to develop this functional concept of printed language as well as the recognition of letters and sounds.

As these concepts of print develop, children begin to associate meaning with written words in stories. They automatically recognize a group of words at sight. They say, "I know a word that starts with *h* and is the same length, so this word must be *hat*." The development of a sight word vocabulary indicates that children are reasoning about the relationship between grahic symbols and meaning. Whether children use sounds, visual features, or background knowledge, their major task is to develop this automatic sight vocabulary, which generally consumes a major portion of their thinking through the middle of first-grade reading level.

TARGETED SKILLS FOR STAGE ONE

Sight Word Vocabulary

Based on
- *Association of prior knowledge with printed words*
- *Ability to remember the visual form (visual memory)*
- *Ability to use the initial letter and word length to remember words*

Typical techniques
- *Language experience method*
- *Sight word method*
- *Word cards*

Stage Two

As children can read more words and longer stories, the major reading tasks change from oral reading to silent reading and from sight word recognition to decoding by analogy. Since they can read longer stories, they encounter new words that are not contained in their sight vocabularies. Therefore, emerging readers develop new skills and strategies to accommodate these new tasks. They begin to decode words by sound analogies (i.e., "I know a sight word that looks similar to this new word; I will try substituting the sounds to see if this new word makes sense in the story"). This stage of reading development is marked by the ability to use the alphabetic principle; that words are made of sounds and letters that have a consistent pattern. Therefore, they match these patterns to known sight words.

This new strategy allows young children to read longer stories; silent reading, therefore, becomes more efficient than oral reading. Now in order to talk about what they read, they retell the story or answer questions. Since the simple stories in graded text place a high demand on literal comprehension, children's attention is focused on the logical development of a story line and proving answers using the text.

These skills occupy children's thinking capacity through the end of second grade, where techniques dealing with word attack and literal comprehension are most appropriately employed.

TARGETED SKILLS FOR STAGE TWO

Word Attack

Based on
- *Ability to blend sounds (auditory synthesis)*
- *Ability to divide words into their sounds (sound segmentation)*
- *Use of sound-symbol word patterns*

Typical techniques
- *Synthetic phonics*
- *Analytic phonics*

Literal Comprehension

Based on
- *Understanding of logical relationships in text (textual organization)*
- *How words go together in a sentence*
- *Background knowledge*

Typical techniques

- *Teacher questioning*
- *Story maps*

Stage Three

As reading development continues, the simple strategies of using known sight words, decoding by sound analogy, and thinking about the facts of a story are no longer sufficient to gain meaning from text. Because sentences are longer and more complex, children must use new strategies to interpret text. Developing readers respond with new strategies. At this stage, fluent word identification is necessary in order to allow more thinking capacity for word, sentence, and idea meaning. Because words with multiple meanings are used in the text, students must use more than decoding by analogy to figure out unknown words. Using sentence context to decode unknown words and to develop word meanings becomes a major task for these readers. Furthermore, this more difficult text has an abundance of new word meanings. Readers at this stage must think about what each new word means and how it is like other words and ideas that they already know. This stage occupies students' thinking capacity through the end of the fifth-grade reading level, where techniques developing fluency, sentence comprehension, and vocabulary knowledge are most appropriately employed.

TARGETED SKILLS FOR STAGE THREE

Chall's Stage 3

Fluency

Based on
- *Automatic association of what words look like with what words mean*
- *Breaking sentences into thought units*
- *Use of background knowledge to predict sentence meaning*

Typical techniques
- *Chunking method*
- *Repeated readings*

Sentence Comprehension

Based on
- *Use of sentence meaning to develop word meanings*
- *Use of context to organize information*
- *Familiarity with the content (background knowledge)*

Typical techniques
- *Cloze instruction*
- *Sentence combining*

Meaning Vocabulary

Based on
- *Requisite background knowledge*
- *Identification of likenesses and differences of word meanings*

Stage Four

As students read more difficult text, they find that the strategies that deal primarily with textual information are no longer sufficient. At this reading level, authors develop complex relationships that require an interpretation of text-based information within a reader's personal world view. Therefore, readers must be able to shift between text-based and reader-based processing to gain meaning from text. They read for a variety of purposes and monitor their own understanding of text. This stage of development continues through adult reading, where techniques emphasizing vocabulary knowledge and literal comprehension (described in Stage Three) are orchestrated with developing nonliteral comprehension and study skills.

TARGETED SKILLS FOR STAGE FOUR

Nonliteral Comprehension

Based on
> • *Integration of background knowledge with textual information*
> • *Self-monitoring (Does that make sense?)*
> • *Self-questioning (I wonder what the author is going to say that is important to remember?)*

Typical techniques
> • *Self-questioning*
> • *Story drama*

Study Skills

Based on
> • *Ability to organize information*
> • *Knowledge of question-answer relationships*
> • *Use of the structure of text*

Typical techniques
> • *SQ3R (survey, question, read, recite, review)*
> • *QAR's (question-answer relationships)*

Conclusion

The instructional techniques in this book have been analyzed as to the major skill developed when they are used in a diagnostic program. The diagnostic teacher identifies students' skill needs and provides mediated instruction showing students how a particular skill fits into their repertoire of reading strategies. Although the techniques can be used to develop different reading tasks, they are most efficient when matched with students exhibiting that instructional need. When selecting skill activities, the teacher must also remember that students might not use a particular skill or strategy due to a deficit. Instruction that begins with students' strengths is often more effective (see Wilson & Cleland, 1985, for an elaboration of skill strengths and weaknesses).

Wean the reader slowly from the strength to the weakness.

For example, Student A uses background knowledge to identify unknown words; however, this is not always an effective strategy. He has a limited ability to manipulate the sounds of language (i.e., he cannot segment sounds and then synthesize them to form words). In this case the diagnostic teacher develops a large sight vocabulary using the impress method (see "Impress Method" in Chapter 6). This allows the student to bypass word attack and use background knowledge and sentence comprehension to identify unknown words.

Although use of word attack knowledge would increase this student's reading performance, instruction in word attack is futile without the ability to synthesize or segment sounds. As the student's reading fluency increases, the diagnostic teacher encourages decoding by analogy using this prompt: "What would make sense (strength) and sounds like another word you know (weakness)?" This latter instructional task is accomplished easily using repeated readings (see "Repeated Readings" in Chapter 6) with an intervention of strategy instruction.

In the preceding example, the diagnostic teacher used the strength of the problem reader to develop a successful reading program. Then she showed the student how to use his weaker skill area at times when using only his strength would not solve the reading problem. It is often necessary to try a variety of instructional techniques for these problem readers. For example, Student B is having difficulty with sight word identification. He is a bilingual student and has limited language development with no skill in sound synthesis. Typical techniques to develop sight word identification (word cards, language experience, etc.) prove futile until the new words are tied to a conceptual base. In this case, vocabulary maps (see "Vocabulary Maps" in Chapter 6) are used to tie background knowledge to the sight words so that the student can associate what the words mean with what the words look like.

Each technique in Table 5–1 has been identified according to the targeted reading skill developed when the technique is implemented in a diagnostic program. Within each major skill area, the techniques differ in the focus of instruction, which will be delineated in subsequent tables.

Table 5–1
Classifying
Techniques by
Reading Skills

	Sight Words	Word Attack	Fluency	Meaning Vocabulary	Sentence Comprehension	Literal Comprehension	Nonliteral Comprehension	Study Skills
Alternate Writing					*	*	*	
Analytic Phonics		*						
Chunking			*		*			
Cloze Instruction				*	*			
Contextual Processing				*	*			
Direct Experience				*				
Directed Reading Activity				*		*	*	
Directed Reading-Thinking Activity						*	*	
Distar Reading		*						
Echo Reading	*		*					
Experience-Text-Relationship				*		*	*	
Feature Analysis Grid				*				
Guided Imagery/Comprehension						*	*	*
Guided Imagery/Language Experience	*		*					
Herringbone Technique						*		*
Impress Method	*		*					
Language Experience	*		*					
Linguistic Method	*	*						
Listening-Thinking Activity						*	*	
Metaphors				*				*
Multisensory Approaches	*	*						
Phonograph Approach		*						
Predictable Language	*		*					
Prediction Maps						*	*	
Question-Answer Relationships						*	*	*
Question-Generation Strategy						*	*	*

73

Table 5–1
continued

	Sight Words	Word Attack	Fluency	Meaning Vocabulary	Sentence Comprehension	Literal Comprehension	Nonliteral Comprehension	Study Skills
Readers Theatre			*			*	*	
Reading Logs						*	*	
Reciprocal Teaching						*	*	*
Repeated Readings		*	*					
ReQuest						*	*	
Secondary Reading Sequence	*		*			*		
Self-Directed Questioning						*	*	
Sentence Combining					*			
Sight Word Approach	*							
SQ3R						*		*
Story Drama						*	*	
Story Maps						*	*	
Story Writing					*	*	*	
Summarization						*	*	*
Synthetic Phonics		*						
Talking Books	*		*					
Triple Read Outline						*		*
Visualization				*			*	
Vocabulary Maps				*		*	*	
Word Cards	*	*	*					

Note: 1) These classifications represent common uses for the techniques. Techniques can be adapted to accommodate the task demands of related skill areas; thus, word attack technique (synthetic phonics) might be used to establish a sight word vocabulary. 2) The lesson frameworks of explicit teaching, implicit teaching, dialogue journals, and sustained silent reading are not classified.

CLASSIFYING TECHNIQUES
BY REASONING STRATEGY

Equally important to skill instruction is instruction in the reasoning strategies that accompany effective execution of reading skills. Readers do not automatically apply skills; instead, they strategically reason about what they are reading, applying skills when necessary. As students read, they select, sort, and evaluate the text against what they know. In essence, readers are involved in an active problem-solving process. They predict what is going to be communicated. Then they select and sort important information from the text and relate it to their prior knowledge. Next they confirm or revise their predictions based on new textual information. Finally, they elaborate their understanding. This reasoning process takes place automatically until readers cannot make sense of what they are reading.

Although children with reading problems exhibit individual variations in the strategies they employ, a body of research indicates that poor readers are not actively involved in constructing meaning (Paris & Myers, 1981). They view good reading as effortless; consequently, they do not make plans or vary their strategies as they read. Effective readers, however, are active. Before reading, "good readers use what they know about the topic, the type of text, the author's purposes and their own purposes to make predictions about the content of the text" (Duffy & Roehler, 1987, p. 416).

Predicting requires guessing about what the author is going to say. It occurs before and during reading.

As they read, effective readers remain tentative and revise their predictions frequently using a variety of reasons for their revisions. They intertwine the sources of information for revision (the text, background knowledge, or both) and the strategies for revisions (ignore the problem and read more, reread to check the facts, read ahead to clarify information, and consult an expert source if necessary) (Collins & Smith, 1980). Effective readers stop, reflect, and flexibly shift between reader-based processing ("Does that make sense?") and text-based processing ("What did the text say?"). This is called *monitoring reading*.

Monitoring requires checking the text or one's experience to see if what one is reading is making sense. Monitoring occurs during reading.

Finally, effective readers fit new information into what they know by elaborating relationships among information. They generate new thoughts by relating what they are reading to what they know, creating new connections among ideas (McNeil, 1987).

Elaborating requires relating new information to what is known in order to remember it. Thus the new information becomes part of what is known. Elaborating occurs during and after reading.

Problem readers, however, are less active. Their reading can break down in the predicting, monitoring, or elaborating phase of the reasoning process. Some readers do not use what they know to think about what the author might say. They read exactly what the text says without thinking about what it might mean. They need instruction that helps them make predictions about what the text would mean. Other readers venture a guess but hold on to the initial prediction even when the text does not support it. Other readers revise their predictions but change

Table 5–2
Classifying
Techniques by
Reasoning Strategy

	Decoding *Print Processing*	Comprehension *Meaning Processing*
Prediction under predictor	Echo Reading Guided Imagery/LEA Impress Method Language Experience Listening-Thinking Activity Predictable Language Secondary Reading Sequence Talking Books	Cloze Instruction Directed Reading-Thinking Activity Experience-Text-Relationship Guided Imagery/Comprehension Listening-Thinking Activity ReQuest Self-Directed Questioning SQ3R Vocabulary Maps
Monitoring over predictor	Chunking Guided Imagery/LEA Language Experience Predictable Language Readers Theatre Repeated Readings	Directed Reading-Thinking Activity Herringbone Prediction Maps Reading Logs Reciprocal Teaching Self-Directed Questioning Triple Read Outline Visualization
Elaboration	Readers Theatre Repeated Readings Secondary Reading Sequence Word Cards	Alternate Writing Experience-Text-Relationship Guided Imagery/Comprehension Herringbone Technique Prediction Maps Question-Answer Relationships Question-Generation Strategy Reading Logs Reciprocal Teaching SQ3R Story Drama Story Maps Summarization Triple Read Outline Visualization

only one part of it, such as the *who, when, where,* or *how* information (Dybdahl, 1983). Some readers rely too heavily on the text or their background knowledge when monitoring their reading. They do not shift between knowledge sources to check their reading. These students need instruction in how to monitor their understanding of text. Other students fail to elaborate the relationship between what they know and the text; therefore, they cannot remember what they read. These readers need instruction in how to reason while they are reading.

Demonstrating reasoning strategies can improve the reading performance of poor readers (Duffy & Roehler, 1987). However, the diagnostic teacher needs to evaluate the various instructional techniques. Some techniques lend themselves readily to talking about the different strategies of effective reading; others do not. Therefore, diagnostic techniques have been classified here according to the reading strategy that they develop: predicting, monitoring, or elaborating. In addition, techniques can teach the reasoning process related to print processing or meaning processing. Table 5–2 classifies techniques for reasoning while processing print and meaning.

CLASSIFYING TECHNIQUES BY IMPLEMENTATION IN THE INSTRUCTIONAL FRAMEWORK AND TEXT TYPE

Another instructional decision involves deciding when to implement a technique within the reading event. The appropriate placement of instructional techniques facilitates students' learning by providing instruction at the precise point in the instructional framework at which the students can no longer learn independently. In other words, the instructional lesson is a planned exchange between independent student learning and teacher-guided learning. If the teacher intervenes at appropriate instructional points, she can move the students to more complex reading strategies. Therefore, the diagnostic teacher analyzes which phase of reading instruction is best to mediate these students' learning.

The diagnostic teacher first identifies the major presenting problem or reading task for the students. To read fluently with comprehension, some students need assistance with print processing because once they can read the words, they will comprehend. Other students call words fluently but need assistance in how to derive meaning from these words once they are recognized. Techniques can be classified, therefore, according to whether the students need assistance in print processing or meaning processing.

Instructional Framework

The diagnostic teacher then analyzes the instructional framework. There are several critical points in the lesson framework for decision making. To increase story understanding, techniques can supplement instruction either before, during, or after reading the text (McNeil, 1987). Sometimes it is most appropriate to provide instruction prior to reading so the students can read the text fluently. For example, students might need instruction in word meanings or word identification as related to the story. Before reading, some students will need assistance to think about how what they already know will help them interpret text.

Another critical point in the instructional framework is during the reading of the text. During this part of the lesson, the teacher needs to encourage inferencing, elaboration, and monitoring of text comprehension. In these instances, she intervenes during reading to build reading strategies such as self-questioning, summarization, visualizing difficult parts, and organizing the information.

The final critical point in the instructional framework is after the reading of the text. To mediate learning here, the diagnostic teacher provides instruction in integrating the text with personal experiences, organizing the information, and self-assessment of reading comprehension. She may also need to reinforce word recognition strategies or develop fluency. In any case, using appropriate diagnostic teaching techniques at the critical points in the instructional framework increases student learning.

Type of Text

The selection of appropriate techniques also depends on the type of text (narrative or expository) that is going to be read (McNeil, 1987). Techniques are often developed for a specific kind of text format. For example, story maps (see "Story Maps" in Chapter 6) are designed for narrative text and teach elements of story grammar, while reciprocal teaching (see "Reciprocal Teaching" in Chapter 6) is designed for expository text and teaches summarizing through the use of topic sentences. Techniques are most effective when used with the appropriate kind

Table 5-3
Classifying Techniques by Instructional Framework and Text Type

	Print Processing	
	Narrative	*Expository*
Readiness	Distar Reading	Contextual Processing
	Guided Imagery/LEA	Language Experience
	Impress Method	Metaphors
	Language Experience	Secondary Reading Sequence
	Linguistic Method	Vocabulary Maps
	Listening-Thinking Activity	
	Secondary Reading Sequence	
	Sight Word Approach	
	Synthetic Phonics	
	Talking Books	
Active Reading	Echo Reading	Secondary Reading Sequence
	Language Experience	
	Predictable Language	
Postreading— Reinforcement of Print Processing	Analytic Phonics	Cloze Instruction
	Chunking	Multisensory Approach
	Multisensory Approach	Repeated Readings
	Readers Theatre	Word Cards
	Repeated Readings	
	Word Cards	

Note: Only the techniques that teach print processing are classified. The lesson frameworks of explicit teaching, implicit teaching, dialogue journals, and sustained silent reading are not classified.

Table 5–4 Classifying Techniques by Instructional Framework and Text Type		
Meaning Processing		
	Narrative	*Expository*
Readiness	Direct Experience	Direct Experience
	Experience-Text-Relationships	Experience-Text-Relationships
	Guided Imagery/Comprehension	Feature Analysis Grid
	Visualization	Guided Imagery/Comprehension
	Vocabulary Maps	Metaphors
		Visualization
		Vocabulary Maps
Active Reading	Directed Reading-Thinking Activity	Herringbone Technique
	Prediction Maps	Reciprocal Teaching
	Reading Logs	ReQuest
	ReQuest	SQ3R
	Self-Directed Questioning	Triple Read Outline
	Story Drama	
	Story Maps	
Postreading— Discussion of Meaning	Directed Reading-Thinking Activity	Experience-Text-Relationships
	Experience-Text-Relationships	Feature Analysis Grid
	Sentence Combining	Question-Answer Relationships
	Story Drama	Question-Generation Strategy
	Story Maps	Summarization
	Summarization	Vocabulary Maps

Note: Only the techniques that teach meaning processing are classified. The lesson frameworks of explicit teaching, implicit teaching, dialogue journals, and sustained silent reading are not classified.

of text. The classification of techniques in Tables 5–3 and 5–4 is based on three instructional decisions: the type of text (expository or narrative), the presenting problem (meaning or print processing), and the phase of instruction where guided instruction is most appropriate (readiness, active reading, or postreading reaction).

CLASSIFYING TECHNIQUES BY MODE OF RESPONSE

An additional decision about instruction is the kind of response mode that will be used. Readers' responses can be either oral or written. The diagnostic teacher assesses students individually by asking herself, "Will discussing or writing help this student's reading performance? Which mode is this student's strength? Which mode will facilitate teaching the skills and strategies that this student needs?" Both a verbal discussion and writing a response change the task. Some students prefer to talk, while others prefer to write about what they read. Both processes are constructive and facilitate reading growth.

Writing and Reading

Much attention has recently been devoted to the writing process as an aid to improving reading. Writing about what they read facilitates reading by giving students a written record of their thoughts so that they can later reflect on how they constructed meaning. The record offers the diagnostic teacher a tool for discussing how the students think. She can talk about the strategies they are using to construct meaning. As writing brings inner thoughts into the open for verification, it facilitates discussing the inner thoughts that happen as readers construct meaning.

Writing also facilitates reading because the instructional focus is on the process of constructing meaning. Reading and writing require similar processes: both readers and writers make plans about how they are going to construct meaning; both monitor their understandings to see if they are making sense; both revise their thinking by rereading, using what was written and comparing it to what they know; both elaborate what was written, making connections between what was written and what is known to create new ideas (Tierney & Pearson, 1983). In these ways, both reading and writing are constructive processes where one facilitates the other.

In addition, writing facilitates reading because both systems use the same writing conventions. Both use letters grouped together to form words, words grouped together to form sentences, and so on. The way the groups are formed follows certain patterns or conventions. Writing heightens students' awareness of how to use these conventions when they read (Duffy & Roehler, 1986). For instance, a young writer trying to spell *mother* thinks about how that word looked in the book *Are You My Mother?* Writing heightens an awareness of the visual features of words. It accomplishes the same task as flashing word cards. Writing facilitates reading through three avenues: reflective thinking, constructing meaning, and using writing conventions.

Discussion and Reading

Much recent attention has also been focused on classroom interactions that facilitate learning. Discussing what students read does facilitate reading growth. When they verbalize their understanding of what they read, students reconstruct the text so that they can communicate their understanding to others. This is a constructive process, not simply a recall process. Readers think to themselves: "What is important and how do I communicate that to the others in the group? What did I learn that I want to communicate to this group? Did I think of something in a new light that would help others understand?"

Social interaction facilitates reading, therefore, because it provides a vehicle for interpersonal communication. The strategies, plans, and processes of meaning construction developed through social interaction later become individual mental processes (Vygotsky, 1978). In other words, thinking about what is read is facilitated by social activities that encourage students to elaborate and explain their thinking. In this social situation, the teacher also explains and elaborates her thinking. This allows the student to use tools for thinking (words, plans, strategies, ideas, etc.). The teacher responds, encouraging a refinement of thinking (use of tools) and showing students how she constructs her answer.

This interaction facilitates students' growth. As they discuss their thoughts and support their ideas by explaining how they construct their answers, the new ideas and strategies that they use become part of their internal thought processes. During discussion, the teacher facilitates reading by discussing interpretations, asking students to justify their interpretations, and sharing her own thought process. As a result, verbal discussion facilitates reading through three avenues: meaning construction, verbalizing plans and strategies for meaning construction, and making social thinking an internal process.

Conclusion

The techniques outlined in this book include a variety of both oral and written response modes. Techniques have been selected that require these different response modes for before reading, during reading, and postreading activities (see Table 5–5). To get the desired results from the experiences, the diagnostic teacher uses the techniques to develop verbal and written responses as meaning construction.

Meaning Processing		
	Discussion	*Written Response*
Readiness	Contextual Processing Direct Experience Experience-Text-Relationships Listening-Thinking Activity Visualization Vocabulary Maps	Guided Imagery/Comprehension Vocabulary Maps
Active Reading	Directed Reading-Thinking Activity Reciprocal Teaching ReQuest Self-Directed Questioning Story Drama	Herringbone Technique Prediction Maps Reading Logs Story Maps Triple Read Outline
Postreading—Elaboration	Experience-Text-Relationships Question-Answer Relationships Readers Theatre Story Drama	Question-Generation Strategy Story Maps Story Writing Summarization

Table 5–5
Classifying
Techniques by
Mode of Response

CLASSIFYING TECHNIQUES
BY TYPE OF STRUCTURE

Instructional decision making also includes an analysis of how mediated instruction will occur. The diagnostic teacher asks how much explicit instruction will be necessary for students to regulate their own learning. Learners differ in how they approach the reading event. Some readers are active, while others are passive.

Active Readers

overpredicting

Active readers automatically structure new learning situations by identifying key features, developing plausible solutions, and evaluating their effectiveness. These readers select key characteristics by sampling several alternatives and flexibly shifting among sources of information. As they solve these problems, they create their own rules for what they observe. This may be an inherent way to process information (Witkin, Moore, Goodenough, & Cox, 1977), or it may be developed through the social interactions that students experience daily. Often the more active, independent learners have had numerous experiences with school-book language when they communicate ideas. To communicate socially, these students use a wide variety of words to describe events and elaborate descriptions to justify their actions. Through previous social interactions, they become more active and explicit when they solve verbal problems (Finn, 1985).

Passive Readers

underpredictive

Passive learners, however, learn by watching how other students and the teacher solve the problem. They have difficulty distinguishing between the context of learning (such as teacher praise and peer approval) and the task of learning. They approach problem solving as a spectator and remain passive toward their own process of learning, preferring to follow the teacher's model whenever possible. This passive stance may be an inherent way to process information (Witkin et al., 1977), or it may be a result of the daily social interactions that the students experience (Finn, 1985).

Often, the more passive students have relied on shared understandings during their social interactions. Communication is often limited to information that refers to events or ideas that are known to the listener; therefore, passive learners use less precise words and nonverbal language to communicate meaning. They rely on their listeners to infer meaning based on shared knowledge rather than speaker explanations. When learning demands a more active verbal stance, these students are unfamiliar with the elaborate language that can be used to justify their actions. They remain passive, therefore, preferring to follow the teacher's model to solve problems.

Previous Experiences

For both active and passive students, previous experience with the task being taught affects the need for explicit instruction. If they have not had prior experiences related to the task, they might need some explicit instruction in the new task. If they have had prior experiences and *failed,* they might profit from explicit instruction that is very different from the initial instructional context.

The diagnostic teacher analyzes the students' need for explicit instruction by evaluating how active they are when solving the reading problem. If the students are active and have positive experiences with the task, the diagnostic teacher chooses a task that focuses on implicit instruction (students read texts rich in language and figure out the underlying consistency as the teacher guides inquiry). However, if students are passive and have few positive experiences with the task, the diagnostic teacher chooses a technique that focuses on explicit instruction (students are directly informed of what they are learning, provided a model, and given directed practice).

Explicit Instruction — Direct teaching

In explicit instruction (see "Explicit Teaching" in Chapter 6), the diagnostic teacher precisely states what is to be learned and models the thinking process that accompanies this new skill or strategy. Students are given reasons why this new skill will help them read better (Tierney, 1982). Minilessons are constructed to show them how to use the reading skill or strategy, with the teacher modeling the steps of the task. Guided practice with a high level of teacher feedback is then provided. The feedback explicitly explains when and where students would use the skill or strategy. In the explicit teaching model, however, there is a gradual release of teacher-directed instruction to allow students to direct their own learning. The diagnostic teacher identifies students who initially lack control of their own learning; then she explicitly teaches the new strategy. Finally, she plans for the independent use of the strategy.

Explicit Instruction

Based on
- *Reasons for learning*
- *Teacher modeling how it works*
- *Directed practice*
- *Gradual release of control*

Typical techniques
- *Synthetic phonics*
- *Reciprocal teaching*
- *Question-answer relationships*

Implicit Instruction

Implicit instruction (see "Implicit Instruction" in Chapter 6) is characterized by an emphasis on the text, the reading event, and the child as informant. Large quantities of text are read that require students to use the targeted skill or strategy. Students apply the skill to make sense of what is read without consciously understanding the principle. Because the context has been carefully arranged, students can readily decide which mistakes make a difference in understanding. From these choices, they reason about text interpretation. The teacher plays the role of linguistic inquirer, asking students, "How did you know that . . . ?" (Haussler, 1985). This role allows students to generate their own rules for text interpretation.

Implicit Instruction

Based on
- *Immersion in reading*
- *Teacher as linguistic inquirer*
- *Student generation of rules*

Typical techniques
- *Language experience*
- *Directed reading-thinking activity*
- *Reading logs*

Conclusion

The reading techniques outlined in this book include both explicit and implicit approaches to instruction. Table 5–6 classifies these techniques according to their tendency to approach learning from either an implicit or explicit instructional framework.

CLASSIFYING TECHNIQUES BY STRENGTHS IN COGNITIVE PROCESSING

Individual differences in problem solving influence how students build their models of meaning as they read. A multitude of theoretical frameworks exist for studying individual differences; however, recent attention has been focused on a model of dichotomous thinking referred to as simultaneous and successive cognitive processing (Das, Kirby, & Jarman, 1979; Luria, 1973). This model refers to *how* students

	Implicit	*Explicit*
Sight Words	Echo Reading Guided Imagery/Comprehension Impress Method Language Experience Listening-Thinking Activity Predictable Language Secondary Reading Sequence Talking Books	Linguistic Method Multisensory Approach Sight Word Approach
Word Attack	Analytic Phonics Repeated Readings	Distar Reading Phonograph Approach Synthetic Phonics
Fluency	Echo Reading Guided Imagery/LEA Impress Method Language Experience Readers Theatre Secondary Reading Sequence Talking Books	Chunking Repeated Readings (with teacher mediation)
Meaning Vocabulary	Cloze Instruction Direct Experience Visualization Vocabulary Maps	Contextual Processing Experience-Text-Relationships Metaphors
Sentence Comprehension	Alternate Writing Cloze Instruction Story Writing	Contextual Processing Sentence Combining
Literal Comprehension	Alternate Writing Listening-Thinking Activity Readers Theatre ReQuest Story Writing	Herringbone Technique Reciprocal Teaching Story Maps Summarization
Nonliteral Comprehension	Guided Imagery/Comprehension Readers Theatre Reading Logs Story Drama Visualization	Experience-Text-Relationships Prediction Maps Self-Directed Questioning
Study Skills	Guided Imagery/Comprehension Question-Generation Strategy SQ3R	Question-Answer Relationships Reciprocal Teaching Summarization Triple Read Outline

Table 5–6
Classifying
Techniques by
Type of Structure

Note: 1) The lesson frameworks of explicit teaching, implicit teaching, directed reading activity, directed reading-thinking activity, dialogue journals, and sustained silent reading are not classified. Of these, explicit teaching and the directed reading activity are explicit techniques. 2) Teacher implementation can change any technique to make it more or less explicit or implicit.

solve problems, recognizing and restructuring information in a problem-solving situation like reading.

As students read, they vary their cognitive processing depending on the nature of the reading task, (i.e., they flexibly shift between simultaneous and successive processing). For example, when constructing a main idea from the text, readers organize important information (successive processing) while drawing relationships among this information (simultaneous processing). When reading requires a step-by-step analysis of text, readers use successive processing and sequentially order the information to solve the problem. Reading tasks such as phonic decoding and sequencing story events require that readers recognize and structure information in a step-by-step sequence. This problem-solving process is referred to as successive processing.

On the other hand, when reading requires the analysis of several ideas at the same time, readers use simultaneous processing; they relate ideas according to a general category to solve the problem. Reading tasks such as predicting the author's purpose and interpreting character motives draw heavily on organizing many aspects of information around their most important characteristics. This process is referred to as simultaneous processing.

Students can be identified as having strengths in one of these ways of processing information. A *simultaneous* preference refers to the propensity to think about multiple relationships among ideas relating the most important characteristics (Kaufman & Kaufman, 1983). Simultaneous students build their models of meaning using large, inclusive categories of meaning. A noticeable characteristic of these students is their well-developed ability to manipulate visual information. These readers often draw visual diagrams or pictures to organize information. Students with a strength in simultaneous processing look for the coherent patterns of text by tying together the underlying relationships implied by the author. They use a minimal amount of textual information and rely heavily on their background knowledge to interpret text. They often comment, "Oh, yeah, that's like a. . . ." Their language is noticeably less precise and characterized by a tendency to draw images with words rather than use specific definitional language.

At the word identification level, these readers prefer using the semantic cueing system over the grapho-phonic or syntactic cueing system because they have a high need to create meaning from what they read. Their reliance on top-down processing often precludes a careful analysis of the text.

Simultaneous strength means that the student thinks first about the overall meaning and then organizes the parts as they relate to the entire meaning.

A *successive* preference refers to the propensity for developing sequential, logical relationships with words. These students prefer to develop models of meaning by arranging information in a logical, hierarchical sequence (Kaufman & Kaufman, 1983). They develop meaning from precise words that are logically organized to form definitional language. Students with a successive processing strength look for the logical organization of the text to gain meaning. After reading a text, they can recall the sequence of story events but often cannot tie together events to form a main idea. Because they rely heavily on text information to fill in unstated meanings, their models seldom reflect personal application of the text. They organize information according to its function; therefore, their comments are flooded with precise text-based references.

At the word identification level, successive readers prefer using the graphophonic or syntactic cueing system because they rely on the logical relationships among and within words. Their reliance on a bottom-up process often precludes using the overall meaning of the text to decode words, creating a word-bound reader. They forget to think about the overall meaning of the selection and to relate the textual information to their previous experiences.

---

*Successive strength means that the student thinks about the parts first
and then orders the parts to form the general meaning.*

Instructional decision making is facilitated by knowing which cognitive process is used in the various techniques. The techniques in this book have been classified by their simultaneous or successive framework. Some techniques initially ask children to consider the overall meaning before analyzing the parts. Other techniques ask readers to learn and use the parts before constructing the general meaning.

Simultaneous Framework

When selecting approaches that mediate learning using a simultaneous framework, the diagnostic teacher identifies techniques that focus on the overall meaning of text. In using these techniques, the diagnostic teacher continually redirects attention by asking how things make sense within the entire passage. Specific facts are presented to show relationships to the overall meaning and to one another. These procedures require the synthesis of information characteristic of simultaneous processing. For example, the predictable language approach (see "Predictable Language Approach" in Chapter 6) requires students to move from understanding the whole (memorizing the story) to identifying the parts (single words). Selecting techniques that focus on simultaneous processing, the diagnostic teacher also evaluates whether learning is mediated through a visual array of the relationships, through tactile/kinesthetic experiences, or through visualization. Techniques that have this focus ask students to look at multiple relationships simultaneously.

Simultaneous Framework over predictive/top/down

Based on
- *Multiple relationships among pieces of information*
- *Visual display of information*
- *Overall generalization*

Typical techniques
- *Predictable language*
- *Vocabulary maps*
- *Guided imagery*

Successive Framework

When selecting approaches that mediate instruction using a successive framework, the diagnostic teacher identifies techniques that focus on discrete parts that form meaning when grouped together. In these techniques, the diagnostic teacher gradually presents the sequential parts of the task, leading students to an overall understanding (see "Story Maps" in Chapter 6). These procedures require that new bits of information are evaluated individually and gradually arranged in a sequence that forms meaning. For example, the instructional emphasis of synthetic phonics (see "Synthetic Phonics" in Chapter 6) moves from knowing the parts (single letter sounds) to sequencing these sounds into words (sound synthesis) and finally to reading the words in stories. Selecting techniques that focus on successive processing, the diagnostic teacher also evaluates whether learning is mediated through auditory/verbal information, functional analysis, or analysis of small amounts of information. Each of these techniques requires a successive processing of individual sections within the text.

Successive Framework underpredictive/bottom-up

Based on
- *Small, discrete parts*
- *Step-by-step arrangement*
- *Verbalizing function*

Typical techniques
- *Synthetic phonics*
- *Self-directed questioning*
- *Question-answer relationships*

Conclusion

Effective readers do not operate exclusively in either the simultaneous or the successive mode. What is necessary for fluent reading is a flexible interplay between simultaneous and successive processing of text. Efficient readers flexibly shift between a succesive analysis of the textual elements and a simultaneous relating of textual and nontextual information to construct a model of meaning. However, inefficient readers often rely too much on their strength in cognitive processing, thus inhibiting fluent reading performance.

To develop a more flexible text processing, the diagnostic teacher begins instruction using readers' strengths in cognitive processing (teach new reading strategies using the strength) and gradually introduces a more intergrated processing of text by showing them how to incorporate their weaknesses into their reading repertoires. Thus, the diagnostic teacher initially uses students' strengths in cognitive processing to mediate learning before introducing other strategies.

The sensitive teacher—understanding the problem-solving demands of the tasks of reading, readers' preferences, and the various ways to teach reading—can modify instruction to facilitate students' learning. To assist in the selection process, Table 5–7 analyzes teaching techniques in terms of the skills and cognitive processing emphasized. The teacher asseses students' strength in cognitive processing and analyzes the requisite task to be taught. She then selects a technique and constructs a diagnostic lesson to verify the appropriateness of the technique. Appropriate techniques increase reading proficiency and task competence. Continued instruction using these techniques encourages integration of simultaneous and successive processing rather than an overreliance on a single process.

SUMMARY

To select the most appropriate technique, the diagnostic teacher analyzes each technique according to its instructional features. First, the diagnostic teacher matches the diagnostic techniques and the children's pattern of skill or strategy development so that mediated instruction results in increased performance. She asks, "Is there a skill or strategy that, if learned, would increase these students' reading?" To increase the specificity in selecting techniques, she uses two broad classifications of text format: narrative and expository. She asks, "What type of text am I using?" Then she decides at what point (before, during, or after reading) she needs to implement diagnostic teaching techniques. She asks, "At what point during the lesson will these students need assistance?"

Next she decides the mode of response that will most benefit the students. She asks, "In order to learn this skill or strategy, will writing or discussing facilitate their reading performance?"

Then she decides on the type of structure that is needed: explicit or implicit. Providing the appropriate type of structure in the learning situation enhances students' reading performance. She asks, "In order to learn this unfamiliar skill or strategy, what kind of structure do these students need?"

Table 5-7
Classifying
Techniques by
Sequence of
Cognitive
Processing

	Simultaneous	Successive
Sight Words	Echo Reading Guided Imagery/LEA Impress Method Language Experience Listening-Thinking Activity Predictable Language Secondary Reading Sequence Sight Words*	Linguistic Method Multisensory Approach Word Cards
Word Attack	Echo Reading Guided Imagery/LEA Impress Method Language Experience Repeated Readings Secondary Reading Sequence	Analytic Phonics Distar Reading Linguistic Method Multisensory Approach Synthetic Phonics
Fluency	Chunking Echo Reading Guided Imagery/LEA Impress Method Language Experience Readers Theatre Repeated Readings	Cloze Instruction
Vocabulary	Direct Experience Metaphors Visualization Vocabulary Maps	Contextual Processing Cloze Instruction Feature Analysis Grid
Sentence Comprehension	Readers Theatre Story Writing	Contextual Processing Cloze Instruction Sentence Combining
Literal Comprehension	Experience-Text-Relationships Question-Generation Strategy Story Maps* Story Writing Visualization Vocabulary Maps	Herringbone Technique Question-Answer Relationships Reciprocal Teaching ReQuest Summarization
Nonliteral Comprehension	Experience-Text-Relationships Guided Imagery/Comprehension Prediction Maps Reading Logs Story Drama	Question-Answer Relationships Reciprocal Teaching Self-Directed Questioning
Study Skills	Guided Imagery/Comprehension Question-Generation Strategy Triple Read Outline	Herringbone Technique Question-Answer Relationships Summarization

*These techniques are less simultaneous than the others in the list.

Note: 1) The lesson frameworks of explicit teaching, implicit teaching, directed reading activity, directed reading-thinking activity, dialogue journals, and sustained silent reading are not classified. Of these, explicit teaching and the directed reading activity are more successive than simultaneous. 2) Teacher implementation can change any technique to make it more or less simultaneous.

Finally, the diagnostic teacher decides which technique matches the students' strengths in cognitive processing. Some techniques incorporate a successive, serial approach to instruction, while others incorporate a global, simultaneous approach. For hard-to-teach children, instruction using their processing strength facilitates the learning of new information. She asks, "What processing sequence works the best for these students when learning this task?" As she answers these questions, the diagnostic teacher makes instructional modifications that increase reading performance.

To date, there has been no one instructional sequence or instructional framework that has proven effective for these problem readers. However, teachers vary in their preferences for teaching, and these preferences often dictate how they conduct the diagnostic session. Effective teachers remember that student learning is not accomplished "by a mindless enthusiasm for a given method . . . [but] by understanding the many moving variables in the process of learning to read . . ." (Finn, 1985, p. 150). Therefore, the diagnostic teacher needs to employ a variety of techniques to meet the individual needs of problem readers, identify the key features of these techniques, and evaluate how these features affect reading acquisition.

The Instructional Techniques

6

In this chapter 50 instructional procedures are presented to help teachers design specialized programs for problem readers. The instructional procedures, or techniques, include a variety of instructional formats, approaches, methods, and specialized remedial techniques. These techniques represent a variety of ways to encourage proficient reading. Each technique is discussed in two parts: (a) a simple procedural description followed by (b) an explanation of specific diagnostic applications.

In field use, this chapter may be used in the following manner. First, the diagnostic teacher consults the general description and its steps. In order to make instructional modifications, the teacher needs to evaluate how he instructs the lesson. As he instructs the lesson, therefore, he evaluates at what point he modified instruction to mediate learning. Consequently, this chapter describes the steps in implementing each technique, thus facilitating a comparison of how instruction occurs when using various techniques. The teacher may then wish to turn to the second part of the discussion, since the knowledge of learner patterns where the technique produces success will be of assistance when matching an appropriate instructional technique to the needs of an individual student. As shown in Figure 6–1, the teacher uses this information to formulate his diagnostic hypotheses. Furthermore, the teacher uses diagnostic lessons to evaluate his hypotheses (see Chapter 9).

The Information for Each Technique

Initially, the explanation is presented in simple terminology and is constructed to assist the transition between prescription and implementation. The following topics are included.

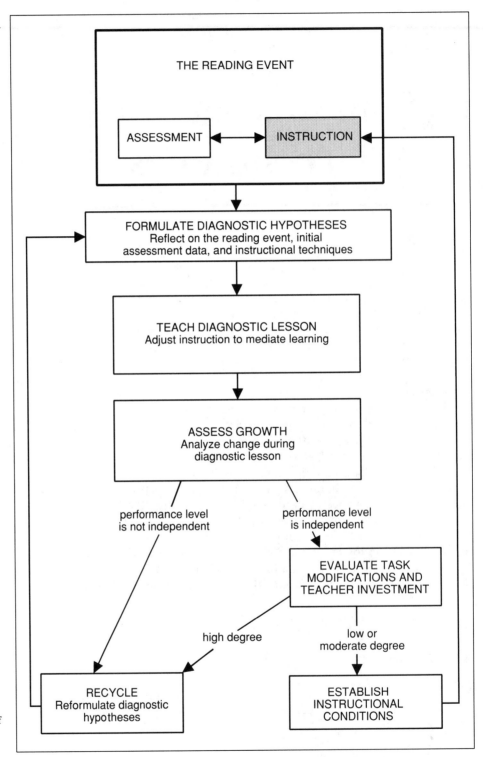

Figure 6–1
The Decision-
Making Cycle of
Diagnostic
Teaching

- *Description.* In an effort to simplify communication, a two- or three-sentence description is presented. This description can be used in report writing or communicating with parents.
- *Major Reading Tasks It Develops.* Although many techniques can serve various purposes, they are usually designed to develop specific reading skills or strategies. This section will focus on the results of the technique so that instruction can develop the specified reading task the student needs.
- *Targeted Reading Levels.* Many techniques were developed for use with students at a particular stage in reading development. This section will facilitate selecting a technique that matches the reading level of the student.
- *Procedures.* This section is a sequential enumeration of the process of instruction for each technique. This explanation serves two purposes. First, it facilitates implementation of the technique so experimenting with new methods of instruction is not overwhelming. Second, by delineating the steps of instruction, the diagnostic teacher can analyze in what part of the instruction the student has incorporated the desired reading behaviors. This knowledge facilitates modifying instruction to increase its efficiency.

The next section specifies the diagnostic applications of each technique and includes the following elements.

- *Basic View of Reading.* Techniques have developed from various views of learning. As individuals formulate views of how learning occurs in young children, they propose teaching techniques that support their views. Therefore, instructional techniques reflect theories about how children learn. It is an assumption of this chapter that the diagnostic teacher can match how a child is learning with a diagnostic technique that reflects that learning process. The major views are bottom-up, where instruction is focused on text-based processing; top-down, where instruction is focused on reader-based processing; and interactive, where instruction is focused on combining reader-based and text-based processing (see Chapter 1).
- *Patterns of Strengths and Strategies.* This section looks specifically at what the student is asked to do when the teacher implements the technique. The underlying strengths and strategies that are necessary to profit from this instructional technique are then presented.
- *Learner Patterns That Produce a High Success Rate.* Techniques can be used in different ways to produce success. This section analyzes the technique as it would be integrated into instruction with different learners. How the technique is implemented is matched to the corresponding learner patterns. Learner patterns (see Chapter 5 for further explanation) that are highlighted in this section are the following:

  1. *Active readers*, who independently solve reading problems by reorganizing new information around its key features. They predict, monitor, and elaborate what they read, using both the text and what they know.

2. *Passive readers*, who rely heavily on cues from their environment to decide what is important to remember. They prefer to follow a teacher's model when predicting, monitoring, and elaborating what they read. When reading, they use either the text or what they know to solve the reading problem.

3. *Readers who have a simultaneous strength* and think first about the overall meaning, then organize the parts as they relate to the entire meaning.

4. *Readers who have a successive strength* and think about the parts first, then order the parts to form the general meaning.

Described first are the learner patterns that represent how the technique matches a learner strength. For these students, the technique can be used to modify the basic lesson during guided contextual reading or for skill and strategy instruction (see Chapter 4 for further explanation of these features of the diagnostic teaching session). The starred items, which appear second, represent how the technique would be used to remediate a weakness during skill and strategy instruction.

• *Using the Technique as a Diagnostic Teaching Lesson.* This section is a short checklist to focus the evaluation of a student's success when using this technique. If the answers are "yes," the technique facilitates learning for this particular student.

Ways to Use This Chapter

The techniques in this chapter are arranged alphabetically so they can be used as a resource rather than procedures to be memorized. The alphabetical arrangement facilitates locating a technique that was selected in Chapter 5.

These pages have been used by preservice teachers, inservice teachers, and school psychologists in many different ways. Preservice teachers follow the procedures step by step as they learn how to teach in different ways. Then they begin reading why they are doing what they are doing. When students do not succeed with a particular technique, these teachers analyze what they asked them to do by reading the second section. This helps preservice teachers understand how children are different. Inservice teachers use Chapter 5 extensively to choose several techniques. They use each of these techniques to help them decide what the students' strengths are. As they identify what technique works best, they also identify their students' strengths. The school psychologist, on the other hand, uses Chapter 5 to match test data with particular techniques. Then he looks up each technique to verify which might be the most beneficial. He then recommends the procedures to the appropriate teacher.

ALTERNATE WRITING

Description. Alternate writing is the composition of a story among a group of students and a teacher. By writing a specified time, each person alternately continues the development of a cohesive story line. Each person's contribution to the story line must build upon prior information in the composition and must lead to the next event.

Major Reading Tasks It Develops

1. Comprehension
2. Sensitivity to story structure

Targeted Reading Levels: 4–8

Text: Students' and teacher's writing

Procedure

1. The teacher selects topics of interest to the students. As the procedure is used, an increasing variety of text types and subject areas needs to be included.
2. Using the story starter or topic selected, the teacher begins writing and continues developing the story line for 2 minutes. In a small group, an overhead can be used.
3. The story is passed to the next student. This student writes for 2 minutes.
4. In order to continue the story, each student must read the previous text and create text that maintains the story theme and moves the story to its conclusion.
5. When the story is completely written, the teacher reads the story as a whole.
6. The teacher revises his own parts of the story for coherence and grammatical clarity. As he is revising, he models the task, asking himself, "Will this make sense to my reader?"
7. The teacher encourages students to revise their writing for coherence and grammatical clarity.

Modifications

1. A story map can be developed prior to writing so that each student adds information that will fit the story map (see "Story Map" in this chapter).

2. A word processing program can be used, and students can write and revise the story on the computer.
3. Cartoons can be used as a framework for the story line.
4. This technique can be used in pairs, small groups, and tutoring situations.
5. This technique can be easily adapted to a writing center, where students add to the story when they attend that center. Students initial their additions.

Further Diagnostic Applications

Basic View of Reading. Reading is an interactive process where the reader uses prior knowledge to construct and monitor understanding. Likewise, writing is an active-constructive process that requires reading, interpreting, and monitoring what was written. Through writing, the reader becomes sensitive to how stories are constructed so that they make sense.

Patterns of Strengths and Strategies. Alternate writing is most appropriate for students who have facility with writing and prefer to communicate through writing rather than discussion. This approach helps students develop a sense of the story line and approach text as a communication between reader and writer.

Learner Patterns That Produce a High Success Rate

1. The successive learner who writes well but does not understand that reading is a communication process. This technique provides a tool for talking about the communicative intent of the author.
2. The simultaneous learner who writes and reads for self-understanding and meaning but does not realize that the text is a contractual agreement between reader and writer. This technique provides a tool for talking about what needs to be in a text in order to make it understandable to a reader.
*3. The nonverbal learner who needs to participate in writing a story to understand story structure. This technique provides an experience in developing writing fluency in a less threatening manner.

Using the Technique as a Diagnostic Teaching Lesson. For alternate writing to be effective, a majority of the following statements must be answered in the affirmative.

YES   NO

_____ _____   **1.** The student writes fluently and can construct text that makes sense.

_____ _____ **2.** The student prefers to write what she thinks rather than contribute to a discussion.

_____ _____ **3.** The student can retell a cohesive story and has an intuitive sense of story structure.

_____ _____ **4.** Composition increases her understanding of the reading process.

For Further Reading

Tiedt, I. M., Bruemmer, S. S., Lane, S., Stelwagon, P., Watanabe, K. O., & Williams, M. Y. (1983). *Teaching writing in K–8 classrooms.* Englewood Cliffs, NJ: Prentice-Hall.

ANALYTIC PHONICS

Description. Analytic phonics is an approach to teaching decoding based on drawing phonic relationships among words that have the same letter patterns. Using words the child already recognizes "at sight," the student identifies the sounds of letter groups by making analogies to known words. In other words, the child says, "I already know a word that looks like this new word. I will match the sounds in that word with the sounds in the new word."

Major Reading Tasks It Develops

1. Word attack
2. Decoding by analogy

Targeted Reading Levels: 1–2

Text: Known sight words and new words that have the same sound pattern

Procedure

1. The teacher selects a text that contains an abundance of the letter sounds to be taught.
2. The teacher presents sight words that represent the targeted sound or sound cluster. For example, he places these words on the board.

green
grass
grow

3. He asks the student to identify how these words are alike. The student responds, "They all have the letters *gr* at the beginning."
4. The teacher directs attention to the sounds by saying, "How does the *gr* sound in these words?"
5. If the student cannot figure out the sound, the teacher says, "Try the *gr-r-r* sound as in *green, grass,* and *grow*"
6. The student reads a text with words that have the *gr* sound.

> In the land of the gremlins, there were gobs of green grapes as big as Grandpa. One baby gremlin loved to eat the green grapes. He began to grow and grow and grow. So his mother said, "You cannot eat anymore. You have grown too big." This made the gremlin grumpy. He growled and growled. He grabbed a great big green grape and gobbled it up. Then he grabbed another green grape and gobbled it up. Then he grabbed another and another and another. He grew and grew and grew until he popped. That was the end of the gremlin.

7. The teacher draws attention to how the student used the strategy of decoding by analogy.

Further Diagnostic Applications

Basic View of Reading. Learning to read is a process where the learner makes inferences about the phonic relationships within words. When a student can read an abundance of words that contain a consistent phonic relationship, she will infer the phonic rule for the target words and similar words. This is called implicit or analytic phonics.

Patterns of Strengths and Strategies. Analytic phonics is most appropriate for students who can segment words into their sounds and readily make phonic inferences about the sound consistency of words. This technique matches their strategies and allows them to develop the strategy of decoding by analogy.

Learner Patterns That Produce a High Success Rate

1. A simultaneous learner who can segment words into their sounds and has established a sight word vocabulary. This technique matches her strengths in knowing the whole word before the parts and finding the patterns between what she knows and what is new.
2. An active reader who does not respond to the direct instruction of other decoding approaches. This technique allows her to develop her own rules for how phonics works.

3. A learner who has an overriding need for meaning and purpose in her learning. Minimal instruction in decoding by analogy makes sense and provides strategies for decoding.

Using the Technique as a Diagnostic Teaching Lesson. For analytic phonics to be effective, a majority of the following statements must be answered in the affirmative.

YES   NO

——— ———   **1** The student is efficient at segmenting sounds.

——— ———   **2.** The student has a well-established sight vocabulary, which facilitates making phonic inferences to new words.

——— ———   **3.** The student can draw sound analogies between known words and new words.

——— ———   **4.** The student checks her new word by asking if it makes sense and looks like what she said.

For Further Reading

Aukerman, R. C. (1984). *Approaches to beginning reading* (2nd ed.). New York: John Wiley & Sons.

Anderson, R. C., Hiebert, E. H., Scott, J. A., & Wilkinson, I. A. G. (1985). *Becoming a nation of readers: The report of the commission on reading.* Washington, DC: National Institute of Education.

CHUNKING

Description. Chunking is a technique to encourage the student to read phrases of language that represent meaning rather than separate words. It focuses on reading phrases of text that represent a thought. Chunking facilitates comprehension and fluency by using thought units rather than word-by-word reading.

Major Reading Tasks It Develops

1. Reading fluency
2. Knowledge that groups of words form chunks of thought
3. Sensitivity to sentence meaning
4. Comprehension by relating words to thoughts

Text: All kinds

Procedure

1. The teacher chooses a passage at an instructional reading level that will take about 3 minutes to read.
2. The teacher tapes the student reading the passage.
3. The teacher and the student echo read (see "Echo Reading" in this chapter) the passage using meaningful phrases. In other words, the teacher reads a sentence modeling appropriate chunks of the sentence, and the student repeats the same sentence using the phrasing. The example that follows illustrates the sequence.

   Text: The bright girl liked to read stories about horses.
   Student reading: The / bright / girl / liked / to / read / stories / about / horses.
   Teacher modeling: The bright girl / liked to read / stories about horses.
   Student echoing: The bright girl / liked to / read stories / about horses.
   Teacher comment: I liked the way you chunked "read stories." Did it make more sense to you to read it that way?

4. The teacher and student continue reading the entire passage. When possible, the teacher increases the number of sentences chunked before the student repeats the model.
5. As the student's ability to chunk thought units increases, the teacher ceases to model the chunking, and the student reads the passage on her own.
6. The teacher tapes the reading of the passage again.
7. The teacher and the student compare fluency, intonation, and phrasing.

Modifications

1. For the extremely slow reader, the teacher may incorporate oral chunking experiences as an intervention with multiple timed, silent readings.
2. For the beginning reader, chunking a language experience story by writing phrases from the story on 3″ × 5″ cards is an effective technique.

Basic View of Reading. Reading is an interactive process whereby a reader thinks about how the words of the text are combined to form the ideas the author intended to convey.

Patterns of Strengths and Strategies. Chunking is most appropriate for students who have facility with word identification and reflect a sequential, bottom-up processing of text. Chunking of text encourages these students to connect the underlying thought with the text as they are reading.

Learner Patterns That Produce a High Success Rate

1. A successive learner who has difficulty relating what is written in the text to her own thoughts. When chunking, the student must use her understanding of the meaning to group the words together.
2. The passive reader who reads words without thinking of their meaning. Chunking uses recognizing the words (a strength) to understand how the words create meaning (a weakness).
*3. A learner who is word-bound because of an overemphasis on phonics or oral accuracy. Chunking increases her fluency and speed.
*4. An extremely slow reader who thinks about every word. Chunking encourages thinking about groups of words rather than individual words.

Using the Technique as a Diagnostic Teaching Lesson. For chunking to be effective, a majority of the following statements must be answered in the affirmative.

YES	NO	
____	____	**1.** The student has accurate word identification skills.
____	____	**2.** The student can model the teacher's chunking of words.
____	____	**3.** The student transfers the chunking to new text.
____	____	**4.** The student finds the technique helpful and responds to instruction.

For Further Reading

Allington, R. L. (1983). Fluency: The neglected reading goal. *Reading Teacher, 36*, 556–561.

Ekwall, E. E., & Shanker, J. L. (1983). *Diagnosis and remediation of the disabled reader* (2nd ed.). Boston: Allyn and Bacon.

Guszak, F. J. (1985). *Diagnostic reading instruction in the elementary school*. New York: Harper & Row.

CLOZE INSTRUCTION

Description. The instructional cloze is a technique that develops comprehension by deleting target words from a text. This encourages the student to think about what word would make sense in the sentence and in the context of the entire story.

Major Reading Tasks It Develops

1. Comprehension
2. Context clues
3. Predicting words using sentence meaning

Targeted Reading Levels: 4–12

Text: Paragraphs and stories that are coherent

Procedure

1. The teacher selects a text of 200–400 words.
2. The teacher decides on the target words.
3. The teacher systematically deletes the words from the paragraph and inserts a blank for the deleted word.
4. The student is instructed to read the entire passage to get a sense of the entire meaning.
5. The student is then instructed to fill in the blanks in the passage.
6. When the student finishes filling in the blanks, the answers are evaluated as to the similarity of meaning between the deleted word and the supplied word.
7. The student reviews her choices and talks about what strategies she used to decide on the word choices.

1. An oral cloze can be used to develop predictive listening in the young child.
2. A cloze exercise can be constructed from language experience stories in order to develop the ability to predict a word by using prior knowledge (what I said) and the text (how I said it).
3. A cloze exercise can be constructed from predictable language books so that the sight words are reinforced.
4. Cloze can be adapted so that pairs of students work together to decide what word fits in the text. This causes a discussion and justification of word choices.

Further Diagnostic Applications

Basic View of Reading. Reading is an interactive process of verifying text expectation by using knowledge of how language works (sentence structure) and what the passage means (overall contextual meaning).

Patterns of Strengths and Strategies. The cloze procedure relies on a well-developed sense of the redundancy of language and a manipulation of sentence structure. For students who have verbal fluency, this technique facilitates comprehension by encouraging the combination of text and meaning cues.

Learner Patterns That Produce a High Success Rate

1. The successive learner who has become word-bound during the process of initial reading instruction and needs to increase the use of context to decode meaning. This technique increases the ability to guess what words are from context.
2. The successive learner who tends to read isolated words rather than using the context and asking what would make sense. This technique helps the reader think about what groups of words mean.
*3. The simultaneous learner who needs to use both sentence structure and overall meaning to read text effectively. The technique focuses attention on sentence meaning.

Using the Technique as a Diagnostic Teaching Lesson. For cloze instruction to be effective, a majority of the following statements must be answered in the affirmative.

YES   NO

_____ _____   **1.** The student fills in the blanks with some degree of certainty.

_____ _____   **2.** The student has verbal facility, which supplements her performance on the cloze.

_____ _____   **3.** The student begins to use not only *word* knowledge but also *world* knowledge to complete the cloze.

_____ _____   **4.** The student is not so frustrated by the procedure that she refuses to fill in the blanks.

For Further Reading

Jongsma, E. A. (1980). *Cloze instruction research: A second look*. Newark, DE: International Reading Association and ERIC/RCS.

Weaver, G. C. (1979). Using the cloze procedure as a teaching technique. *Reading Teacher, 32*, 632–636.

CONTEXTUAL PROCESSING

Description. Contextual processing is a technique used to develop new word meanings as they are found in the context of a selected story. This technique shows the student how to use context to figure out what new vocabulary words mean.

Major Reading Tasks It Develops

1. Meaning vocabulary
2. Sentence comprehension

Targeted Reading Levels: 2–12

Text: Paragraphs three to four sentences long, where the meaning of new vocabulary is apparent from the surrounding context.

1. The teacher selects unfamiliar key vocabulary words to teach.
2. The teacher finds a passage in the text where the meaning of the word is apparent when using the surrounding context. If not available, he creates his own three-sentence paragraph.
3. He writes the paragraph on the overhead or chalkboard.
4. He reads the paragraph aloud to the students.
5. The students reread the paragraph silently.
6. The teacher asks the students about the meaning of the word found in the paragraph, asking, for example, "What does the paragraph tell you about the word . . . ?"
7. The teacher uses the students' answers to probe further understanding, asking, "Why did you think that?"
8. The teacher asks students to write down what the new word might mean.
9. The teacher has students think of other similar situations where they could use the word. He asks, "Who else might be . . . ? Where else might you . . . ?"
10. The students think of other words with similar meanings.
11. The students record target words and a personal definition in their word notebooks.

Modification

The teacher can increase the explicitness of the technique by modeling how to figure out the meaning of the word using the surrounding words in the paragraph. The teacher models Steps 6 (what the paragraph told him), 7 (why he thought that), and 8 (how he came up with the meaning).

Further Diagnostic Applications

Basic View of Reading. Reading is an interactive process where the readers use what they know about how the words in the story are used to interpret what the author is saying.

Patterns of Strengths and Strategies. Contextual processing has students figure out unfamiliar word meanings from the context; therefore, it is most appropriate for students who have facility with sentence meaning but do not use this strength to figure out what new words mean. This is often the pattern of successive learners who have facility with sentence structure but do not combine this strength with what they already know to expand their understanding of word meanings.

1. A successive learner who has the ability to use sentences to figure out new words but does not use her background knowledge to expand word meanings. This technique starts with her strength and then asks her to use background knowledge to tie the meaning to other events in her life.
2. A passive learner who reads the words without actively thinking about what they mean in the new context or other contexts. This technique encourages her to think actively about what words mean. The modification of modeling may be needed.
*3. A simultaneous learner who does not use the sentence context to figure out word meanings. This technique encourages her to use context as well as what she knows to figure out new word meanings.

Using the Technique as a Diagnostic Teaching Lesson. For contextual processing to be effective, a majority of the following statements must be answered in the affirmative.

YES	NO	
___	___	**1.** The student has adequate word identification skills.
___	___	**2.** The student can use sentence comprehension to facilitate learning new word meanings.
___	___	**3.** The student learns to use information from two sentences to define the word easily.
___	___	**4.** The student can use words to define new meanings and does not need a direct experience.

For Further Reading

Gipe, J. P. (1978–1979). Investigating techniques for teaching word meanings. *Reading Research Quarterly, 14,* 624–644.

McKeown, M. (1985). The acquisition of word meaning from context by children of high and low ability. *Reading Research Quarterly, 20,* 482–496.

Tierney, R. J., Readence, J. E., & Dishner, E. K. (1985). *Reading strategies and practices: A compendium* (2nd ed.). Boston: Allyn and Bacon.

DIALOGUE JOURNALS

Description. Dialogue journals use writing as a communication device between the students and the teacher. In small notebooks, the students write about ideas that they want to communicate to the teacher. The teacher responds to these ideas with questions, comments, and personal reactions. Through multiple journal entries, students and teacher carry on a conversation.

Major Reading Tasks It Develops

1. Reading as communication
2. Active comprehension
3. Use of textual and nontextual information

Targeted Reading Levels: All levels

Text: Self-generated dialogue

Procedures

1. The teacher secures writing notebooks. He can use bound composition notebooks, student-made books of stapled pages, or loose-leaf notebooks.
2. The teacher explains that a dialogue journal is like writing a letter to someone.
   a. He talks about how exciting it feels to get a letter from someone.
   b. He explains that the dialogue journal is like writing important things about your life to your teacher.
   c. He tells the students he will comment personally on what is written.
3. The teacher shows the students an example from another journal. (The teacher first secures permission from the writer and reader.)
4. He reminds the students that they can write about any topic.
5. The teacher designates a time for writing and then sets the timer.
6. The students and teacher write in their journals.
7. The teacher reads what the students write.
8. The teacher responds with questions or comments: "Can you describe . . . ? I have felt like that, too."
9. The students read the teacher's comments.
10. The students write a response or choose another topic.
11. The writing cycle continues.

COMMENT: Although this technique is more effective for some students than others, it is recommended as part of the diagnostic teaching session because it releases the structured format of directed and guided instruction.

Further Diagnostic Applications

Basic View of Reading. Reading is a top-down process where readers' personal interpretations focus comprehension. Both reading and writing are constructive processes that are influenced by the desire to communicate.

Patterns of Strengths and Strategies. Dialogue journals are most appropriate for simultaneous, nonverbal students who enjoy communicating ideas through writing rather than talking. In this technique, personal ideas are communicated without an oral explanation or eye contact.

Learner Patterns That Produce a High Success Rate

1. A simultaneous learner who needs time to express her ideas in words. Writing allows her to think through ideas without noticeably lengthy pauses.
2. A nonverbal reader who prefers to communicate her ideas through writing rather than talking. Dialogue journals allow her to put her thoughts into words without talking.
*3. A passive reader who does not realize that reading and writing are constructive processes. This technique allows her to experience reading and writing as communication.
*4. A text-bound reader who does not use her personal understanding of the world to interpret information. Dialogue journals show her how a writer uses personal understanding to compose text.

Using the Technique as a Diagnostic Lesson. For dialogue journals to be effective, a majority of the following statements must be answered in the affirmative.

YES   NO

____ ____   **1.** The student can write (produce letters) fairly easily.

____ ____   **2.** The student likes to communicate her ideas in writing.

____ ____   **3.** The student uses the teacher's model to correct her own writing errors.

For Further Reading

Gambrell, L. B. (1985). Dialogue journals: Reading-writing interaction. *Reading Teacher, 38*, 512–515.
Glazer, S. M. (1984). Liberating students to write. *Early Years, 15*(1), 67–69.

DIRECT EXPERIENCE APPROACH

Description. Direct experience is an approach where actual situations are used to develop word meanings. The actual object is manipulated or the event is enacted in order to develop an understanding of the concept. During the activity, the teacher and students use the new word (label) as they actually experience the concept. This associates the word label with the word concept.

Major Reading Tasks It Develops

1. Word meanings
2. Reading comprehension

Targeted Reading Levels: All levels. Necessary for young children.

Text: The object or event in a situational context

Procedure

1. The teacher makes a list of target words that are not well developed in the students' meaning vocabularies.
2. He secures the objects that these words represent or plans an excursion for the event. To develop an understanding of the word *sour*, for example, the teacher brings lemons to the class.
3. The teacher constructs a situation in which to use the object. In the example, the students would taste the lemons.
4. The students use the objects in the situation and describe the experience. In the example, students could describe how the lemons tasted.
5. The students identify other objects that are similar and tell how they are alike and then how they are different. In the example, students could contrast the taste of the lemon with a pickle, a doughnut, and a hamburger.
6. The students identify other objects that are different and tell how they are different and then how they may be alike. In the example, the students would think of other fruits that are sour and those that are not sour.
7. The teacher writes the words on a card or the chalkboard so that meaning can be associated with what the words look like.

1. Science experiments use activities to develop a concept and follow the activity with a labeling and recording of the information; therefore, they develop meaning through a direct experience.
2. Simulation of social studies concepts provides an activity where words describing a concept are used in a social-interactive context and, therefore, develop meaning through a direct association between the concept and the label.

Further Diagnostic Applications

Basic View of Reading. Reading is a top-down process where a conceptual understanding of words is based on generalizations from specific events that the reader has encountered. Therefore, word meanings are based not only on categorical relationships but also on the knowledge of specific events each person has had. Definitions are developed as the child uses language in social situations.

Patterns of Strengths and Strategies. Direct experience is appropriate for students who learn through sensory motor involvement in their learning. Concrete objects build a store of specific instances from which to develop definitional language. For these students, the approach matches their underlying preference for developing meaning within the context of situations rather than by verbal descriptions devoid of actions.

Learner Patterns That Produce a High Success Rate

1. A simultaneous learner who uses past experiences rather than specific definitional knowledge to comprehend text. Direct experience shows her how to label her environment.
2. A kinesthetic learner who needs to touch and feel concrete objects in order to develop word meanings. The direct experience helps her to develop verbal and concept meaning simultaneously.
*3. A passive but verbal learner who uses word labels without understanding the underlying conceptual meaning of the words. Direct experience makes the connections between the words she uses and their underlying conceptual meaning.

Using the Technique as a Diagnostic Teaching Lesson. For the direct experience approach to be effective, a majority of the following statements must be answered in the affirmative.

—— ——   **1.** The student uses specific examples when defining words.

—— ——   **2.** The student uses *like a* statements rather than definitional language.

—— ——   **3.** The student finds manipulative activities meaningful and not boring.

—— ——   **4.** The student can draw similarities and differences between words and concepts.

For Further Reading

Dale, E. (1969). *Audiovisual methods in teaching* (3rd ed.). New York: Holt, Rinehart & Winston.

Johnson, D. D., & Pearson, P. D. (1984). *Teaching reading vocabulary* (2nd ed.). New York: Holt, Rinehart & Winston.

May, F. (1986). *Reading as communication: An interactive approach* (2nd ed.). Columbus, OH: Merrill.

DIRECTED READING ACTIVITY

Description. A directed reading activity (DRA) is an instructional format for teaching reading where the teacher assumes the major instructional role. He develops background knowledge, introduces new words, and gives the students a purpose for reading. Then he directs the discussion with questions to develop reading comprehension. Finally, he reinforces and extends the skills and knowledge developed in the story.

Major Reading Tasks It Develops

1. Comprehension
2. Word meanings
3. Word identification

Targeted Reading Levels: All levels

Text: Graded stories in basal readers

1. The teacher develops readiness for reading:
   a. He presents new vocabulary words in oral and written context. Children are asked what these new words mean and directed to remember the words by their distinctive visual features.
   b. He develops appropriate background knowledge so that students will understand the general setting of the story.
   c. He gives the students a purpose for reading by telling them to read to find out a particular thing or concept. He develops purposes that require students to read the entire story before an answer is resolved.
2. The students read the story silently.
   a. If necessary, the teacher divides the story into sections. After reading a section, the teacher asks a variety of questions emphasizing literal and nonliteral story understanding.
   b. The teacher asks the students to support their answers by reading the appropriate sections in the text.
3. The teacher reinforces and extends concepts introduced in the story.
   a. Activities to reinforce word recognition and word meanings are used to develop independence in reading.
   b. Activities that develop a creative response to the story are assigned.
   c. Activities that require students to relate the story to their own experiences and to other stories in the basal reader are used.

Further Diagnostic Applications

Basic View of Reading. Reading requires recognizing words and then associating meaning with these new words. Initially, therefore, reading is a text-based process. However, when new words have been learned and purposes have been set, students can read with comprehension.

Patterns of Strengths and Strategies. A directed reading activity is a flexible approach for instructing young children to read stories. Following this format, the text can be narrative or expository, short or long, interrupted or read as a whole. However, it must be remembered that the directed reading activity is just that, reading directed by the teacher and not the student. Therefore, it is most appropriate for young readers who need a substantial amount of teacher direction in order to understand stories.

Learner Patterns That Produce a High Success Rate

1. The active reader who needs new words presented before she reads so that word recognition does not interfere with story comprehension. This approach introduces new words to facilitate story comprehension.

2. The passive reader who needs the teacher to direct her attention to important word recognition and comprehension cues. The teacher can begin with this format but should phase as quickly as possible to strategies that require a more active stance from the reader.

Using the Technique as a Diagnostic Teaching Lesson. For directed reading to be effective, a majority of the following statements must be answered in the affirmative.

YES   NO

_____ _____   **1.** The student comprehends the story and is fairly active when she reads.

_____ _____   **2.** The student needs her attention directed to recognizing words in isolation and context.

_____ _____   **3.** The student is more comfortable answering questions than retelling the story.

For Further Reading

Anderson, R. C., Hiebert, E. H., Scott, J. A., & Wilkinson, I. A. G. (1985). *Becoming a nation of readers: The report of the commission on reading.* Washington, DC: National Institute of Education.

Betts, E. A. (1946). *Foundations of reading instruction.* New York: American Book.

Tierney, R. J., Readence, J. E., & Dishner, E. K. (1985). *Reading strategies and practices: A compendium* (2nd ed.). Boston: Allyn and Bacon.

DIRECTED READING-THINKING ACTIVITY (DRTA)

Description. A directed reading-thinking activity is an instructional format for teaching reading that includes three stages: readiness for reading, active reading comprehension, and reacting to the story (Stauffer, 1975).

Major Reading Tasks It Develops

1. Comprehension
2. Contextual reading

Targeted Reading Levels: All levels

Text: Can be applied to all narrative and expository texts

Procedure

1. The teacher develops readiness for reading by creating an expectation for story theme through the selection of activities to enhance story comprehension. The following activities can serve to develop an expectation for the central theme of a story.
   a. The teacher and the students discuss what they already know about the key concepts.
   b. The teacher and the students discuss the key words and associate them with the key concepts.
   c. The teacher asks the students what they think will happen in the story.
2. The teacher guides active reading, and the students read the story silently. During this step, the teacher encourages active reading by probing students' responses, focusing on important textual information and what the students know about this information. The following questions are used to encourage active, reflective reading of the story.
   a. What do you think is going to happen or is happening?
   b. How do you know that? (On what are you basing your answer?)
   c. Can you support your information or interpretation?
3. The teacher and the students react to the story as a whole.
4. The teacher leads the students to analyze the story in relation to other stories, personal experiences, and the author's purpose.
5. The teacher discusses the strategies that were used to understand the story.

Further Diagnostic Applications

Basic View of Reading. Reading is an active thinking process where a reader uses both important textual information and prior understanding of that information to comprehend the story. The reflective thought process focuses on not only what was understood about the story but also how it was understood.

Patterns of Strengths and Strategies. A DRTA is appropriate for students who readily engage in constructing meaning as they read. They use what they already know to predict what will happen in the story and then select important information from the text to justify their answers. The teacher matches these active strategies by discussing not only what the students think but also how the students think.

1. The active reader who uses what she already knows and the text to construct meaning. A DRTA allows this reader to construct meaning with the guidance of the teacher.
2. The simultaneous reader who uses what she already knows to understand stories but has difficulty justifying her answers with information from the text. This technique requires the reader to justify her thinking with information from the text.

Using the Technique as a Diagnostic Teaching Lesson. For a directed reading-thinking activity to be effective, a majority of the following statements must be answered in the affirmative:

YES   **NO**

_____ _____   **1.** The student directs and monitors her own learning when reading.

_____ _____   **2.** The student uses appropriate text-based and reader-based inferences when evaluating predictions.

_____ _____   **3.** The student is more comfortable summarizing the story than answering questions.

For Further Reading

May, F. (1986). *Reading as communication: An interactive approach* (2nd ed.). Columbus, OH: Merrill.
Stauffer, R. (1975). *Directing the reading-thinking process.* New York: Harper & Row.
Tierney, R. J., Readence, J. E., & Dishner, E. K. (1985). *Reading strategies and practices: A compendium* (2nd ed.). Boston: Allyn and Bacon.

DISTAR READING

Description. Distar reading is a structured synthetic phonics approach to initial reading instruction. It focuses on learning the sounds of letters in isolation before putting them together to form words. It uses symbol-action games to develop attention, blending tasks to develop sound synthesis, and rhythmic tasks to develop sound segmentation.

Major Reading Tasks It Develops

1. Word recognition
2. Decoding
3. Sound blending
4. Attention to the sequential arrangement of letters in words

Reading Levels: K–3

Text: Storybooks to accompany the program that are composed entirely of phonetically consistent but visually different short words

Procedure

(Key components for initial reading instruction only)

1. The teacher introduces the sounds through a structured presentation of isolated letter sounds.
2. The teacher provides sufficient repetition so that the sounds of letters are stabilized. The students say the sounds of letters when cued by the teacher.
3. The students blend sounds of letters into words when cued by the teacher. The teacher focuses attention successively to the individual sounds in words.
4. The students slowly blend the sounds together to form the target word.
5. After slowly blending the sounds into words, the students are directed to ''say it fast.''
6. After the sounds and words are mastered, the teacher introduces the story.
7. The teacher begins each lesson by reviewing single letter sounds. The review is followed by sounding out each word. Finally, the story is read and comprehension questions asked.
8. The students orally reread the story.

CAUTION: This approach encourages a very slow, laborious approach to reading. After two years of the approach, fluency instruction is necessary.

Further Diagnostic Applications

Basic View of Reading. Reading is a bottom-up process where the reader learns the sounds of letters and then blends them into words. Next she reads sentences and short stories. Distar reading is an extremely sequentially structured approach to reading, where learning to decode words precedes understanding stories.

Patterns of Strengths and Strategies. Distar reading is most appropriate for students who have facility with auditory perception, auditory discrimination, and sound blending. For these students, the approach matches their underlying perceptual strengths. Therefore, successive learners profit most from this approach to reading.

Learner Patterns That Produce a High Success Rate

1. The successive learner who can blend sounds but has no visual memory. (The student can always decode the word she has forgotten.)
2. The successive learner who needs many repetitions before the word becomes part of her sight vocabulary. This program provides many repetitions of new words before they are expected to be learned.
3. An extremely inattentive learner who can blend sounds but does not attend to the visual forms of words because of attentional control problems. The procedures for introducing the lesson include hand signals that draw attention to the individual letters in words.
4. The learner who guesses at words and refuses to analyze the distinctive features of letters in words but can blend sounds. Distar reading draws her attention to the sequential nature of sound-symbol associations.

Using the Technique as a Diagnostic Teaching Lesson. For Distar reading to be effective, a majority of the following statements must be answered in the affirmative.

YES	NO	
____	____	**1.** The student can blend sounds.
____	____	**2.** The direct instruction of the teacher focuses the student's attention.
____	____	**3.** The student responds to the repetitious nature of the program.
____	____	**4.** The student has difficulty remembering what the word looks like.

For Further Reading

Bereiter, C., & Englemann, S. (1966). *Teaching disadvantaged children in the preschool.* Englewood Cliffs, NJ: Prentice-Hall.

Bereiter, C., & Englemann, S. (1970). *The Distar reading program.* Chicago: Science Research Associates.

ECHO READING

Description. Echo reading is a form of modeling oral reading where the teacher reads a line of a story and the student echos his model by reading the same line, imitating his intonation and phrasing.

Major Reading Tasks It Develops

1. Oral reading fluency
2. Intonation and phrasing
3. Chunking the text into meaningful thought units

Targeted Reading Levels: 1–4

Text: Any text that is well written

Procedure

1. The teacher selects a text around 200 words long that is near frustration level reading.
2. The teacher reads the first line of the text, accentuating appropriate phrasing and intonation.
3. Immediately, the student reads the same line, modeling the teacher's example.
4. The teacher and the student read in echo fashion for the entire passage, increasing the amount of text when the student can imitate the model.

Modifications

1. Echo reading is an effective intervention when using repeated readings (see ''Repeated Readings'' in this chapter). After the first reading, the

teacher and student can echo read those sentences where there were a string of miscues or errors.

2. Echo reading can also be used in conjunction with chunking (see ''Chunking'' in this chapter) so the student can hear the way the teacher chunks language into thoughts.

Further Diagnostic Applications

Basic View of Reading. Reading is a top-down process where a reader matches what she hears with the text. The reader must read fluently to integrate the meaning with the text on the page.

Patterns of Strengths and Strategies. Echo reading is most appropriate for the student who needs the teacher to model fluent oral reading and needs to repeat that model immediately in order to remember how the text sounded.

Learner Patterns That Produce a High Success Rate

1. A passive and successive reader who has become word-bound and lost the flow of language. This technique allows her to hear fluent oral reading and immediately imitate the model.
2. A simultaneous learner who has become extremely word-bound by an overemphasis in decoding. Echo reading shows her how to use sentence meaning as well as the model to increase oral reading fluency.
3. An extremely slow reader who needs to hear language read fluently. The teacher reads each sentence rapidly and in thought units so this reader can read fluently with intonation.
4. A learner who refuses to follow the teacher when using the impress method or simultaneous reading. Echo reading provides a clear model for this student to follow.

Using the Technique as a Diagnostic Teaching Lesson. For echo reading to be effective, a majority of the following statements must be answered in the affirmative.

YES	NO	
_____	_____	**1.** The student imitates the model of the teacher.
_____	_____	**2.** The student follows the line of print as she reads the text.

For Further Reading

Aulls, M. (1982). *Developing readers in today's elementary school.* Boston: Allyn and Bacon.

Tierney, R. J., Readence, J. E., & Dishner, E. K. (1985). *Reading strategies and practices: A compendium* (2nd ed.). Boston: Allyn and Bacon.

EXPLICIT TEACHING

Description. Explicit teaching is a lesson framework that directly instructs a student in the skills and strategies of reading. The lesson framework is based on making the task relevant to the student and directly teaching the task through examples and modeling. The teacher systematically plans activities to increase independent application of the skill or strategy.

Major Reading Tasks It Develops

1. Various skills or strategies
2. Self-directed learning

Targeted Reading Levels: Depends on the skill being taught

Text: Can be applied to all kinds

Procedure

1. The teacher selects the skill or strategy to be taught.
2. The teacher selects a series of texts to illustrate the skill or strategy.
3. The teacher introduces the skill or strategy. For example, he may choose finding the main idea in paragraphs.
4. He explains the reason why learning this skill or strategy will facilitate reading performance. In this example, he may say that finding the main idea is important because it helps us remember facts using one idea rather than many different facts.
5. He asks students how this is like other skills or strategies that they have learned. This helps them understand the reasons for learning a particular skill. In this example, he may say, "We already studied how to identify key vocabulary words. How did this help us?" The students and teacher discuss how these words were often what the text was mainly about.

6. The teacher explains the process of the skill. For example, he may say, "When deciding on a main idea, you think to yourself, 'What does each sentence tell about and how is the information alike?' How the information is alike becomes the main idea."

7. The teacher demonstrates how to think when using the skill. A sample demonstration might include the steps that follow.

   a. The teacher puts a three- or four-sentence paragraph on an overhead or the chalkboard.

   b. He summarizes each sentence aloud.

   c. He tells how they are related to the main idea.

   d. He explains that the way the sentences are alike is what the paragraph is mostly about, or the main idea.

8. The students and the teacher do the next example together. The students talk through the new example, explaining what they are doing, why they are doing it, and how they are doing it. The teacher explains his thinking to clarify any steps in the process.

9. The students do the next example by talking through how they complete the task. Then the students tell how this will help them read.

10. The teacher provides feedback about what the students say by modeling how he would have completed the task.

11. The students read more paragraphs and use the newly learned task on their own.

Further Diagnostic Applications

Basic View of Reading. Reading is an interactive process where the reader monitors her reading using both skills and strategies. Reading instruction, therefore, should explicitly teach the student to use reading skills and strategies independently.

Patterns of Strengths and Strategies. Introducing the new skill or strategy, the approach systematically leads students through the reasoning process relating to the skill or strategy. It takes the separate parts, explains them, and then integrates the parts into the whole task. It is most efficient for the passive or successive learner who profits from seeing how to fit the parts of reading into the whole process.

Learner Patterns That Produce a High Success Rate

1. A passive learner who does not actively use a particular skill or strategy when reading stories independently. Explicit instruction teaches the skill by showing her how to use it when she is reading.

2. A successive learner who needs to be shown exactly how the strategies of reading affect the entire reading process. Explicit instruction shows her how the parts fit into the whole.

3. An inattentive learner who approaches reading in a trial-and-error fashion, not understanding the exact skills and strategies necessary for consistent reading performance. Explicit instruction gives her a system for approaching learning.

*4. A simultaneous learner who needs to be shown how to control her own learning. (Mediation would be very short.)

Using the Technique as a Diagnostic Teaching Lesson. For explicit teaching to be effective, a majority of the following statements must be answered in the affirmative.

YES	NO	
____	____	**1.** The student has proficient word identification for the passage.
____	____	**2.** The student learns from the examples what the process is.
____	____	**3.** The student learns from the examples how the process works.
____	____	**4.** The student improves her ability to do the skill or strategy.
____	____	**5.** The student can explain how the process works in new situations.

For Further Reading

Tierney, R. J., & Cunningham, J. (1984). Research on teaching reading comprehension. In P. D. Pearson (Ed.), *Handbook of reading research* (pp. 609–656). New York: Longman.

Tierney, R. J., Readence, J. E., & Dishner, E. K. (1985). *Reading strategies and practices: A compendium* (2nd ed.). Boston: Allyn and Bacon.

EXPERIENCE-TEXT-RELATIONSHIP (ETR)

Description. Experience-text-relationship is specifically designed to use children's experiences to teach new concepts and new words in the story. In this technique, the teacher spends time showing students the relationships between what they know and what they are reading, both before and after reading the story. It is specifically designed for use with multiculture students (Au, 1979).

Major Reading Tasks It Develops

1. Comprehension
2. Integrating background knowledge with the text

Targeted Reading Levels: All levels

Text: Stories with an interesting theme or plot that can sustain an in-depth discussion

Procedure

1. The teacher chooses an appropriate text.
2. The teacher reads the selected passage to decide the theme, topic, and important points.
3. The teacher thinks about what the students know related to the theme, topic, and important points.
4. The teacher formulates general questions that will initiate a discussion about what the students know.
5. The teacher begins the instruction with a general discussion of what the students know. (This step is the *experience phase* of the lesson and is student-initiated.)
6. The teacher uses the information that is generated to tie the students' experiences directly to the story. He uses pictures and information that come directly from the story. (This step is teacher-directed.)
7. He asks the students to make a prediction based on the discussion (student input).
8. Then, if necessary, the teacher sets other purposes for reading (teacher input).
9. The students read a portion of the story to see if their predictions are right. This begins the *text phase* of the lesson.
10. The teacher returns to predictions and asks the students what they have learned so far about these predictions.
11. The teacher sets additional purposes.
12. The teacher calls attention to important information in the text if necessary.
13. The teacher alternates periods of silent reading and discussion until the entire story has been read.

14. When the entire story has been read, the teacher directs a discussion of the key ideas in the story.
15. He then compares the key ideas in the text to the key experiences of the students. To do this, he returns to the information gained during the experience phase of the lesson. This is called the *relationship phase* and is teacher-directed.
16. He then contrasts the key ideas in the text with the students' experiences.
17. The teacher summarizes the main relationships after the discussion is complete.
18. Finally, the teacher recommends that the students use the ETR steps when they read on their own.

Further Diagnostic Applications

Basic View of Reading. Reading is an interactive process where the learners use what they know to interpret what the text says. Readers need assistance learning how to figure out what they know that is useful to interpret the text. They also need assistance in making connections between this information and what the text says.

Patterns of Strengths and Strategies. The ETR technique is appropriate for students who need assistance in bringing their background knowledge to the text. It is especially useful for multiculture students who experience a gap between the way they talk about their experiences and the way an author describes those same experiences. This technique helps these students relate their own language and experiences to the text.

Learner Patterns That Produce a High Success Rate

1. A child who experiences a wide gap between what she knows and what she reads. ETR shows the student the relationship between what she knows and how the text explains these same experiences.
2. A passive learner who reads text without relating what she knows. ETR focuses on the student's experience during every step of the lesson.
*3. A passive learner who will not venture a guess while reading. ETR gives her the tools to make a guess.

Using the Technique as a Diagnostic Teaching Lesson. For experience-text-relationship to be effective, a majority of the following statements must be answered in the affirmative:

_____ _____   **1.** The student can express what she knows.

_____ _____   **2.** The student can make a prediction.

_____ _____   **3.** With teacher assistance, the student can see the relationship between her experience and what the text says.

For Further Reading

Au, K. (1979). Using the experience-text-relationship method with minority children. *Reading Teacher, 32,* 677–679.

McNeil, J. D. (1987). *Reading comprehension: New directions for classroom practice.* Glenview, IL: Scott, Foresman.

Mason, J. M., & Au, K. H. (1986). *Reading instruction for today.* Glenview, IL: Scott, Foresman.

FEATURE ANALYSIS GRID

Description. A feature analysis grid is a technique to develop word meanings by graphing the major characteristics of target words. Key words are compared as to how they are alike and how they are different (Johnson & Pearson, 1984).

Major Reading Tasks It Develops

1. Word meanings
2. Categorization of words
3. Using student knowledge to develop word meanings

Targeted Reading Levels: All levels

Text: Isolated words that are associated in categories. It is most advantageous to select key vocabulary words and their respective categories prior to reading a selection.

Procedure

1. The teacher selects categories and words to analyze.

2. The teacher makes a feature analysis grid with a column of words to analyze.

CATEGORY: LANDSCAPES

New and Known Words	Important Characteristics			
	Trees	Water	Rocks	Snow
Mountains	+	+	+	+

3. The teacher and the students discuss the characteristics of the first word.
4. The teacher adds the characteristics across the top of the grid, indicating the important characteristics with a plus in the respective squares of the grid.
5. The teacher and the students then discuss the second target word.
6. The teacher and the students evaluate this word according to the important features on the grid. The teacher puts a plus on those characteristics that the second target word has and a minus on those that it does not have.

CATEGORY: LANDSCAPES

New and Known Words	Important Characteristics				
	Trees	Water	Rocks	Snow	Sand
Mountains	+	+	+	+	−
Deserts	−	+	−	?	+

7. The teacher adds any new important characteristics, indicating those with a plus in the appropriate square on the grid. The teacher and the students discuss any uncertain responses. In the example, deserts consist mainly of sand, but there are some snow deserts.
8. The teacher and the students discuss how the two words are alike and how they are different.
9. The procedure is repeated for other words. The teacher adds important characteristics as needed.

10. The teacher adds other words that are prevalent in the students' oral vocabularies to make comparisons between what is new and what is already known.

Modifications

1. Use a rating scale (1–3) to show the relative importance that each characteristic contributes to the meaning of the words.
2. Use as a prewriting activity for a comparison paragraph among words and concepts.

Further Diagnostic Applications

Basic View of Reading. Reading is an interactive process that is based on what the reader already knows about the words used in the text. Comprehension is facilitated by understanding the specific attributes of the words used in a passage.

Patterns of Strengths and Strategies. The feature analysis grid is most appropriate for students who have a well-developed background of experiences but who overgeneralize word meanings, failing to see the likenesses and differences between specific definitional meanings. For these students, the graphic representation of important characteristics organizes the prior knowledge into specific linguistic categories.

Learner Patterns That Produce a High Success Rate

1. A successive learner who has difficulty drawing comparisons among word meanings but has verbal fluency and analyzes individual words by their major features. This technique allows her to compare and contrast the major features of words at the same time.
2. A divergent thinker who notices features other than the major characteristics but easily understands the grid and the relationships among word meanings. This technique focuses her attention on the key features of the words.
*3. A passive learner who does not think about the differences among words. This technique helps her think and talk about how words are alike and different.
*4. A simultaneous learner who overgeneralizes the meanings of words. This technique helps her specify the features of words by developing more discrete features of word meanings.

Using the Technique as a Diagnostic Teaching Lesson. For a feature analysis grid to be effective, a majority of the following statements must be answered in the affirmative.

YES   NO

_____ _____   **1.** The student can identify important characteristics of words.

_____ _____   **2.** The student understands the purpose of the grid and can visualize the negative and positive aspects of the grid.

_____ _____   **3.** Using the grid, the student develops a clear understanding of the attributes of the target words.

_____ _____   **4.** The student understands likenesses and differences.

_____ _____   **5.** The student can make comparisons among key features of words.

For Further Reading

Anders, P., Bos, C., & Filip, D. (1984). The effects of semantic feature analysis on the reading comprehension of learning disabled students. In J. Niles & L. Harris, (Eds.), *Changing perspectives on research in reading/language processing and instruction* (pp. 62–166). Rochester, NY: National Reading Conference.

Johnson, D. D. (1982). *Three sound strategies for vocabulary development* (Ginn Occasional Papers No. 3). Lexington, MA: Silver, Burdett & Ginn.

Johnson, D. D., & Pearson, P. D. (1984). *Teaching reading vocabulary* (2nd ed.). New York: Holt, Rinehart & Winston.

GUIDED IMAGERY/COMPREHENSION

Description. Guided imagery uses sensory images related to the story line to increase active comprehension and activate background knowledge about (a) situations and characters in a story or (b) key concepts in expository text (Walker, 1985).

Major Reading Tasks It Develops

1. Active comprehension
2. Imagery involvement in reading

Text: Narrative text or concepts in expository text

Procedure

1. The teacher selects a text.
2. He identifies key events and characters or key concepts, depending on the type of text.
3. The teacher writes a guided journey that uses these key items. In the journey, the teacher intersperses calming statements with the story events and character descriptions or the key concepts. The following is an example that might be used prior to reading a narrative story.

   Close your eyes . . . and relax in your chair. . . . Now listen to the noises in the room. . . . Can you hear them? Feel the temperature of the room. . . . Now turn the noises of this room into the sounds of a meadow. . . . What kind of day is it? You are at the foot of a mountain in China . . . begin walking up . . . up . . . up . . . the mountain. . . . As you climb higher . . . and higher . . . you see a lake. . . . Walk toward the lake. . . . Your village needs the water in this lake. . . . Looking for a way to release the water, you walk around . . . and around . . . and around the lake. . . . A wild goose soars toward you. . . . Listen to the goose. . . . She says that you will need the golden key. . . . It will open the gate of the lake. . . . Looking around . . . you see the keyhole in the stone gate . . . but there is no key. . . . You begin searching . . . and searching for the golden key. . . . Something is flying toward you. . . . It says to find the third daughter of the Dragon King. . . . She will help you. . . . I will leave you now to continue searching for the golden key. . . . When you have finished your search . . . you may return to this room . . . and open your eyes.

4. For narrative text, the teacher uses the key events to develop the guided imagery, but he leaves the problem in the story unresolved. The students are to finish the story in their minds.
5. For expository text, the teacher develops a guided imagery that illustrates the attributes of the key concepts.
6. To begin the lesson, the teacher has the students relax in their chairs and think of sounds and smells like the setting. Then he reads the journey in a calm, serene voice, interspersing action statements with calming statements.
7. He tells the students to return to the classroom when they have completed their journeys in the mind.
8. The teacher and students share their images. The students can share their stories in pairs.
9. Students read the selection to compare their journeys with the text.

1. In narrative text, the use of images facilitates comprehension by activating what students already know (images) so they can use this information to understand how the author resolved the problem.
2. In expository text, the use of images helps students remember the key concepts in the text so they can elaborate or compare those images with the text as they read.

Further Diagnostic Applications

Basic View of Reading. Reading is a top-down process that uses personal images (reader-based inferencing) to create meaning. As the student reads, she forms an expectation for meaning that is represented by images of specific events. She refines her model of meaning (basically images) when she reads.

Patterns of Strengths and Strategies. Guided imagery/comprehension is a technique for students who store information in images. It is appropriate for the reflective, simultaneous thinker who refers to specific events and images when discussing text. Using guided imagery prior to discussion helps this learner translate her images into a verbal response.

Learner Patterns That Produce a High Success Rate

1. The simultaneous thinker who uses images to construct meaning that often results in changing the story line to fit her model of meaning. This technique helps her see how her own ideas and images affect her comprehension.
2. An extremely imaginative thinker who enjoys sharing her images and comparing them to the text. This technique allows her to use this strength when comprehending.
3. A simultaneous reflective thinker who uses images instead of words when thinking. This allows images to be connected with words.
*4. The passive reader who does not check what he knows while he reads. Learning to image can increase her elaboration and monitoring of what she is reading.
*5. The extremely literal thinker who seldom constructs images. The guided image technique provides a process for the student to use images when reading.

Using the Technique as a Diagnostic Teaching Lesson. For guided imagery/comprehension to be effective, a majority of the following statements must be answered in the affirmative.

_____ _____ **1.** The student recalls images and enjoys sharing those images.

_____ _____ **2.** The student constructs a coherent and logical ending to the guided journey.

_____ _____ **3.** The student reads with increased involvement comparing her journey with the text.

_____ _____ **4.** The student does not overly rely on the guided journey and make the text fit her predictions.

For Further Reading

Gambrell, L. B., & Bales, R. J. (1986). Mental imagery and the comprehension-monitoring performance of fourth and fifth grade poor readers. *Reading Research Quarterly, 21*, 454–465.

Vaca, R., & Vaca, J. (1986). *Content area reading* (2nd ed.). Boston: Little, Brown.

Walker, B. J. (1985). Right-brained strategies for teaching comprehension. *Academic Therapy, 21*, 133–141.

GUIDED IMAGERY/LANGUAGE EXPERIENCE

Description. Guided imagery/language experience uses sensory images related to a particular situation to create a personal understanding of that experience. In language experience, this created story is dictated and recorded for the reading lesson (Walker, 1982).

Major Reading Tasks It Develops

1. Knowledge that printed words are thoughts and images written down
2. Develop a sight vocabulary by anticipating words
3. Develop oral reading fluency

Targeted Reading Levels: K–3

Text: The child's own language

1. The teacher designs a guided imagery journey that incorporates targeted sight words. He intersperses calming statements with story events. However, he lets the students resolve the problem in their imaginations. For instance, if the targeted sight words are *balloon, climb, sky,* and *wind,*, the journey might contain the events that follow.

   Close your eyes and imagine that you are walking on a narrow pathway. . . . The wind is blowing gently as you walk softly down the pathway. . . . You come to an open meadow, and there is a hot air balloon. . . . A wise teacher offers to take you on a ride in the sky. . . . You climb into the basket. . . . You soar up . . . up . . . up . . . in the sky. Look at the sky . . . the teacher shows you different . . . kinds of clouds. . . . You watch as you float through the clouds. . . . Notice how the sky changes as you float . . . float . . . float . . . through the different kinds of clouds. . . . I will leave you now. . . . You can finish the journey in your mind. . . . When you have finished your journey . . . you may return to the classroom and open your eyes.

2. When conducting the guided imagery, the teacher has the students relax in their chairs and close their eyes. He reads the journey in a calm, serene voice. At the close of the journey, he asks the students to return to the classroom.

3. When all the students have opened their eyes, they share their journeys in pairs. This allows them to verbalize the images.

4. The students dictate the journey while the teacher serves as secretary for the class (or individual student).

5. The students are reminded that the stories represent what happened in their imaginations. Their stories represent their images, just like a published story represents an author's images.

6. If a group story is written, the students are again asked to use general descriptions of the images, so that each time they read the story, they will be reminded of the pictures that were in their minds.

7. The teacher reads the story simultaneously with the students to revise any unclear statements or images.

8. The story is then read *repeatedly* so that the repetition and wholeness will encourage a predictive set for the story.

9. Chunk cards (cards with phrases from the story) are made by dividing the entire story into meaningful chunks of language, starting from the beginning of the story.

10. These chunk cards are flashed in story order so that the students can use their images of the whole story to decode unrecognized words.

11. To reinforce the recognition of sight words, the chunk cards are shuffled and the story reassembled in order.

12. Later cloze exercises (see "Cloze Instruction" in this chapter) are constructed so that unknown words are reinforced within language structures.
13. The teacher collates the stories into anthologies that create the initial reading material for the students.

Further Diagnostic Applications

Basic View of Reading. Reading is a top-down process where the personal images of meaning precede verbal expression and the decoding of written language. The students use their images to remember the words in the story.

Patterns of Strengths and Strategies. Guided imagery/language experience is an imaging technique. It is most appropriate for students who need a sense of the whole before proceeding to the parts of language. It is appropriate for the reflective, simultaneous thinker who needs time to construct an image in order to remember words. If she uses vivid images in her drawing or speaking and predicts words using her background knowledge, then language experience matches her natural processing style and facilitates word learning by asking her to recognize words using her personal images.

Learner Patterns That Produce a High Success Rate

1. A simultaneous thinker who uses images to construct meaning, which often results in overpredicting or guessing from pictures without identifying words by what they look or sound like. This technique helps her use her images to remember what words look like.
2. An extremely imaginative thinker whose expressive language is vivid and elaborate. This allows her to use her imagination as she learns what words look like.
3. A simultaneous reflective thinker, who uses images instead of words when thinking. This technique allows her time to connect words with these images.

Using the Technique as a Diagnostic Teaching Lesson. For guided imagery/language experience to be effective, a majority of the following statements must be answered in the affirmative.

YES   NO

_____ _____   **1.** The student can image and enjoys sharing those images.

____ ____   **2.** The student can remember the story she told.

____ ____   **3.** The student tells a fairly coherent story.

____ ____   **4.** The student uses her images to predict words she does not remember. (She closes her eyes as she tries to remember a word.)

____ ____   **5.** The student responds correctly when prompted, using the preceding context and story theme to encourage identifying a forgotten word.

For Further Reading

Walker, B. J. (1985). *Using guided fantasy to teach reading.* Paper presented at the Second Ruperstsland Regional Reading Conference of the International Reading Association, Regina, Saskatchewan, Canada. (ERIC Document Reproduction Service No. ED 253 850)

Walker, B. J. (1982). A new approach to language experience. *Journal of Language Experience, 5,* 25–30.

HERRINGBONE TECHNIQUE

Description.   The herringbone technique develops comprehension of the main idea by plotting the *who, what, when, where, how* and *why* questions on a visual diagram of a fish skeleton. Using the answers to the *wh* questions, the student writes the main idea across the backbone of the fish diagram (Tierney, Readence, & Dishner, 1985).

Major Reading Tasks It Develops

1. Comprehension
2. Main idea
3. Important details

Targeted Reading Levels: 5–12

Text: Particularly suited for expository text. Can be used for narrative text.

1. The teacher selects a text at the appropriate reading level.
2. The teacher constructs a visual diagram of the herringbone.
3. The teacher tells the student to record the answers to the questions on the diagram. She will look for answers to:
    a. Who is the author talking about?
    b. What did they do?
    c. When did they do it?
    d. Where did they do it?
    e. How did they do it?
    f. Why did they do it?
4. The student reads to find the answers and records the answers on the diagram.
5. After the information is recorded, the teacher shows the student how each answer fits into a slot in a main idea sentence.
6. The student writes a main idea, using the information from the herringbone diagram.
7. The teacher duplicates sheets with the herringbone diagram, and students complete the diagram on their own.
8. The diagram becomes a tool for story discussion. During the discussion, the teacher and students compare their answers and their rationales.

Modification. The implementation of the herringbone can be changed from finding the facts first to writing the main idea and then looking for the facts that support this main idea.

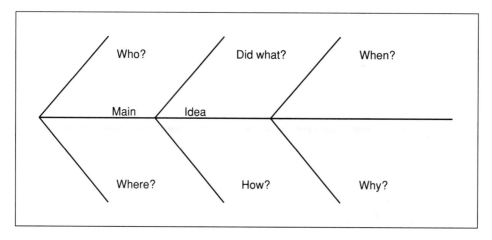

Note. From Robert J. Tierney, John E. Readence, and Ernest K. Dishner, READING STRATEGIES AND PRACTICES: A COMPENDIUM, Second Edition. Copyright © 1985 by Allyn and Bacon, Inc. Reprinted with permission.

Further Diagnostic Applications

Basic View of Reading. Reading is a bottom-up process where the reader uses the facts in the text to construct a main idea.

Patterns of Strengths and Strategies. The herringbone technique is most appropriate for students who need a visual structure to draw relationships between the facts in a text and the main idea. For these students, the technique records the information so that it can be organized into a whole.

Learner Patterns That Produce a High Success Rate

1. A successive learner who has difficulty organizing factual information to form a main idea. This technique shows her how the facts fit together to form the main idea.
2. A passive learner who has difficulty identifying the important facts that are used to form a main idea. This technique gives her an active strategy to use while she is reading.
3. A simultaneous learner who has difficulty identifying the factual information that she used to construct a main idea. This technique can be modified so that first the student writes the main idea and then rereads the text to find the facts that support the main idea.

Using the Technique as a Diagnostic Teaching Lesson. For the herringbone technique to be effective, a majority of the following statements must be answered in the affirmative.

YES	NO	
____	____	**1.** The student can find the facts in the text and record them on the diagram.
____	____	**2.** The student can construct a main idea from the facts.
____	____	**3.** The student finds the visual diagram helpful when reading.
____	____	**4.** The student is more active in a group discussion after using the herringbone diagram.

For Further Reading

Herber, H. L. (1978). *Teaching reading in content areas* (2nd ed.). Englewood Cliffs, NJ: Prentice-Hall.

Tierney, R. J., Readence, J. E., & Dishner, E. K. (1985). *Reading strategies and practices:*
  A compendium (2nd ed.). Boston: Allyn and Bacon.

139

The Instructional
Techniques

IMPLICIT TEACHING

Description. Implicit teaching is a nondirective approach to instruction where the teacher creates an instructional environment that stimulates thinking about specific reading tasks. The teacher participates only as a cognitive inquirer, asking the student, "How did you know that?" The student makes generalizations because she is immersed in a literate environment.

Major Reading Tasks It Develops

1. Active learning
2. Can be applied to all skills or strategies

Targeted Reading Levels: All levels

Text: Carefully selected to demonstrate the skill or strategy that is targeted for instruction

Procedure

1. The teacher decides on the targeted learning outcome.
2. The teacher strategically arranges the physical environment so that students can discuss with the teacher what they read in a relaxed atmosphere.
3. The teacher arranges attractive books or printed materials that incorporate the skill or strategy in prominent places in the room.
4. The teacher creates a social activity that causes the students to use the targeted skill or strategy in a meaningful way.
5. When the students use print to make sense of their environment, the teacher asks, "How did you know that?"
6. The teacher creates the expectation of the learning outcome by discussing informally the learning outcome. He says, "Did you notice . . . ?"
7. When appropriate, the teacher models reading the text for meaning and enjoyment. He says, "When I read that I thought. . . . "

8. The teacher creates a similar experience that causes the students again to use the targeted skill or strategy in a meaningful way.

COMMENT: Implicit instruction is an instructional format where the teacher takes a more indirect role in mediating learning. Techniques fall along a continuum, ranging from *less teacher intervention* to *more teacher intervention.* Implicit instruction has less teacher intervention and more student participation in the learning activity.

Further Diagnostic Applications

Basic View of Reading. Reading is a top-down process where the reader uses what she knows to make sense of her environment. Reading instruction, therefore, should consist of creating a literate environment where a child can use print to make sense of her environment.

Patterns of Strengths and Strategies. This format presents skills and strategies in the whole learning context. The teacher asks the student what she did to make sense of her environment. The student who actively restructures her environment so that it makes sense learns easily through this method.

Learner Patterns That Produce a High Success Rate

1. An active learner who needs learning activities to make sense. This method allows her to use her thinking strategies in natural learning environments.
2. An active learner who prefers to learn without teacher direction. This method allows her to direct her own learning.
3. A simultaneous learner who needs to experience the whole before understanding the parts. This method allows her to use the social-interactive experience to understand the parts of reading.

Using the Technique as a Diagnostic Teaching Lesson. For implicit teaching to be effective, a majority of the following statements must be answered in the affirmative.

YES   NO

_____ _____   **1.** The student can read most of the words in the text.

_____ _____   **2.** The student actively explores the context to make sense of her reading.

_____ _____   **3.** The student can explain her reasons for the way language works.

For Further Reading

Duffy, G. G., & Roehler, L. R. (1986). *Improving classroom reading instruction.* New York: Random House.

Haussler, M. M. (1985). A young child's developing concepts of print. In A. Jaggar & M. T. Smith-Burke (Eds.), *Observing the language learner* (pp. 73–81). New York: International Reading Association & National Council of Teachers of English.

IMPRESS METHOD

Description. The impress method uses unison oral reading between the teacher and the student. The teacher and student sit side by side, with the teacher reading out loud slightly louder and ahead of the student, modeling fluent and expressive oral reading (Heckelman, 1969).

Major Reading Tasks It Develops

1. Oral reading fluency
2. Sight word identification through contextual reading
3. Intonation and phrasing

Targeted Reading Levels: K–5

Text: Self-selected text is recommended

Procedure

1. The teacher selects text that is near frustration-level reading and around 200 words long.
2. The teacher and the student read the text in unison. The teacher reads slightly ahead of and slightly louder than the student.
3. The teacher sits on the right side of the student and reads into the right ear to impress the language structure on the left side of the brain.
4. The teacher moves his finger along the line of print so that the student's eyes can follow his reading.
5. The student's eyes follow the line of print as she reads.
6. As the student gains success through understanding the context, the teacher gradually lets her take the lead.
7. At this time, the teacher releases his lead in reading; however, he supplies difficult words when needed.

Modification. The textual characteristics seem to influence the effectiveness of impress reading. Rhythmic and repetitive texts seem to increase the student's participation. A good source is Shel Silverstein's *Where the Sidewalk Ends.*

Further Diagnostic Applications

Basic View of Reading. Reading is a process of accurate word identification, where automatic word identification precedes understanding. Therefore, reading is a bottom-up process. An abundance of reading errors contributes to an incorrect visual form being imprinted in memory. Therefore, accurate word identification is increased by unison reading, with the teacher modeling fluent oral reading.

Patterns of Strengths and Strategies. Impress method is most appropriate for students who make a series of word identification errors without using passage meaning to self-correct the errors. This is often the result of reading at frustration level for an extended period of time. By hearing the correct intonation and phrasing by a teacher, the student senses the rhythm and flow of language.

Learner Patterns That Produce a High Success Rate

1. A simultaneous learner who relies heavily on background knowledge when orally reading and who does not attend to the graphic cues. The impress method establishes accurate identification of words using overall textual meaning.
2. A nonfluent reader who is word-bound because of a heavy emphasis on phonic instruction. This method can rapidly increase oral reading fluency.
3. A nonreader who has not established a sight vocabulary. Using high interest material, this technique develops a sight vocabulary.

Using the Technique as a Diagnostic Teaching Lesson. For the impress method to be effective, a majority of the following statements must be answered in the affirmative.

YES   NO

_____ _____   **1.** The student is sufficiently motivated to read along with the teacher.

_____ _____   **2.** The student rapidly learns the words in the selected text.

_____ _____ **3.** The student begins to track with the teacher and
follows the model.

_____ _____ **4.** There is an increase in sight word accuracy as a result
of using the method.

For Further Reading

Heckelman, R. G. (1969). A neurological-impress method of remedial reading instruction.
Academic Therapy, 4, 277–282.

Memory, D. M. (1981). The impress method: A status report of a new remedial reading
technique. *Journal of Research and Development in Education, 14,* 102–114.

LANGUAGE EXPERIENCE APPROACH (LEA)

Description. The language experience approach is a technique that is used for
beginning reading instruction where the child dictates a story to the teacher. The
story becomes the text for instruction and a collection of the stories becomes the
child's first reader (Stauffer, 1970).

Major Reading Tasks It Develops

1. Understanding that printed words are thoughts written down
2. A sight word vocabulary
3. Fluency of oral reading

Targeted Reading Levels: K–3

Text: The child's own language

Procedure

1. The teacher engages students in dialogue about a particular topic. A
stimulating, engaging, and concrete topic tends to elicit more
language from the students.
2. The students dictate a story while the teacher serves as secretary for
the class.

3. Using leading questions, the teacher guides the students to develop a story line by using questions like these: "What happened next? Is this what you wanted to say? How can you make a story using this information?"

4. The students and the teacher read the story simultaneously to revise any statements or phrases that are unclear to the students. The story is to follow the natural language patterns of the students.

5. Then the teacher and the students read the story *repeatedly* so that repetition of the entire story will encourage a predictive set for the story.

6. The students are asked to read the story independently.

7. Activities to reinforce word identification are constructed from the story.

8. Word cards or chunk cards are developed using the words in the story. It is recommended that chunk cards (made by dividing the entire story into meaningful phrases) be used.

9. Initially, these chunk cards are flashed in the order in which they appear in the story. Later, they are mixed up. This activity maintains the sense of the whole while the whole is being broken into parts.

10. To continue the instructional process, cloze exercises (see "Cloze Instruction") can be developed to reinforce sight word identification.

11. Stories are collated into anthologies that create the initial reading material for the student.

12. As words are learned, progress is monitored by checking the words off a word list.

Further Diagnostic Applications

Basic View of Reading. Reading is a top-down process. By reading her own story, the child will infer the consistency of printed language patterns. Since the story is based on her own experience, she continually uses this experience to remember the words in the story.

Patterns of Strengths and Strategies. Language experience is most appropriate for students who have facility with language and are simultaneous, top-down thinkers. If a student predicts from her own experiences rather than the words in the text, then language experience matches her strategies (using what she knows); therefore, this technique facilitates word learning by asking the student to identify words using her own experiences.

Learner Patterns That Produce a High Success Rate

1. A simultaneous thinker who uses prior knowledge to construct meaning, often resulting in overpredicting or guessing without identifying

words by how they are written. LEA uses the student's strength (using prior knowledge) to facilitate word identification.

2. An extremely verbal, creative student whose verbalization interferes with the mundane task of looking at words. LEA uses the strength (verbalization) to facilitate word identification.
3. A student who is unwilling to take a guess unless very certain that the response will be correct. LEA provides a text that allows the student to take a safe guess, using both what is on the page and what she remembers was written.
4. A learner who has had an overemphasis on phonics. Language experience can increase her fluency and the predictive set.

Modifications

1. The extremely imaginative, creative learner can use guided imagery as a medium for creating stories.
2. The extremely concrete learner can use field trips and science activities as a medium for creating stories.
3. The student who deals most effectively in visual-spatial relationships can use mapping as a medium for developing a story.
4. The shy, simultaneous learner who has difficulty developing a coherent story can use wordless picture books to boost her confidence in developing a story.

Using the Technique as a Diagnostic Teaching Lesson. For LEA to be effective, a majority of the following statements must be answered in the affirmative.

YES   NO

_____ _____   **1.** The student can remember the story she told.

_____ _____   **2.** The student focuses on the words and story line.

_____ _____   **3.** The student tells a fairly coherent story.

_____ _____   **4.** The student remembers the story well enough to predict the words she does not remember.

_____ _____   **5.** The student responds correctly when prompted using the preceding context and story theme.

For Further Reading

Aukerman, R. C. (1984). *Approaches to beginning reading* (2nd ed.) (pp. 368–371). New York: John Wiley & Sons.

Stauffer, R. G. (1970). *The language experience approach to the teaching of reading.* New York: Harper & Row.

LINGUISTIC METHOD

Description. The linguistic method is an approach for instructing a beginning reader that is based on word patterns. The word families have a minimal contrast in the word patterns. Therefore, this approach emphasizes decoding by visual analogy.

Major Reading Tasks It Develops

1. Word recognition
2. Decoding by analogy
3. Analysis of distinctive visual features

Targeted Reading Levels: K–2

Text: Isolated words that have the same word patterns and designated text that introduces the word patterns.

Procedure

1. The teacher introduces a word pattern by presenting three new words in the word family. For example:

   cat
   mat
   fat

2. The teacher spells each word. Then he says each word. For example:

   c-a-t spells *cat*
   m-a-t spells *rat*
   f-a-t spells *fat*

3. The teacher asks the students how the words are alike. He elicits the response that the words have the same ending pattern of *at.*
4. The teacher asks the students how the words are different. He elicits the response that the words are different because they have a different letter at the beginning.
5. The students read the text that uses the word pattern.

   The cat is fat.
   The cat is on the mat.
   The fat cat is on the mat.

Further Diagnostic Applications

Basic View of Reading. Reading is a bottom-up process where the reader masters a set of word patterns that have a minimal visual contrast. Meaning is stressed after the code is broken. Since the student comes to school with a well-developed oral language, initial reading instruction should focus on decoding.

Patterns of Strengths and Strategies. The linguistic word structure approach to reading is most appropriate for students who have extremely high visual discrimination skills and need a directed approach to word learning.

Learner Patterns That Produce a High Success Rate

1. A successive learner who visually discriminates difference among wholes and has a well-developed visual memory. This technique shows her the parts in whole words.
2. A student who has good visual memory but needs her attention drawn to the patterns in words. This technique shows her how to form decoding analogies.

Using the Technique as a Diagnostic Teaching Lesson. For the linguistic method to be effective, a majority of the following statements must be answered in the affirmative.

YES	NO	
____	____	**1.** The student can visually discriminate the differences in words.
____	____	**2.** The student recognizes letter names and patterns easily.
____	____	**3.** The student transfers the visual patterns to new words; therefore, she decodes using visual analogies.
____	____	**4.** The student finds the simple stories exciting because she is breaking the code.

For Further Reading

Bloomfield, L., & Barnhart, C. (1961). *Let's read: A linguistic approach.* Detroit: Wayne State Press.

Ray, D. D. (1971). Specificity in remediation. In B. Batemen (Ed.), *Learning Disorders* (pp. 180–191). Seattle, WA: Special Child Publications.

LISTENING-THINKING ACTIVITY

Description. A listening-thinking activity (LTA) is an instructional format for teaching children how to listen to stories. It involves predicting what will happen, talking about what happened, and talking about how you know what is happening. As the teacher reads aloud, he communicates the message by adding intonation and gestures to facilitate understanding.

Major Reading Tasks It Develops

1. Listening comprehension
2. Comprehension monitoring
3. Making predictions

Targeted Reading Levels: All levels

Text: An interesting, well-written text. Picture storybooks are excellent.

Procedure

1. Using the title, the teacher has the students brainstorm what the story might be about.
2. He reads to a turning point.
3. The teacher models his questions about what is happening thus far in the story: "I wonder why the author said . . . ?"
4. The teacher summarizes what he has read so far, relating it to the *I wonder* statements.
5. From the summary, he develops a prediction or bet. He says, "Oh, I know, I bet. . . ."
6. Then the students make predictions or bets.
7. The teacher continues reading to the next turning point in the story.
8. He asks the students to talk about what they are thinking using *I wonder* statements. The teacher models his thinking also.
9. The teacher asks the students to tell what has happened so far to make them curious. The teacher adds his own interpretation.
10. The teacher and the students review previous predictions. Then they decide if they still want to keep all the predictions.
11. The students revise or make a new prediction.
12. The teacher alternates reading and discussing until the end of the story.

13. The teacher uses nonverbal cues from the students to check their understanding. When students are confused, the teacher stops to discuss the story line and how they arrived at their interpretations.
14. The teacher and the students discuss the story as a whole, relating various interpretations.

Further Diagnostic Applications

Basic View of Reading. Reading is an interactive process where the student thinks about what she reads, using what she knows and the text. Listening is also an active process where the student interprets the story as she listens. In a listening activity, there is the interpersonal communication during reading, where the teacher can use nonverbal cues and intonation to convey the author's message.

Patterns of Strengths and Strategies. A listening-thinking activity is appropriate for developing readers who need the added input of social interaction to learn either the strategy of predicting or monitoring comprehension. This technique allows the teacher to model these active reasoning strategies and to check students' understanding.

Learner Patterns That Produce a High Success Rate

1. A passive reader who needs to learn how to make predictions. The LTA provides a short lesson where the student can be involved in making predictions.
2. A passive reader who needs to check his understanding. The LTA provides a short lesson where the teacher can model comprehension monitoring.
3. The severe reading disabled student. This technique allows the student to practice active thinking strategies without having to read the words. The LTA leads the student to more active thinking strategies that she can use when she can read the words.
*4. A simultaneous reader who needs to experience the steps of active thinking to clarify her thinking.

Using the Technique as a Diagnostic Teaching Lesson. For LTA to be effective, a majority of the following statements must be answered in the affirmative:

YES   NO

_____ _____   **1.** The student listens to stories and can remember what was read.

_____ _____ **2.** The student can maintain attention for an extended period of time.

_____ _____ **3.** The student can construct an oral response after listening.

_____ _____ **4.** The student likes listening to stories that are read orally.

For Further Reading

Baker, L., & Brown, A. (1984). Metacognitive skills and reading. In P. D. Pearson (Ed.), *Handbook of reading research* (pp. 353–394). New York: Longman.

Gillet, J. W., & Temple, C. (1986). *Understanding reading problems* (2nd ed.). Boston: Little, Brown.

METAPHORS

Description. Metaphors are used to relate words and concepts to already known objects by identifying their likenesses and differences. For young children, common concrete objects can be used to develop metaphors.

Major Reading Tasks It Develops

1. Meaning vocabulary
2. Using what is known to remember new concepts or words

Targeted Reading Levels: 4–8

Text: Isolated words or concepts

Procedure

1. The teacher selects a key word or concept from the assigned text.
2. The teacher creates a metaphor which would describe the key attributes of the word or concept.
3. The teacher describes how the metaphor is like the key word and how it is different from the key word. For example, "A cloud is a puddle in the sky. It is like a puddle because a cloud is made of water droplets.

It is not like a puddle because the water droplets have become water vapor."

4. Then the students create a metaphor within a particular class. For example, "What can you think of that is like a volcano? What animal is like a volcano?"
5. The students decide on a metaphor. For example, "A dragon is like a volcano."
6. The students explain the similarity. For example, "A dragon is like a volcano because they are both hot and spit fire."
7. The students explain how it is different from the metaphor. For example, "A dragon is not like a volcano because it has four legs, and can run very, very fast."
8. The students discuss the meaning of the words.

Modification. A brainstorming or listing of options in group situations can facilitate understanding. In this situation, students would justify their metaphors and decide on one or two metaphors to use as the concept is developed in class.

Further Diagnostic Applications

Basic View of Reading. Reading is an interactive process where a reader's prior knowledge influences her comprehension of the text. Word knowledge is based on conceptual knowledge that is related by analogous relationships among prior experiences.

Patterns of Strengths and Strategies. Metaphors are most appropriate for students who have facility with verbal language but draw unspecific relationships among concepts. The words *like a* are often prevalent in their conversations. For these students, creating metaphors elaborates the relationships they draw between what they already know and the new information.

Learner Patterns That Produce a High Success Rate

1. A simultaneous learner who relates many concepts at once but is often unaware of the relationship or the precise words used to associate them. This technique helps her label and categorize word relationships.
2. A highly verbal student whose facility with words needs to elaborate the analogous relationships between what she already knows and new words. This technique helps her relate what she knows into more inclusive categories.

*3. A successive learner who uses words without drawing relationships between the word concepts and the word label. This technique helps her explain relationships among words and experiences.

Using the Technique as a Diagnostic Teaching Lesson. For metaphors to be effective, a majority of the following statements must be answered in the affirmative.

YES   NO

_____ _____   **1.** The student understands how a metaphor is con-structed and can readily draw analogous relationships.

_____ _____   **2.** The student enjoys creating new ways to explain the meaning of words.

_____ _____   **3.** The student can rationally explain the similarities and differences of the metaphors she creates.

_____ _____   **4.** The student creates more elaborate definitions of words as a result of explaining the relationships.

For Further Reading

Delain, M. T., Pearson, P. D., & Anderson, R. C. (1985). Reading comprehension and creativity in black language use: You stand to gain by playing the sounding game! *American Educational Research Journal, 22,* 155–173.

Johnson, D. D., & Pearson, P. D. (1984). *Teaching reading vocabulary* (2nd ed.). New York: Holt, Rinehart & Winston.

Readence, J. E., Baldwin, R. S., & Rickelman, R. J. (1983). Instructional insights into metaphors and similes. *Journal of Reading, 27,* 109–112.

MULTISENSORY APPROACHES

Description. Multisensory approaches or VAKT (visual/auditory/kinesthetic-tactile) techniques reinforce learning by tracing the letters and words to develop mastery. Relying on tactile-kinesthetic reinforcement, these techniques provide a multisensory stimulation for word learning.

Major Reading Tasks It Develops

1. Letter recognition
2. Word recognition

3. Attention to the sequential arrangement of letters in words

Targeted Reading Levels: K–3

Text: Varies with approach; however, a generic VAKT can be used to reinforce any word that is difficult to learn.

Procedure

1. The teacher selects the key words to be learned and writes them with a crayon on cardboard or large paper. (A rough surface is better for the tactile reinforcement.)
2. The teacher models writing the word one letter at a time, saying the letter name, syllable, or letter sound.
3. The student traces each word letter by letter, saying either the letter name or letter sound. Then the student says the entire word.
4. The procedure is repeated with each word until the word can be written (not copied) from memory.
5. At any point that an error is made, the procedure is stopped and the teacher models the correct form of writing and saying the word.
6. This structured presentation continues until the student has mastered a sight vocabulary sufficient to read the stories.

Modifications. Many variations of the generic VAKT exist. The following approaches are a few examples of how the variations can be used to differentiate instruction.

1. The Fernald Technique moves from self-selected word learning to creating personal stories from individual word banks. Words are presented by syllables, maintaining more of a sense of the whole than other VAKT procedures. Therefore, the technique is highly personalized and motivational for students who like to structure their own language.
2. The Orton-Gillingham-Stillman Method, the Herman Method, the Cooper Method, and the Spaulding Method use the generic VAKT to reinforce the sounds of letters and require the student to blend sounds of letters to form words. Therefore, words are selected that are decodable and follow an extremely structured presentation of phonic generalizations. This variation is most appropriate for a student who guesses at words and has poor visual memory but can blend sounds to form words.

Further Diagnostic Applications

Basic View of Reading. Reading is a bottom-up process where the reader learns a basic sight vocabulary through repetitious, multisensory reinforcement of letters in words before reading complete stories.

Patterns of Strengths and Strategies. Multisensory approaches are most appropriate for students who have strong tactile-kinesthetic preferences for learning and exhibit difficulty in initial word learning. This approach focuses the attention of the learner to the key features of each word.

Learner Patterns That Produce a High Success Rate

1. A successive learner with tactile-kinesthetic preferences who has difficulty remembering sight words that have been taught. This technique reinforces those words that are difficult to learn.
2. An extremely passive learner with tactile-kinesthetic preferences who does not attend to the key features of words but instead makes wild guesses. This technique draws attention to what words look like and the key features of the words.
3. The simultaneous learner who has difficulty remembering key sight words. Multisensory techniques reinforce words that are difficult for her to remember.

Using the Technique as a Diagnostic Teaching Lesson. For multisensory techniques to be effective, a majority of the following statements must be answered in the affirmative.

YES	NO	
_____	_____	**1.** The student guesses at words without using their graphic or phonic cues.
_____	_____	**2.** Tracing the word facilitates recognition of sight words or sounds.
_____	_____	**3.** Tracing the words focuses attention on the key features of words.

For Further Reading

Fernald, G. (1943). *Remedial techniques in basic school subjects.* New York: McGraw-Hill.

Orton, J. (1966). The Orton-Gillingham approach. In J. Money (Ed.), *The disabled reader* (pp. 119–146). Baltimore: Johns Hopkins University Press.

PHONOGRAPH APPROACH

Description. The phonograph approach is a structured program to introduce phonic principles by using sound clusters within whole words. As whole words are introduced, the student is directed to look at the sound clusters in the words. Then the student finds similar letter clusters in new words and associates them with the known cluster words (Glass, 1973).

Major Reading Tasks It Develops

1. Decoding by analogy
2. Word recognition
3. Perception of sound clusters

Targeted Reading Levels: 1–3

Text: Isolated words only; purchased materials or teacher-made word cards

Procedure

1. The teacher presents isolated words that contain the letter cluster. For the *an* sound cluster, these words could be presented:

fan	can	candy
man	pan	fancy
ran	Stan	candle

2. The teacher pronounces the whole word and identifies letter names and letter sounds of that target cluster. For example:

   "In the word *fan*, the letter *f* goes *f-f-f* and the letters *a-n* go *an*."

3. The teacher pronounces the letter sound or cluster sounds and asks the student for its name. For example:

   "In the word *fan*, what letter goes *f-f-f?*"
   "In the word *fan*, what letters go *an?*"

4. The teacher pronounces the letter name or cluster and asks the student for its sound. For example:

   "In the word *fan*, what sound does the *f* make?"
   "In the word *fan*, what sound do *a-n* make?"

5. The teacher asks the student, "What is the word?"
6. Steps 2, 3, 4, and 5 are continued until the pattern is learned.
7. The teacher presents the words in sentences, and the student reads the sentences. For example:

    The man canned the fancy candy.
    Stan ran to fan the candle.

8. If a word cannot be decoded, the teacher directs the student to the letter cluster and asks for its name and sound. For example:

    "Look at the word. Where is the *a-n*? What sound does it make? What's the first letter? What sound does it make?"

9. The teacher returns to the list of words and asks the student, "How are *can, candy,* and *canopy* alike and how are they different?"

Modifications

1. The target words can be selected to teach the word patterns that are causing the student difficulty.
2. The target words can be selected to teach a particular letter sound. For example, if short *a* words are difficult for the student, the teacher can choose the patterns of *an, at, am, ab,* and *ap* so she can generalize the concept of short *a* without separating the individual letter sound from its pattern.

Further Diagnostic Applications

Basic View of Reading. Reading is a bottom-up process where the student must learn to decode printed words before she can read for meaning. As such, the learner is explicitly taught the analogous sound relationships to enhance decoding.

Patterns of Strengths and Strategies. Looking for sound clusters in whole words is most appropriate for a simultaneous learner. For this student, the approach facilitates word identification using the similarity among sounds in already known words.

Learner Patterns That Produce a High Success Rate

1. A simultaneous learner who needs direct instruction in forming phonic analogies among the word she already knows and new words. This technique uses her strength in identifying patterns.

2. An older student who needs to add a decoding strategy to supplement contextual analysis. This technique helps her use what she knows about context and word identification.

Using the Technique as a Diagnostic Teaching Lesson. For the phonograph approach to be effective, a majority of the following statements must be answered in the affirmative.

YES   NO

_____ _____   **1.** The student can segment sounds.

_____ _____   **2.** The student responds to the repetitious nature of the program.

_____ _____   **3.** The student applies the analogies to both known and unknown words.

_____ _____   **4.** The student applies the strategy when reading connected text and encountering an unknown word.

For Further Reading

Glass, G. (1973). *Teaching decoding as separate from reading.* Garden City, NY: Adelphi University Press.

Glass, G., & Burton, E. (1973). How do they decode: Verbalization and observed behaviors of successful decoders. *Education, 94,* 58–63.

PREDICTABLE LANGUAGE APPROACH

Description. The predictable language approach uses the rhythmic, repetitive language structures of young children's stories to develop a predictive set for facilitating word identification.

Major Reading Tasks It Develops

1. Sight word recognition
2. Sensitivity to printed context
3. Prediction of sight words from the redundancy of language

Targeted Reading Levels: K–2

Text: Predictable books with patterned language like:

> Run, run, as fast as you can
> You can't catch me; I'm the Gingerbread Man.

Procedure

1. The teacher chooses a predictable book or story.
2. The teacher and the students talk about the story to develop a predictive set.
3. The teacher reads the first few pages or lines to the child. The teacher uses his finger above the line of print to mark the flow of language.
4. The teacher asks the student to join him. The teacher and student read together.
5. The teacher continues to read using an oral cloze. The student supplies the missing word in the language pattern.
6. When the student knows the language pattern, she reads the rest of the story on her own.
7. The student reads the whole story again on her own. The teacher assists her when necessary.
8. The teacher develops chunk (phrase) cards with the patterned language (e.g., "as fast as" or "as fast as you can"). For the very young reader, sometimes it is necessary to put the entire story on chunk cards and flash them in story sequence.
9. Using the predictable pattern, the student writes her own story, changing the characters and the setting.

Further Diagnostic Applications

Basic View of Reading. Reading is a top-down process where the reader's knowledge of language structures drives the word recognition process. Through rhythmic, repetitious language patterns, the student recognizes the printed forms of words and infers the graphophonic rule system.

Patterns of Strengths and Strategies. The predictable language approach encourages the student to associate printed words with the predictive patterns of language; therefore, it is most appropriate for students who laboriously try to decode words to derive meaning from text. Because a repetitive sentence pattern is used in this technique, the student can easily predict both what the words are and what they mean at the same time.

Learner Patterns That Produce a High Success Rate

1. A simultaneous thinker who has facility with verbal language but does not attend to the key features of short similar words found in basal

readers. This technique allows her to identify words using the repetitive pattern.

2. A learner who needs a sense of the whole story before reading. The predictable language approach provides her with a brisk, paced reading of the entire story prior to word identification.

*3. An extremely slow, laborious letter-by-letter reader. The predictable language approach can restore her sense of the whole and the predictive nature of reading.

*4. The learner who reads in a monotone. This approach can restore her sense of rhythm and cadence in reading.

Using the Technique as a Diagnostic Teaching Lesson. For the predictable language approach to be effective, a majority of the following statements must be answered in the affirmative.

YES	**NO**	
____	____	**1.** The student identifies the language patterns easily.
____	____	**2.** The student models the teacher's fluent reading and intonations readily.
____	____	**3.** The student can complete the oral cloze.
____	____	**4.** The student enjoys repetitive language and does not find it boring.

For Further Reading

Bridge, C. (1979). Predictable materials for beginning readers. *Language Arts, 50,* 503–507.

Leu, D. J., DeGroff, L. C., & Simons, H. D. (1986). Predictable texts and interactive-compensatory hypotheses: Evaluating individual differences in reading ability, context use, and comprehension. *Journal of Educational Psychology, 78,* 347–352.

McClure, A. A. (1985). Predictable books: Another way to teach reading to learning disabled children. *Teaching Exceptional Children, 17,* 267–273.

PREDICTION MAPS

Description. The prediction map uses a conceptual, flowchart to visually map the comprehension process of prediction and revision. In using the map, teacher questioning focuses on what the reader is understanding about the text and the sources of information she is using. The teacher suggests that she can revise or expand her prediction according to what she has read and what she already knows (Walker, 1985).

Major Reading Tasks It Develops

1. Active comprehension
2. Prediction
3. Using text and nontextual information

Targeted Reading Levels: 4–8

Text: Short narrative stories

Procedure

1. The teacher selects a narrative text at the appropriate reading level.
2. The teacher identifies the key turning points in the story. (A story map can help.)
3. The teacher designates the story intervals that reveal enough of the story line to encourage logical inferences, but not enough to draw exact conclusions.
4. Using the title, the student makes a prediction and places it in the center of the circle on the left side of the page.
5. The teacher and the student record important information and what she already knows about it as illustrated.
6. The student reads the first section.
7. The student is asked to evaluate her prediction and to revise or change it if needed. The new prediction is written in the center circle.
8. The teacher asks, "What in the text made you think that?" The student records important information to support or revise the prediction.
9. The teacher asks, "What do you know about the important information that made you think that?" The student writes what she knows about the important information on the map to support the revised prediction.
10. The prediction/revision process is mapped at the designated intervals in the story, using important information from the text and what is already known about the important information.
11. Initially, the teacher takes an active role by mapping his own process of comprehending as the story is read.

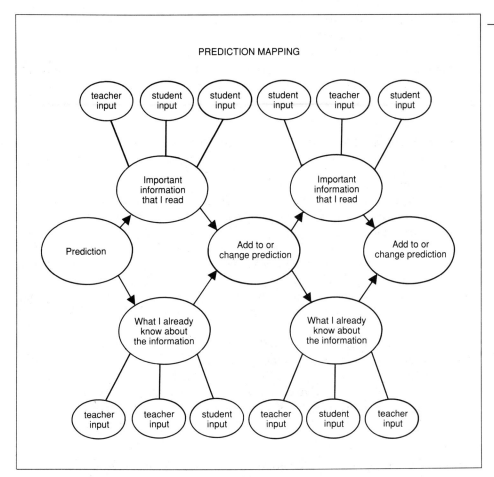

PREDICTION MAPPING

Note. From "Right-Brained Strategies for Teaching Comprehension" by Barbara J. Walker, 1985, *Academic Therapy, 21*, p. 137, Novato, CA: Academic Therapy Publications. Copyright 1985 by Academic Therapy Publications. Reprinted by permission of the author and publisher.

12. The predictions, important textual information, and personal interpretations are mapped interchangeably in the flowchart, with the
teacher modeling how the comprehending process is restructured
during the reading of a story.

Further Diagnostic Applications

Basic View of Reading. Reading is an interactive process where a reader uses
both textual and nontextual information to build a model of meaning. The reader
actively builds her model of meaning by predicting what the author is going to
say, selecting important information from the text, and evaluating her interpretation of the text using prior knowledge (reader-based inferencing) and the text (text-
based inferencing).

Patterns of Strengths and Strategies. Prediction mapping is most appropriate for the simultaneous nonverbal student who tends to overrely on what she already knows about the text rather than the textual information. In this technique, the information is displayed in a spatial orientation and offers the reader more flexibility of options, revisions, and additions during the reading of a story.

Learner Patterns That Produce a High Success Rate

1. A simultaneous learner who relies heavily on what she already knows to form a model of meaning. Visually adding what the text says to the prediction map shows her how to use the text in combination with what she knows.
2. A nonverbal reader who needs to see a map of how to use the information she knows and the text. The map provides a tool for verbalizing how she is thinking.
*3. A passive reader who maintains her initial prediction without revising it even when conflicts develop between the prediction and important new information from the text and what she already knows about it. The map helps her see when she needs to revise a prediction because of new information presented in the text.
*4. A text-bound reader who does not use background knowledge when reading a story. The map helps her see how she can use what she knows to interpret what she is reading.

Using the Technique as a Diagnostic Teaching Lesson. For prediction maps to be effective, a majority of the following statements must be answered in the affirmative.

YES   NO

____ ____   **1.** The student has no problem with word identification.

____ ____   **2.** The student will make a prediction and fill in the circle.

____ ____   **3.** The student responds to the teacher model and adds information of her own.

____ ____   **4.** The student retells the story in more detail, relating important information and background knowledge.

____ ____   **5.** The student can answer more questions with increasing specificity.

For Further Reading

Walker, B. J. (1985). Right-brained strategies for teaching comprehension. *Academic Therapy,
21,* 133–141.

QUESTION-ANSWER RELATIONSHIPS (QAR)

Description. Question-answer relationships (QAR) is a technique used to identify the type of response necessary to answer a question. Questions are the most
prevalent means of evaluating reading comprehension; therefore, knowledge about
sources of information required to answer questions facilitates comprehension and
increases a student's ability to participate in teacher-directed discussion and answer
questions in textbook exercises (Raphael, 1982).

Major Reading Tasks It Develops

1. Reading comprehension
2. Study skills

Targeted Reading Levels: 4–8

Text: Any text with accompanying questions

Procedure

1. The teacher selects a text that represents different kinds of questions.
2. He introduces *text explicit* and *script implicit sources* of information.
   a. Text explicit means that the answers are "right there" on the page
      and the words from the text can be used to answer the question.
      This source must often be used in answering a teacher's questions
      and in completing textbook exercises.
   b. Script implicit means that the students must fill in missing informa-
      tion using what they know about what is in the text to answer the
      question. In this instance, the students must realize that they are
      "on their own" when they answer the question.
3. The teacher completes an example lesson identifying the kind of
   answer that is required by the question as well as the answer. He

models the strategy of finding answers to questions and identifying the sources of information used.

4. The teacher introduces the *text implicit* question-answer relationship. Here the student must read the text carefully and then "think and search" different parts of the text to find the answers that fit together to answer the question.

5. The teacher completes an example lesson, identifying the kind of answer that is required by the questions as well as the answer. He models by using all three sources of information and telling why and how the answers were obtained.

6. The students complete a third example lesson using a paragraph, the questions, and the answers. The students as a group identify the question-answer relationships. The students talk about reasons for a particular answer and the strategy used to obtain the answer.

7. The students complete a fourth example lesson using a paragraph, the questions, and the answers. Individually, the students identify the question-answer relationship. Then the students tell why they chose an answer, based on textual and nontextual information and the strategy used to obtain the answer.

8. Steps 5, 6, and 7 are extended to longer passages in progressive steps until the procedure can be used with basal readers or content area text.

Further Diagnostic Applications

Basic View of Reading. Reading is an interactive process where a reader's interpretation of text is based on textual and nontextual information. Readers shift between the text and what they already know to construct answers to questions. Therefore, not only do students figure out answers to questions, but they also know the source of information they are using to construct the answer.

Patterns of Strengths and Strategies. QAR is most appropriate for students who rely heavily on one source of information to answer questions or who cannot answer questions. For these students, the technique requires them to distinguish when it is appropriate to use their background knowledge and/or textual information to answer questions.

Learner Patterns That Produce a High Success Rate

1. A passive learner who is unaware of the various sources of information used when answering questions. This technique increases her active reading by asking her to evaluate how she got an answer.

2. A simultaneous learner who relies heavily on background knowledge about the subject to answer questions. This technique shows her when and how she can use background knowledge effectively and when she needs to use the text.

3. A successive text-bound learner who does not use what she already knows to answer questions. This technique shows her how to fill in missing information using what she knows.

Using the Technique as a Diagnostic Teaching Lesson. For QAR to be effective, a majority of the following statements must be answered in the affirmative.

YES   NO

_____ _____   **1.** The student can understand the differences between reader-based answers and text-based answers.

_____ _____   **2.** The student can explain which source of information was used when she answered the question.

_____ _____   **3.** The student elaborates her responses to questions.

For Further Reading

Pearson, P. D., & Raphael, T. E. (1985). Increasing student's awareness of sources of information for answering questions. *American Educational Research Journal, 22,* 217–235.

Raphael, T. E. (1982). Question-answering strategies for children. *Reading Teacher, 36,* 186–190.

QUESTION-GENERATION STRATEGY

Description. Writing postreading questions uses student-generated questions to develop an understanding of the important information in the text. By deciding what to ask in their questions, students think about what is important in the text.

Major Reading Tasks It Develops

1. Study skills
2. Comprehension

Targeted Reading Levels: 4–12

Procedure

1. The teacher selects a text at the appropriate level.
2. She discusses how to write questions:
   a. A question has an answer.
   b. A good question begins with a question word like *who, what, when, where,* or *why.*
   c. A good question can be answered using information in the story.
   d. A good question asks about important information in the story.
3. The teacher selects a short paragraph and models writing questions about the important information in the text.
4. The students write questions after they read a short paragraph.
5. The students answer their questions.
6. The students compare their questions and answers with the teacher's questions and answers.
7. The teacher gives feedback about the importance of the questions.
8. The students write questions about the important information in their assigned text.
9. The students answer their questions.
10. The students compare their questions and answers with the teacher's questions and answers.

Modifications

1. Instead of Step 2, the teacher uses story grammar questions (e.g., "Who was the leading character?"). Then, he has the students make story-specific questions.
2. Instead of Step 10, the teacher allows the students to share their questions and answers in small groups.
3. The teacher uses postgenerated questioning with book reports. After reading a book, the student writes her questions on cards. Then other students who have read the same book can use the cards to answer questions for their book reports.

Further Diagnostic Applications

Basic View of Reading. Reading is an interactive process where the reader selects important textual information by constructing questions using her background knowledge.

Patterns of Strengths and Strategies. Postgenerated questioning is most appropriate for students who have facility with word identification and word meaning but have difficulty studying for tests. For these students, this approach requires them to read text in order to formulate questions about the important information in the text or important parts of the story organization.

Learner Patterns That Produce a High Success Rate

1. A passive learner who tries to remember all the details rather than focusing on the important facts. By writing and comparing questions, she thinks about what is important to remember.
2. A successive learner who knows the meanings of words but depends on teacher questioning to interpret the important information. This technique helps the student become more independent by having her write the questions before comparing them with the teacher's questions.
3. A simultaneous learner who has not learned to ask herself questions to monitor what she needs to remember when she reads. This technique encourages her to monitor her understanding by asking herself questions.

Using the Technique as a Diagnostic Teaching Lesson. For question-generation strategy to be effective, a majority of the following statements must be answered in the affirmative.

YES	NO	
————	————	**1.** The student can recognize and understand the individual words in the text.
————	————	**2.** The student does not ask herself what information is important enough to remember.
————	————	**3.** The student does not rehearse important information.

For Further Reading

Barr, R., & Sadow, M. (1985). *Reading diagnosis for teachers.* White Plains, NY: Longman.

Cohen, R. (1983). Self-generated questions as an aid to reading comprehension. *Reading Teacher, 36,* 770–775.

King, J. R., Biggs, S., & Lipsky, S. (1984). Student's self-questioning and summarizing as reading study strategies. *Journal of Reading Behavior, 15,* 205–218.

READERS THEATRE

Description. Readers theatre is a dramatic interpretation of a play script through oral interpretive reading. The story theme and character development are conveyed through intonation, inflection, and fluency of oral reading.

Major Reading Tasks It Develops

1. Oral reading fluency
2. Intonation and chunking of language
3. For younger students, identifying sight words

Targeted Reading Levels: 2–5

Text: Scripts designed for the appropriate number of readers

Procedure

1. The teacher selects a narrative text at the appropriate reading level.
2. The teacher presents a brief description of the characters, setting, events, and problem.
3. The students select or are assigned appropriate parts to read.
4. The students preview the scripts silently.
5. Standing in a line in front of a seated audience, the students read the scripts orally.
6. No props or costumes are used.
7. The students convey the story line by their intonation and phrasing.
8. Listeners must use their imaginations to interpret the story line.

Modifications

1. A readers theatre can be developed from the text that the student is reading. This provides additional reinforcement for word recognition. For example, when deciding how to write a script from a preprimer, the students and teacher reread parts of the text numerous times as they write the scripts on chart tablets.
2. Writing a readers theatre script from a story can also improve comprehension. The students must decide what important dialogue and narration are necessary to understand the story.

3. Different reading levels can be included in a script to allow readers of varying reading abilities to participate in the same activity.

Further Diagnostic Applications

Basic View of Reading. Reading is a top-down process where the reader interprets the author's intended meaning through dramatic oral interpretative reading.

Patterns of Strengths and Strategies. Readers theatre is most appropriate for students who have a dramatic flair and when given the stage will perform. Often a quiet, nonverbal student will perform in a readers theatre because the expectation is performance.

Learner Patterns That Produce a High Success Rate

1. A simultaneous learner who communicates through drama and needs to develop oral reading fluency. This is a natural way to develop fluency for this reader.
*2. The highly efficient decoder who is word-bound and does not identify with characters. This student benefits from the naturalness of character identification forced by the readers theatre script.
*3. A student who has difficulty tracking. She develops a purposeful reason to track when reading *short* readers theatre scripts.

Using the Technique as a Diagnostic Teaching Lesson. For readers theatre to be effective, a majority of the following statements must be answered in the affirmative.

YES	NO	
____	____	**1.** The student has enough oral reading fluency to convey the message.
____	____	**2.** The student likes to perform.
____	____	**3.** The student becomes more fluent as she identifies with the character.
____	____	**4.** The student becomes more fluent as the story develops.

For Further Reading

Aulls, M. (1982). *Developing readers in today's elementary school.* Boston: Allyn and Bacon.

Sloyer, S. (1982). *Readers theatre: Story dramatization in the classroom.* Urbana, IL: National Council of Teachers of English.

Wertheimer, A. (1974). Story dramatization in the reading center. *English Journal, 64,* 85–87.

READING LOGS

Description.   Reading logs are written journals of students' thoughts as they are reading. At designated points, the students write a summary, make a prediction, and construct a reason for their prediction. As they read and write about the story, they evaluate new information in relation to their previous predictions. The written record of their previous thoughts allows the students to analyze how they construct meaning.

Major Reading Tasks It Develops

1. Nonliteral comprehension
2. Comprehension monitoring

Targeted Reading Levels: 4–12

Text: Narrative text

Procedure

1. The teacher selects interesting stories so that the readers can make predictions.
2. He decides on key turning points in the story and marks them for the students.
3. The teacher prepares log sheets with the following information:

Name of story: _____

Author: _____

Segment: _____

Summary:

Prediction:

Reason for prediction:

How my comprehension is happening:

4. After the story is read, the reading logs are used as a basis for discussing the story.
5. The students discuss how their interpretation developed through the story.
6. The students discuss the influence of personal understanding on comprehension.

Further Diagnostic Applications

Basic View of Reading. Reading is an interactive process where the reader builds a model of meaning based on textual and nontextual information. As the reader builds her model of meaning, she predicts, monitors, and evaluates her interpretation in relation to the context of the situation.

Patterns of Strengths and Strategies. Reading logs are most appropriate for the reflective student who needs to evaluate how she forms her model of meaning. She often does not realize what information she uses from the text and what she already knows. Furthermore, she has difficulty thinking about how she forms her conclusions about a story. Reading logs provide a method for analyzing how she constructs meaning.

Learner Patterns That Produce a High Success Rate

1. A simultaneous, reflective learner who understands the story but does not understand how she constructs a response. Reading logs provide a record of her thoughts so that she can analyze them.
2. A successive learner who cannot tie story events together using what she already knows and the story events. Reading logs provide written summaries of events so that she can relate events to one another.
*3. A passive learner who needs actively to engage in forming and revising her model of meaning. Reading logs have the student elaborate her understanding during the reading of the story.

Using the Technique as a Diagnostic Teaching Lesson. For reading logs to be effective, a majority of the following statements must be answered in the affirmative.

YES   NO

____ ____ **1.** The student can write a summary selecting important information.

____ ____ **2.** The student gets the answers to questions but cannot tell how she got the answer.

____ ____ **3.** The student passively reads the story, recalling events but not relating those events to one another.

For Further Reading

Smith-Burke, M. T. (1982). Extending concepts through language activities. In J. Langer & M. T. Smith-Burke (Eds.), *Reader meets author/bridging the gap* (pp. 163–180). Newark, DE: International Reading Association.

RECIPROCAL TEACHING

Description. Reciprocal teaching is a technique to develop comprehension of expository text by modeling and practicing how to read and understand the text. The teacher and students take turns leading a discussion about sections of the text. The teacher provides the initial model by thinking aloud about *how* he constructs a summary, makes up questions, clarifies what is difficult, and predicts what else the text will discuss (Palincsar & Brown, 1984).

Major Reading Tasks It Develops

1. Reading comprehension
2. Summarizing
3. Predicting

Targeted Reading Levels: 5–12

Text: Expository text is preferred

1. The teacher selects a text from a content area.
2. The teacher explains the four tasks: (a) question generating, (b) summarizing, (c) clarifying the difficult parts, and (d) predicting what the next section will discuss.
3. Both the students and the teacher read silently the first section of the text.
4. The teacher talks about the four tasks of reading for that section.
   a. He constructs several good questions.
   b. He constructs a summary of the section using the main idea and supporting details.
   c. He clarifies difficult parts by stressing vocabulary and organization.
   d. He predicts what the next section will discuss by using the title and headings.
5. The students help revise the summary, answer the questions, clarify unclear parts of the summary and the text, and evaluate the prediction (agree or disagree and add a rationale for doing so).
6. After a few models by the teacher, a student takes the turn of teacher. She thinks aloud using the four steps.
7. The teacher becomes a student and assumes the student's role.
8. Students take turns playing "teacher."
9. Periodically the teacher reviews the four activities with the student.
   a. Rule for good questions: They should be clear and stand by themselves.
   b. Rule for summaries: Look for the topic sentence, make up a topic sentence if there is none, name lists, and delete what is unimportant.
   c. Rule for clarifying: Look for difficult vocabulary, incomplete information, unclear references, and unusual expressions.
   d. Rule for predictions: Use the title and headings, use questions in the text if present, and use text structures (references to *two kinds, four levels,* etc.).
10. As the students play "teacher," the teacher does the following:
    a. He provides feedback about the quality of summaries or questions. When necessary, he models his thinking for the student. For example, he might comment, "That was a start on a summary, but I would summarize by adding. . . ."
    b. He provides encouragement to the student playing "teacher." For example, he may say, "I liked the way you identified the important information."

Further Diagnostic Applications

Basic View of Reading. Reading is an interactive process where a reader's interpretation of the text is based on textual and nontextual information. By thinking aloud, the student becomes more aware of how to integrate knowledge sources when reading.

Patterns of Strengths and Strategies. Reciprocal teaching is most appropriate for students who have verbal fluency and experiential knowledge of the topics but need to focus on their understanding of text. These students read and retain information, but the complexities of content area reading often produce an overload of unorganized facts rather than important related information.

Learner Patterns That Produce a High Success Rate

1. A passive yet verbally fluent learner who needs to organize the information read. By leading the discussion, the student actively thinks about her section of the text. She also can follow the teacher's model.
2. A sequential learner who tries to memorize a string of unrelated facts rather than focus on the important points and how the facts relate to these points. This technique encourages her to use only the important information in her summary.
3. A passive reader who does not monitor information learned and relate it to an organized whole. This technique helps her actively summarize text and clarify the difficult parts.

Using the Technique as a Diagnostic Teaching Lesson. For reciprocal teaching to be effective, a majority of the following statements must be answered in the affirmative.

YES   NO

____ ____   **1.** The student can read the words in the text; in other words, word identification is not a concern.

____ ____   **2.** The student has enough expressive language that constructing a summary is not terribly time-consuming.

____ ____   **3.** The student increases her ability to ask good questions.

____ ____   **4.** The student increases her ability to predict what kind of information the text will contain.

____ ____   **5.** The student increases her ability to summarize information.

For Further Reading

Palincsar, A. S., & Brown, A. L. (1984). Reciprocal teaching of comprehension-fostering and comprehension-monitoring activities. *Cognition and Instruction, 1,* 117–175.

Pearson, P. D. (1985). Changing the face of reading comprehension instruction. *Reading Teacher, 38,* 724–738.

175

The Instructional Techniques

REPEATED READINGS

Description. Repeated readings is the oral rereading of a self-selected passage until accuracy and speed are fluent and represent the natural flow of language.

Major Reading Tasks It Develops

1. Fluency
2. Word recognition
3. Speed

Targeted Reading Levels: 1–4

Text: Self-selected

Procedure

1. The student selects a text that she wants to read. The teacher segments the text into manageable passages for oral reading.
2. The teacher makes a copy of the text so he can mark errors as the student reads.
3. The teacher explains that rereading a passage is like practicing a musical instrument or practicing a football play. The repetition helps us read more smoothly and automatically.
4. The student reads the passage orally while the teacher records errors and speed.
5. The errors and speed are charted on a graph.
6. The student practices silently rereading the passage while the teacher listens to other students.
7. The student rereads the passage to the teacher while he records errors with a different colored pen.
8. The errors and speed are charted on a graph for the second reading Progress toward the reading goals is discussed.
9. The procedure is continued until a speed of 85 words per minute is reached.

1. The teacher can select a text that corresponds to instructional needs.
2. Instead of Step 4, the following interventions have been successfully used.
   a. Discussion of the errors and process of self-correction. The teacher suggests that the student say to herself, "Did that make sense? Can we say it that way?"
   b. Echo reading (see "Echo Reading") of sentences where the most errors occur.
   c. Discussion of the author's use of language and intended meaning of the paragraph.
   d. Tape-recording the readings. Then the student listens to the recording, marks errors, and records her time.
   e. Chunking (see "Chunking") the selection to improve fluency and the interaction of thought and language.
3. Only one or two rereadings are used. All readings are charted.

Further Diagnostic Applications

Basic View of Reading. Reading is both a decoding and a comprehension process. Comprehension is dependent on the automatic decoding of printed language. Therefore, speed and accuracy of decoding are necessary requisites for efficient comprehension. Thus initially, reading is a bottom-up process.

Patterns of Strengths and Strategies. Repeated readings are most appropriate for students who read word by word and do not use contextual clues to confirm anticipated words as they read. For this learner, the repeated readings encourage the use of overall contextual meaning and sentence structure to predict words and correct mistakes.

Learner Patterns That Produce a High Success Rate

1. A simultaneous learner who has a great deal of difficulty with word recognition because of an overemphasis on isolated word drill. This technique uses the overall textual meaning to increase word recognition accuracy.
2. A simultaneous learner who cannot blend sounds and must rely, therefore, on the context for word recognition accuracy. If progressively difficult text is used, this technique allows the student to read more complex text, where words can be recognized by using context rather than what the word looks or sounds like.

*3. A successive learner who has become word-bound with a heavy phonics instruction and needs to develop fluency and use of contextual cues for word identification. This technique emphasizes using context to identify words rather than sounding out individual words.

Using the Technique as a Diagnostic Teaching Lesson. For repeated readings to be effective, a majority of the following statements must be answered in the affirmative.

YES	NO	
___	___	**1.** The student's errors decrease on a second reading.
___	___	**2.** The student's speed increases on a second reading.
___	___	**3.** The student's pattern of errors includes more self-corrections as fluency increases.
___	___	**4.** Over several interventions, the student decreases the number of errors on an initial at-sight reading.

For Further Reading

Kahn, R. (1983). The method of repeated readings: Expanding the neurological impress method for use with disabled readers. *Journal of Learning Disabilities, 16,* 90–92.

Moyer, S. B. (1982). Repeated reading. *Journal of Learning Disabilities, 15,* 619–623.

Samuels, S. J. (1979). The method of repeated readings. *Reading Teacher, 32,* 403–408.

REQUEST (RECIPROCAL QUESTIONING TECHNIQUE)

Description. The ReQuest technique develops comprehension by having the teacher and the student take turns asking and answering questions. At turning points in the text, the teacher models effective question-asking strategies. The student, in turn, asks appropriate questions by following the model. The goal is to develop self-questioning strategies for the student (Manzo, 1969).

Major Reading Tasks It Develops

1. Comprehension
2. Self-questioning

Text: Particularly suited for narrative text but can be used with expository text

Procedure

1. The teacher selects a text that is at the student's reading level and that is predictive in nature.
2. The teacher identifies appropriate points for asking questions.
3. The teacher introduces the ReQuest procedure in terms the student will understand. He tells her that they will be taking turns asking questions about the sentence and what it means. The student is to ask questions that a teacher might ask. Then the teacher emphasizes that questions must be answered fully and that they sometimes require support from the text.
4. The student and teacher read silently the first sentence.
5. When the teacher closes his book, the student asks questions. The teacher answers the question, integrating background knowledge and textual information. He also tells how he decided on his answer.
6. The procedure continues for the next sentence. This time the teacher asks the questions, modeling integrating information and the predictive nature of the reading by using questions like the following: "What do you think will happen next? Why do you think so?"
7. The teacher provides feedback about the student's questioning behavior during the procedure.
8. The procedure is used to develop purposes for reading and employs only the first three paragraphs.
9. The student reads the rest of the story silently to see if she answers her questions.
10. Follow-up discussion and activities can be used.

Further Diagnostic Applications

Basic View of Reading.   Reading is an interactive process that requires the reader to monitor her behavior by asking herself questions about the important information in the text and answering these questions, using both textual and nontextual information.

Patterns of Strengths and Strategies.   The ReQuest procedure is most appropriate for the sequential learner who likes to ask questions but does not always attend to the text for answers. For these students, the approach matches their desire to ask questions, but it focuses on the relevant information in a story and develops an active question-answering role rather than a passive question-asking role.

1. A successive learner who asks questions and enjoys breaking a story into parts, reading only sections at a time. This technique uses her strength to show her how to elaborate her understanding using the text and what she knows.
2. A successive learner who asks irrelevant questions when reading and fails to comprehend the main points of the story. This technique focuses her attention on asking important questions and justifying answers.
*3. A passive learner who reads words fluently but does not ask herself, "What does this mean?" This technique develops self-questioning and monitoring of comprehension.
*4. A passive reader who reads words fluently but does not use her prior knowledge to interpret text. This technique asks the student to use both textual and nontextual information to ask and answer questions.

Using the Technique as a Diagnostic Teaching Lesson. For the ReQuest technique to be effective, a majority of the following statements must be answered in the affirmative.

YES   NO

_____ _____   **1.** The student likes to ask questions.

_____ _____   **2.** The student can answer questions.

_____ _____   **3.** The student can follow the teacher's model in question-answering behavior.

_____ _____   **4.** The student enjoys being teacher.

For Further Reading

Manzo, A. V. (1969). The request procedure. *Journal of Reading, 2,* 123–126.
Tierney, R. J., Readence, J. E., & Dishner, E. K. (1985). *Reading strategies and practices: A compendium* (2nd ed.). Boston: Allyn & Bacon.

SECONDARY READING SEQUENCE (SRS)

Description. SRS is designed to integrate story understanding with word recognition. The teacher develops background knowledge by reading the story aloud and discussing its main points prior to the student's reading the story. The lesson sequence involves four comprehensive steps: listening comprehension, choral reading, oral reading, and review (Fass, 1980).

Major Reading Tasks It Develops

1. Word recognition in context
2. Listening comprehension
3. Use of background knowledge to identify words

Targeted Reading Levels: 2–5; content level 6–12

Text: Adaptable to all contents. Particularly useful for content area reading. The newspaper and magazines are also good sources.

Procedure

1. The teacher selects a text that matches the student's listening comprehension level.
2. The teacher follows a listening comprehension sequence:
   a. The teacher reads the passage aloud. If the passage is long, an interrupted predictive listening format may be followed.
   b. The teacher either asks questions or has the student retell what was read to assess comprehension. Both literal and nonliteral information needs to be stressed.
   c. The teacher asks interpretative questions like these: "What would happen if? How is this character or idea similar to another character?" (VARIATION: Vocabulary maps or story maps of listening comprehension can be used.)
3. The teacher and the student chorally read the same passage. The teacher models correct intonation and phrasing. Errors are ignored as the teacher continues to read fluently.
4. Then the student reads the same passage orally. The teacher records errors on a copy of the text. Errors are reviewed and skill activities developed around these errors.
   The steps are as follows:
   a. The student reads the passage orally.
   b. The teacher records errors.
   c. The teacher and student review the errors, making a list of target words.
   d. Sentences are reread in an echo format. The teacher reads the correct form. The student reads following the teacher's model.
   e. The student rereads the passage.
   f. The teacher records errors in different colored pens.
   g. A comparison is made of the errors.
5. The teacher makes a collection of the passages and target words. This booklet provides the text for weekly review and independent reading.

1. During Step 4, the teacher uses the repeated readings format. This would involve charting progress toward the goal of fluent reading.
2. During Step 4, the teacher tape-records the student's reading. He then has the student listen to the tape and mark her errors on a copy of the text.

Further Diagnostic Applications

Basic View of Reading. Reading is a top-down process where the reader's background knowledge assists the recognition of words and fluent reading. Comprehension precedes decoding. The ultimate goal is a reader who will simultaneously apply the decoding skills of reading while comprehending text.

Patterns of Strengths and Strategies. SRS is most appropriate for adolescent readers who are simultaneous and have a high drive for meaning when reading. For these students, the approach uses their strengths of listening and thinking; then it transfers these strengths to word identification.

Learner Patterns That Produce a High Success Rate

1. A simultaneous learner with a high listening comprehension and minimal (second grade) word identification skills. This technique uses her strength in listening to develop an anticipation of what the text will say. This facilitates word identification.
2. A passive learner with adequate listening comprehension skills and minimal word identification skills. The teacher needs to emphasize self-talk in error correction.
3. An extremely word-bound, successive reader who lacks fluency. This technique uses what the student hears to develop expectations for what words will be in the text.

Using this Technique as a Diagnostic Teaching Lesson. For SRS to be effective, a majority of the following statements must be answered in the affirmative.

YES	NO	
_____	_____	**1.** The student can listen and comprehend.
_____	_____	**2.** The student follows the teacher's model when choral reading.

_____ _____ **3.** The student discusses errors with the teacher.

_____ _____ **4.** A repeated reading improves word identification.

For Further Reading

Chomsky, C. (1978). When you still can't read in third grade: After decoding what? In J. Samuels (Ed.), *What research has to say about reading instruction* (pp. 13–30). Newark, DE: International Reading Association.

Faas, L. A. (1980). *Children with learning problems: A handbook for teachers.* Boston: Houghton Mifflin.

SELF-DIRECTED QUESTIONING

Description. Self-directed questioning uses student-generated questions to develop active reading. By following the sequence of self-directed questions, the student learns to monitor her undertanding as she reads (Walker & Mohr, 1985).

Major Reading Tasks It Develops

1. Comprehension
2. Comprehension monitoring
3. Integrating background knowledge with textual information

Targeted Reading Levels: All levels but most appropriate for 4–12

Text: Narrative text is most appropriate

Procedure

1. The teacher selects a text at the appropriate level that has a fairly cohesive story line.
2. He decides on key prediction points. A story map (see "Story Map" in this chapter) can facilitate this process.
3. The teacher models the steps below with a short passage.

   STEP A: Problem Definition
   "What must I do? . . . I must guess what the author is going to say. . . . A good strategy is to use the title. . . . From the title, I bet that. . ."

STEP B: Plan of Action
"Now, let's see what's my plan for betting. . . . To make my bet, I already know that . . . To prove my bet, I must look for hints in the text. . . ."

STEP C: Self-Instruction in the Form of Self-Questioning
"I wonder how it fits?. . . The _____ must be important because the author keeps talking about it. . . . It fits because _____ ."

STEP D: Ways of Coping with Frustration and Failure
"Oops, that doesn't make sense. . . . I need to check the hints. . . . So far, I'm right about . . . but wrong about . . ."

"Oops, I was wrong. . . . It's OK to make a mistake. . . . I can change my bet as I get more information."

"From the new information, I bet that . . . or I wonder if . . . "
The student then recycles to Step A.

STEP E: Self-Reinforcement
"I knew it, that sure fits. . . . So far I'm right!"
"Now I bet the author. . . ." The student then returns to Step A.*

4. The teacher emphasizes self-correcting behavior and self-reinforcement.
5. The student reads another example passage, talking aloud using the steps.
6. When comprehension breaks down, the teacher models his own thinking rather than asking questions. He says, "When I read that I thought . . . "
7. The teacher phases in and out of the story discussion as necessary, using questions like these: "Have you defined your problem? What is your plan? Does that make sense?"
8. At the end of the story, the student and the teacher discuss the story content and how they constructed meaning.

Further Diagnostic Applications

Basic View of Reading. Reading is an interactive process where the reader builds a model of meaning based on textual and nontextual information. As the reader builds her model of meaning, she predicts, monitors, and reinforces her own learning.

Patterns of Strengths and Strategies. Self-directed questioning is most appropriate for students who have facility with word identification and word meaning but difficulty monitoring reading comprehension and relating textual infor-

---

*Procedure 3 (steps A-E) adapted from *The Effects of Self-Questioning on Reading Comprehension* (pp. 9–10) by B. J. Walker and T. Mohr, 1985. Paper presented at the Washington Organization for Reading Development—Research Conference, Seattle, WA. (ERIC Document Reproduction Service No. ED 262 392) Adapted by permission.

mation to prior knowledge. For this student, the approach matches the textual level emphasis while moving her beyond the text.

Learner Patterns That Produce a High Success Rate

1. A passive learner who needs to actively engage in forming and revising her interpretations of the text. This technique gives her a plan for thinking and checking her understanding.
2. A successive learner who knows the meanings of words but depends on teacher questioning to interpret the important information in the text. This technique gives her the steps to develop her own questions.
3. A successive learner who cannot tie story events together using what she already knows and these events. This technique asks the student to check both the text and what she knows to see if they fit together.
*4. A simultaneous learner who understands the story but cannot recall the textual information used to construct her answer. The technique has her check the text. This will facilitate memory.
*5. A simultaneous learner who does not use self-talk to monitor the sources of information used to construct her answers. This technique encourages the internal dialogue that accompanies effective comprehension.

Using the Technique as a Diagnostic Teaching Lesson. For self-directed questioning to be effective, a majority of the following statements must be answered in the affirmative.

YES   NO

_____ _____   **1.** The student can recognize and understand the individual words in the text.

_____ _____   **2.** The student does not monitor important information when reading.

_____ _____   **3.** The student does not use background knowledge when reading.

_____ _____   **4.** The student does not use key events to predict outcomes.

For Further Reading

Helfeldt, J. P., & Lalik, R.(1979). Reciprocal student-teacher questioning. In C. Pennock (Ed.), *Reading comprehension at four linguistic levels* (pp. 74–80). Newark, DE: International Reading Association.

Meichenbaum, D. (1977). *Cognitive-behavior modification: An integrative approach.* New York: Plenum Press.

Walker, B. J., & Mohr, T. (1985). *The effects of self-questioning on reading comprehension.* Paper presented at the Washington Organization for Reading Development—Research Conference, Seattle, WA. (Eric Document Reproduction Service No. ED 262 392)

SENTENCE COMBINING

Description. Sentence combining is a technique designed to help students write and understand complex sentences. The student is shown how to combine short sentences to make increasingly more complex sentences.

Major Reading Tasks It Develops

1. Sensitivity to sentence structure
2. Awareness of the influence of context on word and sentence meaning
3. Use of context to increase comprehension

Targeted Reading Levels: 3–7

Text: Structured programs of short sentences, the student's own writing, or short sentences from the text

Procedure

1. The teacher introduces the concept of combining sentences by using short sentences which the student can read.
2. The teacher explains that simple sentences can be combined and still have the same meaning.
3. He begins by writing sentences on the board. For example:

   The dog is brown.
   The dog is in the park.
   The dog bit the man.

4. Then he shows the students how to delete repeated words or phrases. For the example in Step 3, the following process would take place.
   a. The teacher might say, "If the dog is brown, we can call it a brown dog." On the board, the teacher would write
   brown + dog = brown dog.

b. The teacher explains that the sentence can be expanded by adding a phrase to tell where the dog is—"in the park." The teacher then shows the change: *The brown dog + in the park = The brown dog in the park.*

c. He also explains that sentences can be further combined by telling what the dog did as the action in the sentence. Therefore, he adds *bit the man* as the action. The teacher writes: *The brown dog in the park + bit the man = The brown dog in the park bit the man.*

d. The teacher states that here the combined sentences would be "the brown dog in the park bit the man."

5. The teacher points out to the student that by combining ideas into one sentence, reading and writing become more interesting.

Modifications

1. Phrases can be placed on cards and then combined and recombined to form new sentences.

2. Closed sentence combining, where cued words are provided to indicate how the sentence is combined, can be used to increase sensitivity to a particular sentence structure. For example, the following two sentences might be combined.

I know ——————.
Chris stole the cookie.

The teacher supplies the cue word *that*, and the sentences are combined with the following result.

I know that Chris stole the cookie.

Further Diagnostic Applications

Basic View of Reading. Reading is a text-based process that involves the action of constructing meaning with words in sentences. The sequence of how words are linked in sentences affects reading comprehension; therefore, learning how the words are related in sentences facilitates both reading and writing.

Patterns of Strengths and Strategies. Sentence combining is most appropriate for students who can read short sentences but have difficulty following sentence order in longer sentences. Usually these students have verbal skills but lack the ability to link information in more complex frameworks.

1. A successive learner who speaks in short choppy sentences without signal words to combine ideas. The technique shows her how short sentences are combined to form longer sentences.
*2. A simultaneous learner who has difficulty with sentence order as exhibited by continued failure with a cloze activity. Using sentence cards helps this student because she can visually manipulate the words in the sentence.

Using the Technique as a Diagnostic Teaching Lesson. For sentence combining to be effective, a majority of the following statements must be answered in the affirmative.

YES	NO	
———	———	**1.** The student can easily see the connection between the short sentences and the complex sentences.
———	———	**2.** The student likes to manipulate words.
———	———	**3.** The more complex sentences appear in her writing.

For Further Reading

Combs, W. (1980). Sentence-combining practice aids in reading comprehension. In D. Sawyer (Ed.), *Disabled readers—Insight, assessment, instruction* (pp. 104–112). Newark, DE: International Reading Association.

O'Hare, F. (1973). *Sentence-combining* (NCTE Report No. 15). Urbana, IL: National Council of Teachers of English.

Straw, S. B., & Schreiner, R. (1982). The effect of sentence manipulation on subsequent measures of reading and listening comprehension. *Reading Research Quarterly, 17,* 339–352.

SIGHT WORD APPROACH

Description. The sight word approach is a technique for beginning reading instruction that uses what words mean to develop what the word looks like. By using pictures and oral context, meaning is associated with isolated sight words. After a sight vocabulary is learned, decoding by analogy is taught to expand reading acquisition.

Major Reading Tasks It Develops

1. Word recognition
2. Decoding by analogy

Targeted Reading Levels: K–2

Text: The basic preprimers and primers of published reading series that contain a regular and controlled introduction of sight words in simple text. Decoding by analogy is taught through known sight words.

Procedure

1. The teacher selects a text that has a controlled sight word vocabulary.
2. He introduces sight words for the story by presenting them in isolation, supplemented by oral context and/or pictures.
3. The teacher reviews the words by placing words on cards and flashing the words in various orders (see "Word Cards" in this chapter). If the student cannot recall the words, a meaning or semantic prompt is used. If the student cannot recall the word *dog*, the teacher might prompt her by saying, "It rained cats and _____."
4. The student reads the story that contains the words. (The teacher uses the format for directed reading activity or directed reading-thinking activity to direct discussion.)
5. The teacher reinforces sight words by using cloze exercises, games with the word cards, and repetitive reading of stories with the controlled vocabulary.
6. After the student can recognize selected words at sight, the teacher uses an analytic phonics (see "Analytic Phonics") to introduce how to decode new words by using analogies to known sight words. For example, the teacher might write *green, grass,* and *grow* on the board. He might then ask the students the following series of questions (the appropriate student answers are supplied in parentheses): "How are they alike? (They have *gr* letters.) What can we say about the *gr* sound? (It goes *gr-r-r*.) The next time you see *gr*, what sound are you going to try? (*gr-r-r*.)"

Further Diagnostic Applications

Basic View of Reading. Reading is an interactive process where the reader learns words by associating them with meaning. Therefore, learning to read is a process of accumulating enough words recognized at sight that a student can decode new words in a story by using the written context and decoding analogies to known words. Initially, this approach places a high demand on visual feature analysis and phonemic segmentation.

Patterns of Strengths and Strategies. The sight word approach is most appropriate for students who have developed a systematic way of analyzing the key visual features of words. At the readiness level, this strength is often indicated by letter naming.

Learner Patterns That Produce a High Success Rate

1. A simultaneous learner who attends to the key features of words. She notices what visual features are alike and what visual features are different.
2. The average learner who exhibits no divergent processing characteristics.

Using the Technique as a Diagnostic Teaching Lesson. For sight word approach to be effective, a majority of the following statements must be answered in the affirmative.

YES	NO	
____	____	**1.** The student easily remembers the sight words taught.
____	____	**2.** The student analyzes the words, noticing visual differences among words.
____	____	**3.** The student can segment sounds so that applying decoding analogies is easy.
____	____	**4.** The student uses meaningful oral and written context to decode unknown words.

For Further Reading

Anderson, R. C., Hiebert, E. H., Scott, J. A., & Wilkinson, I. A. G. (1985). *Becoming a nation of readers: The report of the commission on reading.* Washington, DC: National Institute of Education.

Aukerman, R. C. (1984). *Approaches to beginning reading* (2nd ed.). New York: John Wiley & Sons, 368–371.

Ray, D. D. (1971). Specificity in remediation. In B. Batemen (Ed.), *Learning disorders* (pp. 180–192). Seattle, WA: Special Child Publications.

SQ3R

Description. SQ3R is a procedure for studying content area text that includes the five steps of *survey, question, read, recite,* and *review*. It is designed as a procedure for students to use to monitor their comprehension and learning as they read and study expository text.

Major Reading Tasks It Develops

1. Study skills
2. Self-questioning
3. Comprehension

Targeted Reading Levels: 5–12

Text: Expository

Procedure

1. The teacher selects a content-area text at an appropriate reading level.
2. He introduces the five steps in a short minilesson.
3. *S—Survey*. The teacher explains how to skim (briefly read) the entire passage to construct an overall framework for the information. He directs the student to use the paragraph headings as key information in understanding the overall framework.
4. *Q—Question*. After surveying the text, the teacher directs the student to develop questions that she thinks will be answered in the passage. The teacher helps the student focus on the key concepts of the text as she develops the questions. He directs the student to use paragraph headings and italics to form the questions for each *section*.
5. *R—Read*. The student reads the text section by section to answer the questions posed at the beginning of each section. After a section has been read, the student proceeds to the next step.
6. *R—Recite*. The teacher explains that the student now is to answer the questions she posed for the section just read. The teacher encourages the student to construct an answer rather than read word for word from the text. At this point, the student may need to write down her answer to facilitate recall.
7. The three steps (question, read, and recite) are repeated for each section.

8. *R—Review*. After the last section is read, the student reviews the questions and answers for the entire text. At this time, the student tries to relate the information into an overall framework that will facilitate recall.

Further Diagnostic Applications

Basic View of Reading. Reading comprehension is a bottom-up process where information from the text forms the framework for learning and recalling facts and concepts in content-area texts.

Patterns of Strengths and Strategies. SQ3R is most appropriate for students who have facility with word recognition and comprehension but lack an overall method for organizing factual information in a content-area text. For these students, the approach provides a systematic method for studying the information.

Learner Patterns That Produce a High Success Rate

1. A passive learner who can use the steps to develop a procedure for studying and remembering text. This gives her a tool for active reading.
2. A successive learner who asks questions but forgets to look for the answers. This gives her a tool for finding answers to the important questions in the text.
3. A successive learner who questions and recalls facts without using an organizational framework so that facts can be conceptually related. The survey and review steps provide a means for relating information into an overall framework.
4. The student who develops self-control easily. This technique gives her the steps to manage her own learning.

Using the Technique as a Diagnostic Teaching Lesson. For SQ3R to be effective, a majority of the following statements must be answered in the affirmative.

YES   NO

—— ——   **1.** The student has automatic word recognition skills.

—— ——   **2.** The student reads expository text without a clear organizational framework of the information.

—— ——   **3.** The student can construct questions from the subtopics.

____ ____   **4.** The student reads and reflects on her questions.

____ ____   **5.** The student follows the procedures and easily incorporates the steps.

____ ____   **6.** The student remembers text better when using the steps.

For Further Reading

Adams, A., Carnine, D., & Gersten, R. (1982). Instructional strategies for studying content area texts in the intermediate grades. *Reading Research Quarterly, 18,* 27–55.

Pauk, W. (1974). *How to study in college* (2nd ed.). Boston: Houghton, Mifflin.

Robinson, F. P. (1946). *Effective study*. New York: Harper and Bros.

STORY DRAMA

Description. Story drama is a method for developing reading comprehension by using the natural dramatic abilities of students. The student thinks about how a story will end by role playing scenes from the story. By taking the roles of the various characters, the student uses her knowledge of similar experiences, her affective response to the characters, and key information to act out her interpretation of the story (Walker, 1985).

Major Reading Tasks It Develops

1. Reading comprehension
2. Kinesthetic expression

Targeted Reading Levels: 2–6

Text: Various kinds of literature. Picture storybooks and adventure stories with an intriguing plot lend themselves to dramatic interpretation.

Procedure

1. The teacher selects a story with an intriguing plot.
2. The teacher or the students read until there is enough information about the characters to role play the story.

3. The teacher assigns the students the character roles from the story.
4. The teacher uses key props to engage the students in the drama in a concrete way.
5. The teacher and the students begin the drama at the point of interruption.
6. The students dramatize their predictions through role playing.
7. In the process of the dramatization, the teacher may stop the drama and have students exchange roles.
8. The students discuss their predictions and the information used to make the predictions.
9. After the dramatization, the students write an ending for the story.
10. Finally, the students finish reading the story.
11. The students discuss and compare both the drama and the story ending.
12. The teacher and the students discuss their personal interpretations evidenced in the drama and how their individual viewpoints influence those interpretations.

Further Diagnostic Applications

Basic View of Reading. Reading is a top-down process where the reader's personal interpretation focuses comprehension. Reading requires a personal identification with the story's characters, problems, and events; therefore, the affective purposes of the reader and situational variables influence her model of meaning.

Patterns of Strengths and Strategies. Story drama is most appropriate for students who are extremely expressive, divergent, and simultaneous when thinking. For these students, the powerful influence of personal, kinesthetic imagery is used to analyze the constructive comprehension process. This strategy encourages active involvement in analyzing not only the story line and character development but also the effect that personal identification with story characters has on comprehension.

Learner Patterns That Produce a High Success Rate

1. A nonverbal student who uses dramatic expression and body language to communicate. Story drama uses this strength to aid the student in verbally communicating her ideas about the story.
2. A passive learner who needs to engage in active interpretation of the story line. Story drama concretely demonstrates how to be actively involved in a story.
*3. A simultaneous learner who relies too heavily on personal identification with story characters and has difficulty establishing a sense of

distance when reading. Story drama helps her analyze how her personal identification affects her interpretation.

*4. The dramatic, impulsive learner who needs to attend to the important information in the text. Story drama focuses her attention on character traits and story theme in order to portray a character.

Using the Technique as a Diagnostic Teaching Lesson. For story drama to be effective, a majority of the following statements must be answered in the affirmative.

YES   NO

____ ____   **1.** The student enjoys a dramatic presentation and can easily portray characters.

____ ____   **2.** The student makes predictions as a result of the drama.

____ ____   **3.** The student discusses important information and how it is used by the author.

____ ____   **4.** The student analyzes her personal identification with characters more objectively.

For Further Reading

Galda, L. (1982). Playing about a story: Its impact on comprehension. *Reading Teacher, 36,* 52–58.

Miller, G. M., & Mason, G. E. (1983). Dramatic improvisation: Risk-free role playing for improving reading performance. *Reading Teacher, 37,* 128–131.

Pellegrini, A. D., & Galda, L. (1982). The effects of thematic fantasy play training on the development of children's story comprehension. *American Educational Research Journal, 19,* 443–452.

Walker, B. J. (1985). Right-brained strategies for teaching comprehension. *Academic Therapy, 21,* 133–141.

STORY MAPS

Description. Story maps are visual representations of the logical sequence of events in a narrative text. The elements of setting, problem, goal, events, and resolution are recorded visually on a sheet of paper (Beck & McKeown, 1981; Pearson, 1982).

1. Reading comprehension
2. Visual diagram of story events and their relationships
3. Sensitivity to story structures and sequences

Targeted Reading Levels: 1–8

Text: Any narrative text with a fairly coherent story line

Procedure

1. The teacher selects a narrative passage of sufficient length to have a cohesive story line.
2. The teacher prepares questions to lead students through the story map.
3. The teacher discusses the organization of a story by explaining that every story has a beginning, middle, and an end.
   a. The beginning tells the place and who the characters are.
   b. During the middle of the story, the central character has a problem and makes a plan to solve it. Certain events in the story lead to solving the problem.
   c. The end of the story tells how the character(s) solved the problem.
4. The teacher explains the visual story map (see example on page 196) and relates it to story organization.
5. The students read the story.
6. The teacher and the students fill out the map together. The teacher uses the prepared questions to guide the completion of the map.
7. The teacher and the students compare this story with other stories that they have read.

Further Diagnostic Applications

Basic View of Reading. Reading is an interactive process where the reader's understanding of the elements of a story affects reading comprehension.

Patterns of Strengths and Strategies. Story mapping is most appropriate for the learner who profits from a visual representation of story organization in order to develop adequate comprehension. Often the abundance of facts overwhelms the young reader, who needs a simple structure like a story map to apply to stories to help her organize and remember events.

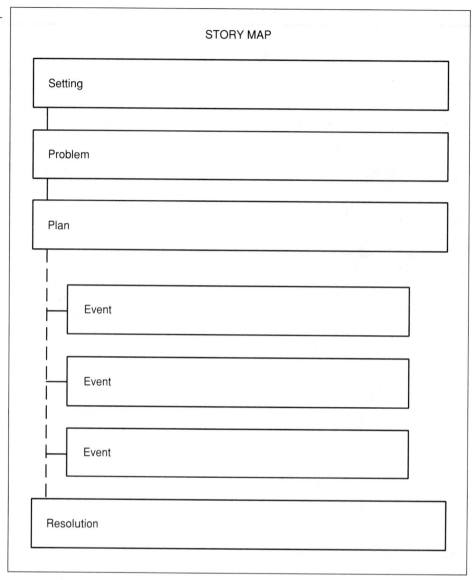

STORY MAP

Setting

Problem

Plan

Event

Event

Event

Resolution

Note. Adapted from *Asking Questions About Stories* (Ginn Occasional Papers No. 15, p. 7) by P. David Pearson, 1982, Lexington, MA: Silver Burdett & Ginn. Copyright 1982 by Silver Burdett and Ginn. Reprinted by permission of the publisher.

Learner Patterns That Produce a High Success Rate

1. A simultaneous learner who has difficulty organizing sequential events of the story and remembering factual detail. The story map uses her visual strengths to develop the text-based skill of story development.

2. The passive learner who has difficulty retelling the story and often leaves out key events or characters in the retelling. The story map gives a structure to the retelling and reasons for the facts to be remembered.

*3. The fact-bound learner who lacks a cohesive sense of story. The map provides her with an overall view of the story.

Using the Technique as a Diagnostic Teaching Lesson. For story maps to be effective, a majority of the following statements must be answered in the affirmative.

YES   NO

_____ _____   **1.** The student understands the story map elements.

_____ _____   **2.** The student improves her ability to retell the story.

_____ _____   **3.** The student improves the number of questions about story events she can answer.

_____ _____   **4.** The student improves her inferences about the character's motives.

For Further Reading

Beck, I. L., & McKeown, M. G. (1981). Developing questions that promote comprehension: The story map. *Language Arts, 58*, 913–918.

Fowler, G. L., & Davis, M. (1985). The story frame approach: A tool for improving reading comprehension of EMR children. *Teaching Exceptional Children, 17*, 296–298.

Pearson, P. D. (1982). *Asking questions about stories* (Ginn Occasional Papers No. 15). Lexington, MA: Silver Burdett & Ginn.

STORY WRITING APPROACH

Description. Story writing is an instructional format for teaching narrative writing that includes three stages: prewriting, writing, and evaluating. By writing their own stories, students increase their awareness of story parts.

Major Reading Tasks It Develops

1. Comprehension of story organization
2. Sentence comprehension
3. Reading as communication

Targeted Reading Levels: 3–6, but can be used at all levels

Text: Student's own writing

Procedure

1. The teacher introduces the structure of a story. Stories have a beginning (the characters and place), middle (problems and the events), and an end (solution of the problem).
2. The teacher and the students brainstorm ideas to select a topic and information that might go into the story.
3. Using the information collected, the students write their stories. The teacher emphasizes that the story needs to flow from one idea to the next and make sense.
4. The teacher has the students reread their stories to see if they make sense. He uses the following questions.
   a. Does the story make sense?
   b. Do I have all the story parts?
   c. Have I left out any information that the reader might need to know in order to understand my story?
5. The students revise any unclear information.
6. The students make a final copy of their stories.

Modifications

1. Prewriting can use a visual story map to form the outline of the story.
2. For the student who has a great deal of difficulty, the teacher might use a story frame with only minimal ideas deleted.
3. Guided imagery journeys may be used as a prewriting activity.
4. A story can be composed by a small group of students. Each person writes a segment of the story and then passes the text to the next person. Each student's contribution to the story line must build upon prior information and make sense.
5. Pairs of students can read and edit each other's stories.

Further Diagnostic Applications

Basic View of Reading. Reading is a top-down process where the reader interprets the author's intended meaning. An author writes a text that allows a clear interpretation by the reader but assumes that a certain amount of inferencing will occur on the part of the reader.

Patterns of Strengths and Strategies. The story writing approach is most
appropriate for students who need to write in order to experience how a story
is organized so that it makes sense. This approach emphasizes the constructive
nature of reading and that the text needs to "make sense."

Learner Patterns That Produce a High Success Rate

1. The simultaneous learner who writes and reads for self-understanding
   and meaning but does not realize that a story is a contractual agreement between reader and writer. This technique helps her think
   about what the author wants her to understand.
2. The passive learner who does not understand story organization. By
   writing her own parts of a story, she learns to attend to these story
   features when she reads.
*3. The reader who relies on her own background knowledge to inter-
   pret text and does not attend to sentence meaning. By writing her
   own stories and listening to others interpret them, she becomes more
   sensitive to the function that text structure has in developing
   meaning.

Using the Technique as a Diagnostic Teaching Lesson. For story writing
to be effective, a majority of the following statements must be answered in the
affirmative.

YES   NO

_____ _____   **1.** The student prefers to write what she thinks rather
than contribute to a discussion.

_____ _____   **2.** The student writes fluently and can construct text that
makes sense.

_____ _____   **3.** The student understands the parts of a story well
enough to be able to construct a coherent story.

_____ _____   **4.** Composition increases her understanding of the read-
ing process.

For Further Reading

Aulls, M. (1982). *Developing readers in today's elementary school.* Boston: Allyn & Bacon.
Tiedt, I. M., Bruemmer, S. S., Lane, S., Stelwagon, P., Watanabe, K. O., & Williams,
M. Y. (1983). *Teaching writing in K–8 classrooms.* Englewood Cliffs, NJ: Prentice-Hall.

SUMMARIZATION

Description. Summarization teaches the student how to write summaries of what she reads. She is shown how to delete unimportant information, group similar ideas, decide on or invent topic sentences, and list supporting details. These procedures culminate in a short paragraph that reflects the most important information.

Major Reading Tasks It Develops

1. Comprehension
2. Comprehension monitoring

Targeted Reading Levels: 6–12

Text: Most appropriate for expository text

Procedure

1. The teacher selects an expository text.
2. He describes a summary as a short version of the text that contains all the important information.
3. The teacher explains that the purpose of writing summaries is to put all the important information together so it can be remembered better.
4. The students read a short selection.
5. The students reread the selection and ask themselves, "What is this mainly about?"
6. The teacher reads his summary of the selection and presents it on the overhead.
7. Each student finds the summary statement in the original text. The student marks the information that each statement represents.
8. The teacher talks about the rules for writing summaries by telling the students how he wrote his summary.
9. The teacher demonstrates the rule of deleting trivial information. He points out that many writers tell us interesting information that is not a key idea. He tells them to ignore this information when writing a summary.
10. The teacher demonstrates the rule for deleting repeated information. He explains that many writers repeat information to make their point.

When writing a summary, students should use this idea only once and ignore repeated information.

11. The teacher demonstrates the rule for combining details into a generalization. When possible, students should combine details that fit into the same category and rename that category with a bigger category. For example, *pigs, horses, cows,* and *chickens* can be renamed to *farm animals*.

12. The teacher demonstrates how to select the topic sentence. He points out that the topic sentence is the author's one sentence summary. It usually comes at the beginning or the end of the paragraph.

13. The teacher demonstrates how to invent a topic sentence when there is not a summary sentence. In this case, he shows how to organize all the important information into one category. Then he writes a sentence that tells what it is mainly about. He shows how to think about how the important information relates.

14. The students write a summary for the demonstration selection and check their summaries individually with the rules.

15. The students compare their summaries in small groups.

16. The students write a summary for another selection.

17. When they have finished, the students describe how they constructed their summaries.

18. The teacher shows them his summary and talks about how he constructed it.

19. The students write summaries for several more selections on their own.

Further Diagnostic Applications

Basic View of Reading. Reading is an interactive process where the reader decides what is important about the text in order to summarize and remember what it says.

Patterns of Strengths and Strategies. Summarization is most appropriate for students who like to think about what a text mainly says but have difficulty remembering the facts that support this decision. The approach helps this student focus on relating all the textual information that is important to the key idea.

Learner Patterns That Produce a High Success Rate

1. A simultaneous reader who understands the key ideas but often does not remember the important details. Summarization helps her put the details into her overall framework.

2. A passive reader who needs to be actively engaged in interpreting the text. This gives her a written record of what she thinks and how her strategies work when she reads.

*3. A successive reader who cannot tie important information together in order to remember information. Summarization helps her decide on general categories that relate details.

*4. A successive reader who thinks everything in the text is important to remember. Summarization helps her learn to delete unimportant and repeated information.

Using the Technique as a Diagnostic Teaching Lesson.   For summarization to be effective, a majority of the following statements must be answered in the affirmative.

YES	NO	
____	____	**1.** The student can recognize and understand the individual words in the text.
____	____	**2.** The student can write fairly fluently; therefore, writing the words on paper does not interfere with the task.
____	____	**3.** The student learns to distinguish what is important and what is unimportant fairly easily.
____	____	**4.** The student learns to group individual information of like categories easily.

For Further Reading

Hare, V. C., & Borchardt, K. M. (1984). Direct instruction of summarization skills. *Reading Research Quarterly, 20,* 62–78.
King, J. R., Biggs, S., & Lipsky, S. (1984). Students' self-questioning and summarizing as reading study strategies. *Journal of Reading Behavior, 16,* 205–218.

SUSTAINED SILENT READING

Description.   Sustained silent reading (SSR) is the designation of an uninterrupted time where both the students and the teacher read self-selected reading materials for their own purposes. The teacher models his own enjoyment of reading. In turn, the students begin to define their interests and read for their own enjoyment.

Major Reading Tasks It Develops

1. Reading for individual purposes
2. Self-selection of appropriate text
3. Identification of reading interest
4. Practicing the whole act of reading

Targeted Reading Levels: All levels

Text: Self-selected

Procedures

1. Before beginning SSR, the teacher collects a variety of reading materials that represent a wide range of reading levels and text types (magazines, newspapers, novels, and informational texts).
2. Next, the teacher reads aloud favorite parts of books or talks about books other students have enjoyed to stimulate students' interest.
3. The teacher designates a specific time for reading each day. (After lunch is a good time; students select their books before lunch so they can be ready to read as soon as lunch is over. Another good time is at the end of the day.)
4. The students select their books prior to the designated time.
5. The teacher explains the "rule of thumb," which aids in book selection. According to this rule, the student selects a book and reads a page at random. When she reaches the first word she does not know, she places her little finger on it. On the next difficult word, she places the next finger, and so on. If she reaches her thumb before the end of the page, the book is too difficult and she must find another book.
6. The students do not change books during the designated time span.
7. Initially, the teacher sets aside a short time period (5 to 10 minutes) and then increases the amount of time each day.
8. The teacher uses a timer to monitor the time so everyone is free to read.
9. The students read silently for the time period.
10. The teacher and anyone else in the room read silently for the time period.
11. The teacher does not keep records or have students make reports on what they read. The students are in control of what and how much they read.
12. Initially, the teacher allows pretend reading, browsing through books, and looking at pictures. He also initially provides a narrow range of selection choices.

13. The teacher reiterates some key principles of sustained silent reading.
    a. Read what you want.
    b. Getting all the words right is not necessary.
    c. If it meets your needs, skipping pages is OK.

COMMENT: Although this technique is more effective for some children than others, it is recommended as part of the diagnostic teaching session because it allows students to read for their own purpose, practice their reading skills, and experience "wanting to read."

Further Diagnostic Applications

Basic View of Reading. Reading is a top-down process where the readers' personal interpretations and enjoyment are the focus of reading instruction. By the teacher's modeling his own enjoyment of literature, he shares "wanting to read."

Patterns of Strengths and Strategies. Sustained silent reading is most appropriate for the successive, independent reader who enjoys reading for her own purposes rather than the teacher's purposes. In this technique, personal enjoyment is gained while reading for individual purposes.

Learner Patterns That Produce a High Success Rate

1. A successive learner who needs to identify her own reasons for reading. Sustained silent reading allows her to identify her own interests and reasons for reading.
2. An active reader who likes to read for her own purposes and reasons rather than the teacher's. This technique gives her the freedom to take what she wants from reading.
*3. An inattentive reader who cannot read long sections of text silently. This technique allows her to increase her attention during silent reading.
*4. A passive reader who views herself as a failure when reading. This technique allows her to feel success when reading because she controls the reasons for reading.

Using the Technique as a Diagnostic Teaching Lesson. For SSR to be effective, a majority of the following statements must be answered in the affirmative.

YES   NO

_____ _____   **1.** The student selects books she wants to read.

_____ _____ **2.** The student observes the rules of silent reading and is
not disruptive during that time.

_____ _____ **3.** The student increases her own task reading time and
asks for longer time for sustained silent reading.

_____ _____ **4.** The student decreases her responses to distractions and
increases her concentration.

CAUTION: Be persistent in expecting success. Even though some students will pretend to be reading, it is the model and message that they can read what they like
that is important.

For Further Reading

Berglund, R. L., & Johns, J. L. (1983). A primer on uninterrupted sustained silent reading.
Reading Teacher, 36, 534–539.
Trelease, J. (1985). *The read-aloud handbook.* New York: Penguin Books.

SYNTHETIC PHONICS APPROACH

Description. Synthetic phonics teaches sound-symbol relationships in words to
facilitate word identification. The student is systematically instructed to say the
letter sounds in words and then blend the sounds together to decode the unknown
word. Rules for the phonic relationships are presented with examples. The rapid
transfer of decoding principles to new words is expected as the text includes many
words that follow the rule but were not presented before reading.

Major Reading Tasks It Develops

1. Phonic decoding
2. Sight word identification by sounding out words

Targeted Reading Levels: 1–2

Text: Decodable words in meaningful text and some isolated drill

1. The teacher selects phonic rules to be taught.
2. He selects texts and words to illustrate the rule.
3. The teacher directly teaches the letter sounds.

   The letter *s* goes *s-s-s*.
   The letter *t* goes *t-t-t*.
   The letter *n* goes *n-n-n*.
   The letter *m* goes *m-m-m*.

   In short words that have a consonant at the beginning and the end and an *a* in the middle, the letter *a* says *ă-ă-ă*

4. The student blends the sounds together to form words.

   S-ă-m says *Sam*.
   S-ă-t says *sat*.

5. The student reads the words in a text that uses the sound-symbol relationships that the teacher has introduced.

   Sam is on the mat.
   The man is on the mat.
   Sam sat on the man on the mat.

6. The teacher facilitates the transfer of rules to new words. He teaches the sounds for *d*, *h*, and *c*. Then he asks the student to read the following story:

   The man has a hat. The hat is in the sand.
   The man sat on the mat in the sand.
   Dan sat on the mat in the sand.
   Sam is a cat. Sam ran in the sand.
   Sam ran to Dan. Sam ran to the man.
   Sam ran in the sand. Sam sat in the sand.
   Sam sat on the man's hat.
   The man is mad at Sam. Sam ran.

Further Diagnostic Applications

Basic View of Reading. Reading is a bottom-up process where effective reading is based on accurate decoding of words. Learning sounds of letters and sounding out words precedes reading stories; therefore, decoding precedes comprehension.

Patterns of Strengths and Strategies. Synthetic phonics is a process of successive blending of sounds requiring the child to hold a sequence of sounds in her memory while synthesizing them to form a word. Young children who have facility with sound blending and can hold oral sequences in memory will have the greatest success with this method.

Learner Patterns That Produce a High Success Rate

1. A successive learner who can rapidly and flexibly apply the rules to new words in new contexts. This technique allows her to apply phonic rules to the stories that she reads.
2. A successive learner who has facility with language so that the systematic decoding of words becomes a tool rather than an end by itself. For this reader, the phonics facilitates word identification without interfering with fluency.
3. A passive learner who can blend sounds and profits from direct instruction in the sound system. This technique directly shows her how to decode new words as well as directs her attention to individual letters.

Using the Technique as a Diagnostic Teaching Lesson. For synthetic phonics to be effective, a majority of the following statements must be answered in the affirmative.

YES	NO	
____	____	**1.** The student can blend sounds.
____	____	**2.** The student can segment sounds.
____	____	**3.** The student can hold a sequence of letter sounds in memory long enough to blend the sounds to form a word.

For Further Reading

Aukerman, R. C. (1984). *Approaches to beginning reading* (2nd ed.). New York: John Wiley & Sons, 368–371.

Ray, D. D. (1971). Specificity in remediation. In B. Bateman (Ed.), *Learning disorders* (pp. 180–191). Seattle, WA: Special Child Publications.

TALKING BOOKS

Description. The talking books method uses tape-recorded readings of selected stories to increase word recognition and reading fluency. The student repeatedly reads along with a tape until she can read the text fluently with comprehension (Carbo, 1978).

Major Reading Tasks It Develops

1. Oral reading fluency
2. Sight word identification through contextual reading
3. Intonation and phrasing

Targeted Reading Levels: K–5

Text: Stories with specially prepared tape recordings

Procedure

1. The student selects a text that is interesting to her.
2. The teacher secures or makes a tape recording of the story.
3. If he makes a tape, he includes the following:
   a. He segments the story so that the student can easily finish a tape in one sitting.
   b. He cues the page numbers so the student can easily find the page.
   c. He records the text using the natural phrases of language.
4. The student follows the line of print with her finger.
5. The student listens to the tape recording to develop an overall understanding of the story.
6. Then the student listens and reads along with the tape as many times as necessary until she can read the text fluently.
7. The student rehearses the text by herself.
8. The student reads the text to the teacher.
9. The teacher evaluates fluency and comprehension.
10. If she reads the passage fluently with comprehension, the student listens and reads the next segment of the story or another story.

Further Diagnostic Applications

Basic View of Reading. Reading is a top-down process where the reader's personal understanding of the story drives the word recognition process. By repeatedly listening to the story, the reader gains an understanding of the story meaning, story structure, and sentence structure. She uses this understanding to facilitate recognizing the words in the story.

Patterns of Strengths and Strategies. The talking books technique is most
appropriate for the beginning reader or the nonfluent reader who easily memorizes
stories. This memorization facilitates fluent reading of text and allows the student
to attend to both meaning and print simultaneously. By memorizing stories, the
student is exposed to lots of words in context, enabling her to apply phonic knowledge, recognize sight words, and self-correct as she meaningfully reads text.

Learner Patterns That Produce a High Success Rate

1. A simultaneous learner who relies too heavily on background knowledge when orally reading; therefore, she does not self-correct using
   graphic cues. This technique develops word identification by using
   the overall textual meaning (prior knowledge) to identify words.
2. A nonfluent reader who has had an overemphasis of synthetic or explicit phonic instruction and, therefore, has become word-bound.
   This technique develops reading in meaningful phrases.
3. A passive reader who reads word by word without attention to
   meaning. This technique restores reading for meaning by learning to
   read whole stories with expression and allows the student to experience success.
*4. A slow reader who has not developed either decoding skills or a
   recognition vocabulary. Talking books use memorizing whole stories
   so that the student can read lots of words before developing either
   phonic knowledge or a sight word vocabulary.

Using the Technique as a Diagnostic Teaching Lesson. For talking books
to be effective, a majority of the following statements must be answered in the
affirmative.

YES   NO

_____ _____ **1.** The student is sufficiently interested in the text to
                listen and read the story repeatedly.

_____ _____ **2.** The student memorizes the story fairly easily, requiring
                only a minimal number of listen-and-read sessions.
                (More than a week on the same story is too long.)

_____ _____ **3.** As the story is read, the student follows the text and
                associates the words she hears with the words on the
                page.

_____ _____ **4.** There is an increase in fluent reading with comprehen-
                sion as a result of using this method.

For Further Reading

Carbo, M. (1978). Teaching reading with talking books. *Reading Teacher, 32,* 267–273.

Chomsky, C. (1978). When you still can't read in third grade: After decoding what?'' In J. Samuels (Ed.), *What research has to say about reading instruction* (pp. 13–30). Newark, DE: International Reading Association.

TRIPLE READ OUTLINE

Description. Triple read outline is the rereading of expository text to develop an organizational framework of main ideas and supporting details. By reading the information three times, the student focuses on different purposes for organizing information during each reading.

Major Reading Tasks It Develops

1. Comprehension (main ideas and details)
2. Study skills

Targeted Reading Levels: 7–12

Text: Expository

Procedure

1. The teacher selects a short expository passage to demonstrate the triple read outline.
2. He makes an overhead of the passage and copies for the students.
3. The teacher states the purpose for the first reading—identify the main idea—and models the step by reading a paragraph out loud and identifying the main idea. Then he writes or illustrates the main idea in the paragraph margins. He continues the procedure for the entire passage, identifying the main idea of each paragraph in the passage.
4. The teacher models the second procedure—identify supporting details—by talking out loud as he rereads the entire passage and underlining the key details that support the main idea for the first paragraph. He continues the procedure for each paragraph in the entire passage.

5. On the third reading, the teacher models the third step—organize the information into an outline. He puts the notes that he wrote in the margins and the key details into an outline of the passage. Some of the key ideas will not fit into the overall outline. He writes those on a separate page.

. The teacher writes a summary of the passage. He uses the main idea as the topic sentence and puts in the details that support the main idea. He leaves out information that is not important.

. Next the teacher distributes copies of a passage from the textbook to be read.

. This time the students read the passage, looking for the main idea of each paragraph and writing the main idea in the margin. He tells them that some paragraphs will not have a main idea.

. The students compare their margin "main ideas" with the teacher's margin "main ideas."

10. The students revise the information as necessary.

11. The students read the passage again, looking for and underlining the supporting details for the main ideas in the margin.

12. The students compare the facts they underlined with the facts the teacher underlined.

13. The students revise the underlining as necessary.

14. The students read the passage a third time to organize the information into an outline of main ideas and supporting details. Unimportant information is to be forgotten.

15. The students compare their outlines with the teacher's outline. They discuss the differences and similarities.

16. If the students have left out important information, the teacher models his thinking about why something is important enough to leave in the outline.

17. Using the outline, the students write a three- to four-sentence summary of passage.

Note: From *The Triple Read Method for Expository Text* by P. D. Pearson, 1985. Seminar presentation, Eastern Montana College, Billings, MT. Adapted by permission.

Further Diagnostic Applications

Basic View of Reading. Reading is an interactive process that requires the reader to select information and organize this information so it can be remembered. Organizing the information into a logical structure facilitates recall, as does rereading the text with different purposes for selecting information.

Patterns of Strengths and Strategies. The triple read outline is most appropriate for students who read expository text rapidly and fluently but remember very little of the information when they have finished. Frequently these students

The Instructional Techniques

do not understand how the author organized the information, so they passively read the words without a reason for gaining information. They think that good readers read the text once rapidly and are somehow able to remember an enormous amount of facts with this simple strategy.

Learner Patterns That Produce a High Success Rate

1. The simultaneous reader who remembers main ideas but forgets the facts. This gives the student a strategy for remembering facts within an overall framework.
2. The passive reader who lacks the strategy to read for different purposes as she is reading. This shows her how to read information for different purposes and the results of these rereadings.
*3. The successive reader who verbalizes the words, remembers some facts, but does not organize the facts by relating them to the key ideas. This gives her a tool for organizing information.

Using the Technique as a Diagnostic Teaching Lesson. For the triple read outline to be effective, a majority of the following statements must be answered in the affirmative.

YES   NO

____ ____ **1.** The student is able to read the passage rapidly enough that the technique is not too time-consuming.

____ ____ **2.** The student learns how to find a main idea rather easily.

____ ____ **3.** The student learns how to find the supporting details for each main idea without much difficulty.

____ ____ **4.** The organizing of the information facilitates recall of the information.

For Further Reading

Giordano, G. (1982). Outlining techniques that help disabled readers. *Academic Therapy, 17*, 517–522.

Santa, C., Danner, M., Nelson, M., Havens, L., Scalf, J., & Scalf, L. (1986). *Content reading in secondary school: Learning across the curriculum.* Unpublished manuscript, Kalispell School District No. 5, Kalispell, MT.

VISUALIZATION

Description. Visualization is an approach for improving comprehension by suggesting to children that they form a mental image of the setting and characters as they are reading. It is used to develop word meaning by asking the students to form mental images of words, relating descriptors with the new word.

Major Reading Tasks It Develops

1. Comprehension
2. Word meaning

Targeted Reading Levels: All levels

Text: Isolated words, narrative text, or expository text

Procedure for Word Meaning

1. The teacher selects target words for developing meanings.
2. The students look at the word and then close their eyes.
3. The teacher reads a definition and *like a* statements and asks the students to form a mental picture of the word. For example, if the target word is *geyser*, the teacher could say, "Think about a geyser as a large whistling teapot just about to boil. The water is bubbling and the pressure is mounting. When enough pressure builds up, the teapot begins to whistle and blow steam into the air. The geyser is a large teapot in the ground."
4. The teacher and the students discuss their mental pictures.
5. In some cases, the students draw their images.

Procedure for Comprehension

1. The teacher selects the text.
2. The teacher tells the students that forming pictures in their minds can increase their understanding of the text. These mind pictures are like illustrations within the text that can help the reader remember the text.
3. The teacher introduces the story setting.

4. The students close their eyes and imagine what the story is going to be about by using the title and the story setting.
5. The students read the selection up to a designated turning point.
6. The students and the teacher discuss both images and story line.
7. The students close their eyes and imagine what is going to happen next.
8. The students finish reading the selection.
9. The students and the teacher compare and contrast images and what the text said.
10. The teacher uses these questions to guide discussion: How did the characters resolve the problem in the story? How is their resolution like what you imagined? How is it different?

Further Diagnostic Applications

Basic View of Reading. Reading is an interactive process where information is stored in images as well as words. Reading involves inferencing from the text by using words and images that are stored in memory.

Patterns of Strengths and Strategies. Visualization is most appropriate for the highly visual, simultaneous learner who initially searches visual images to comprehend text. This approach activates these students' strength in representing knowledge in its visual-spatial relationships and encourages them to relate this information to verbal comprehension.

Learner Patterns That Produce a High Success Rate

1. A simultaneous learner who uses elaborate and imaginative descriptions of words and events. This technique matches her strength of visualization.
2. The passive reader who does not check her past experiences to see if what she is reading makes sense. Visualization enhances her active comprehension and monitoring as she learns to check her interpretation with her images.
3. The extremely nonverbal student who codes information in images rather than words. Visualization links her visual images to verbal descriptions.
*4. The highly successive learner who needs to embellish the definitional meanings of words. Visualization offers her a tool for elaboration.

Using the Technique as a Diagnostic Teaching Lesson. For visualization to be effective, a majority of the following statements must be answered in the affirmative.

YES	NO	
——	——	**1.** The student is relatively nonexpressive.
——	——	**2.** The student prefers drawing to talking.
——	——	**3.** The student sees pictures in her mind.
——	——	**4.** The student has difficulty verbalizing ideas.

For Further Reading

Gambrell, L. B., & Bales, R. J. (1986). Mental imagery and the comprehension-monitoring performance of fourth and fifth grade poor readers. *Reading Research Quarterly, 21*, 454–465.

McNeil, J. D. (1987). *Reading comprehension: New directions for classroom practice* (2nd ed.). Glenview, IL: Scott, Foresman.

Peters, E., & Levin, J. R. (1986). Effects of a mnemonic imagery strategy on good and poor readers' prose recall. *Reading Research Quarterly, 21*, 179–192.

VOCABULARY MAPS

Description. This is a technique for developing word meanings by visually mapping the relationships among words. The target vocabulary word is placed in the center of the map. Related words and concepts are arranged around this word to show relationships between what the student already knows and the new word (Johnson & Pearson, 1984).

Major Reading Tasks It Develops

1. Word meaning
2. Using known words to develop new relationships among words
3. Labeling conceptual relationships based on personal experience

Targeted Reading Levels: All levels

Text: Key vocabulary words. (Often this technique is used to introduce vocabulary words for a story.)

Procedure

1. The teacher chooses a word or concept that is a key element of what is to be read.

2. He places the word inside a circle in the middle of a blank page or chalkboard.
3. The students and the teacher brainstorm what is already known about this word and place the information in conceptual relationships, making a visual array of the relationships.
4. The teacher adds each new word that describes the central word to the map by drawing lines and new circles that indicate their relationships to the words. For the word *image*, for example, some relationships involve similes of what an image is like, some suggest the composition of an image, and others look at how an image might be useful.
5. The students read the story.
6. The students and the teacher add additional story information to the map.
7. The students and the teacher discuss new meanings to known words and new relationships among the words that were gained by reading the story.

Modification. For the student who needs to build a meaning vocabulary, vocabulary cards can be made with vocabulary maps on one side of the card and the word in a sentence on the reverse side. These words are then reviewed periodically for comprehension.

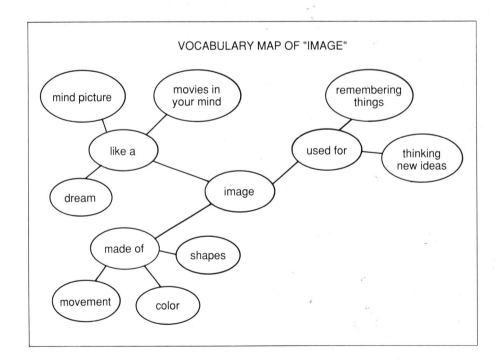

VOCABULARY MAP OF "IMAGE"

Further Diagnostic Applications

Basic View of Reading. Reading is an interactive process where readers use their background knowledge to map relationships between word knowledge (verbal labels) and world knowledge (concepts).

Patterns of Strengths and Strategies. Vocabulary mapping encourages the student to use her experiential knowledge to expand her definitional knowledge; therefore, it is most appropriate for the student who tends to think visually about the relationship of information without describing these relationships in words. This strategy facilitates learning for this student because it begins by showing the visual relationships and then uses words to explain that relationship.

Learner Patterns That Produce a High Success Rate

1. A simultaneous thinker who perceives visual-spatial relationships rather than definitional relationships. This technique helps the student use her visual understanding of relationships to increase her understanding of what words mean.
2. A bilingual student who has a well-developed conceptual base but nonspecific word usage. The visual mapping of words and relationships helps her make specific comparisons between the events of her life and the words that are commonly used to express them.
*3. A student with verbal weaknesses who needs to develop word knowledge in order to read and understand. This technique helps her develop conceptual relationships among words as well as the verbal labels used to express those relationships.

Using the Technique as a Diagnostic Teaching Lesson. For vocabulary maps to be effective, a majority of the following statements must be answered in the affirmative.

YES   NO

_____ _____   1. The student has a sound experiential base but is unable to express it.

_____ _____   2. The student often has a general understanding but does not know specific words to express that understanding.

_____ _____   3. The student's elaboration of ideas is marked with the word *thing* instead of a specific word.

_____ _____   4. The student has a facility with visual mapping activities.

For Further Reading

Heimlich, J. E., & Pittleman, S. D. (1986). *Semantic mapping: Classroom applications.* Newark, DE: International Reading Association.

Johnson, D. D., & Pearson, P. D. (1984). *Teaching reading vocabulary* (2nd ed.). New York: Holt, Rinehart & Winston.

Sinatra, R. C., Berg, D., & Dunn, R. (1985). Semantic mapping improves reading comprehension of learning disabled students. *Teaching Exceptional Children, 17,* 310–314.

WORD CARDS

Description. The word card technique is a systematic recording of sight words introduced during the reading lesson. These words are placed on individual cards so that they may be used to review and reinforce a recognition vocabulary.

Major Reading Tasks It Develops

1. Word recognition
2. Identification of words by key visual features

Targeted Reading Levels: PP–2

Text: Isolated words

Procedure

1. The teacher selects target sight words (including easy words too) for each lesson. (CAUTION: Word cards are most effective when concrete words are selected.)
2. He writes these words on 3″ × 5″ cards.
3. On the back of the card, he places the word in a sentence taken from the child's own vocabulary or the story.
4. To reinforce sight word recognition, the teacher flashes the word cards with a semantic cue from the story. For example, when the target word *play* is forgotten, the teacher uses the semantic cue, "We like to run and _____."
5. The teacher counts the correct word cards and records the student's responses on a graph (see the example) so that she can monitor her progress.

JANE'S PROGRESS					
Word	*M*	*T*	*W*	*Th*	*F*
door	✔	✔	✔	✔	✔
window			✔		✔
shade		✔	✔	✔	✔
visitor				✔	✔

6. The teacher keeps two file boxes of cards. One box is for those words that are mastered; it can be used to construct activities that reinforce learning and as a spelling dictionary for creative writing. The other box is for those words that need to be reinforced through repetition.

Modifications. A multitude of ideas are available for using word cards to reinforce and stimulate word learning. These are a few of the most popular.

1. The teacher uses the word cards to form a word bank that can be used to write and combine sentences. This bank becomes a spelling dictionary of known words for writing during uninterrupted sustained silent writing.
2. The teacher uses word cards to construct games to reinforce learning.
3. Students quiz each other using the word cards.
4. Students classify the word cards according to categories and make a feature analysis grid.

Further Diagnostic Applications

Basic View of Reading. Reading is a bottom-up process where the reader initially masters a set of words that are automatically recognized "at sight." These sight words are mastered in isolation, then read in sentences, and finally read in stories.

Patterns of Strengths and Strategies. Word cards are most appropriate for the young reader who is developing a recognition vocabulary. For these students, the isolated drill of sight words draws attention to the key visual features of words. This reinforces the learning of word features and aids the automatic recognition of words.

1. A simultaneous learner who needs more than the average contextual repetitions before a word is mastered. Presenting the word card with a semantic cue helps the student focus on meaning and visual cues at the same time.
2. An inattentive learner who attends more to the pictures and context when reading stories than the important features of the words. Word cards isolate the word so the student can identify and remember the key visual features.
3. A passive learner who needs direct instruction in how to select the key features so she can remember what the words look like. Word cards provide a tool for the teacher to talk about what words look like.

Using the Technique as a Diagnostic Teaching Lesson. For the word card technique to be effective, a majority of the following statements must be answered in the affirmative.

YES	NO	
____	____	**1.** The student can remember the words flashed.
____	____	**2.** The student needs a minimal number of trials to remember the word visually.
____	____	**3.** The student needs a minimal amount of prompting when the word is flashed.

For Further Reading

Stauffer, R. (1970). *The language experience approach to teaching of reading.* New York: Harper & Row.

Wilson, R. M., & Cleland, C. J. (1985). *Diagnostic and remedial reading for classroom and clinic* (5th ed.) (pp. 233–234). Columbus, OH: Merrill.

Gathering
Diagnostic Data

7

The diagnostic teacher gathers data to formulate her hypotheses about the strategies a reader uses to interpret text (see Figure 7–1). Diagnostic decisions are made based on data gathered without prior instruction and also after instructional adjustments have been made. This chapter focuses on data acquired when the student does not receive instruction. Such data provide needed information about the independent problem-solving strategies of the learner.

In the decision-making cycle of diagnostic teaching, data are gathered to make initial decisions and to monitor changes in reading performance. The initial decisions are made using informal reading inventories, including the selection of a text that is moderately difficult for the student. The diagnostic teacher then chooses a story and conducts an assessment using the first section of the story. This is referred to as an on-level assessment. The data gathered from it are used to monitor the student's changes. This assessment can be taken from the first phase of the diagnostic lesson, which establishes baseline data (see "Establishing Baseline Data" in Chapter 9), or it can be the information that is continuously gathered (see "Continuous Diagnostic Assessment" in Chapter 4). These procedures provide detailed information about the reader's strategies for regaining meaning when text interpretation becomes difficult. The diagnostic teacher uses these data to formulate hypotheses about a particular student's instructional needs. This chapter elaborates the sources of data: the level of text needed for instruction, the major presenting problem, and the reader's strategies.

ESTABLISHING THE LEVEL
OF STUDENT PERFORMANCE

To begin gathering data, the diagnostic teacher samples reading behavior across levels of text difficulty to identify the student's performance without assistance. To make this assessment, the teacher uses an informal reading inventory, a series

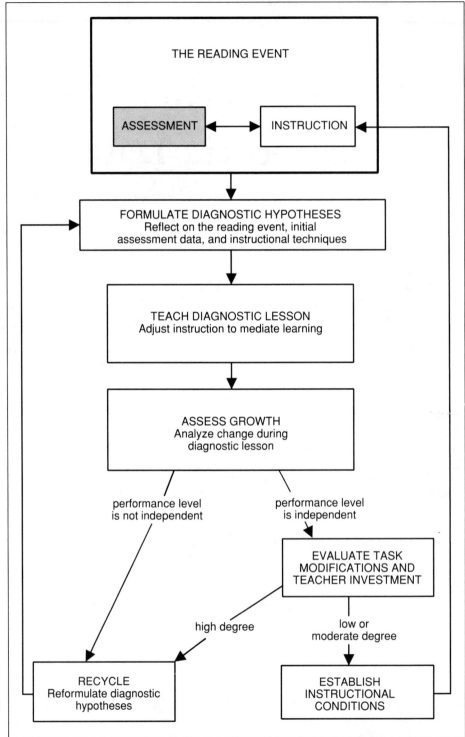

Figure 7–1
The Decision-
Making Cycle of
Diagnostic
Teaching

of graded passages that range in difficulty from first grade to junior high. Information from each passage, therefore, allows the teacher to estimate how the student would perform when reading other selections of the same difficulty level.

The diagnostic teacher uses the inventory to assess a number of potential problem areas. In a standarized inventory, there are equivalent passages. Therefore, the diagnostic teacher administers one form for the oral reading analysis and another form for the silent reading analysis. After each passage has been read, comprehension is evaluated by computing the percentage of correct answers to various types of comprehension questions, such as main idea, supporting details, inferences, and vocabulary. As the student reads orally, errors (deviations from the text) are recorded. These errors are used to compute an error rate or percentage of word recognition. Although variation exists in what constitutes an error, substitutions, mispronunciations, omissions, insertions, and unknown words are usually used to compute the error rate. Other reading behaviors such as repetitions, punctuation errors, and self-corrections are analyzed when conducting a qualitative assessment of oral reading performance. (Further directions for conducting informal reading assessments can be found in the Appendix.)

From the information derived from the informal reading inventory, the diagnostic teacher identifies a level that would be moderately difficult for the student. She thinks again about the criteria for frustration and independent reading level and mentally pictures the ranges shown in Figure 7–2. Word recognition and comprehension criteria for *independent* reading are 1 error in 100 words (1/100 or 99% accuracy) and 90% comprehension accuracy. Word recognition and comprehension criteria for *frustration* reading are 1 error in 10 words (1/10 or 90% accuracy) and 50% comprehension accuracy. The diagnostic teacher identifies the level where the student will experience a moderate amount of difficulty but is not frustrated. She choose a text that is near the frustration reading level (90% oral accuracy and/or 50%–60% comprehension) to continue her analysis. It is at this *borderline* level that she will be able to observe how the student surmounts problems when he encounters difficulties in reading.

IDENTIFYING THE
MAJOR PRESENTING PROBLEM

Based on an informal reading inventory, the diagnostic teacher decides whether print processing or meaning processing is the major inhibiting factor in fluent reading performance. She asks, "In order to develop hypotheses, what do I need to observe? Do I need to observe how the student fixes mistakes when he reads orally (print processing) or when he corrects miscomprehension (meaning processing)?" She knows that fluent reading requires that the student use both printed words and background knowledge to interpret the text. She also realizes that oral reading is a different task from silent reading.

When reading orally, the reader must attend not only to meaning but also to the oral production of the text. According to Allington (1984b, p. 853), "the instructional setting for oral reading imposes different demands from that of silent

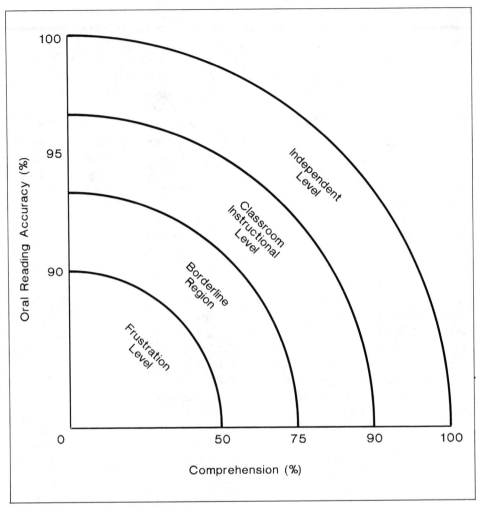

Figure 7–2
Performance
Ranges

reading (e.g., public vs. private performance, personal vs. external monitor of performance, emphasis on accuracy of production vs. accuracy of meaning construction)." Therefore, if the diagnostic teacher needs information on print-processing ability, she uses an oral reading assessment. Then she can observe how the student attends to print when reading breaks down. If the diagnostic teacher needs further information on meaning processing, she uses silent reading analysis and asks the student to think aloud at critical points in the story. Figure 7–3 illustrates this relationship.

In order to formulate hypotheses, the diagnostic teacher selects a text that is suspected to be in the borderline area, or moderately difficult (90% oral accuracy or 60% comprehension), for the student. She also decides if the major inhibiting factor is print processing or meaning processing. Then she prepares an extended passage that is read either orally or silently. In either case, she constructs

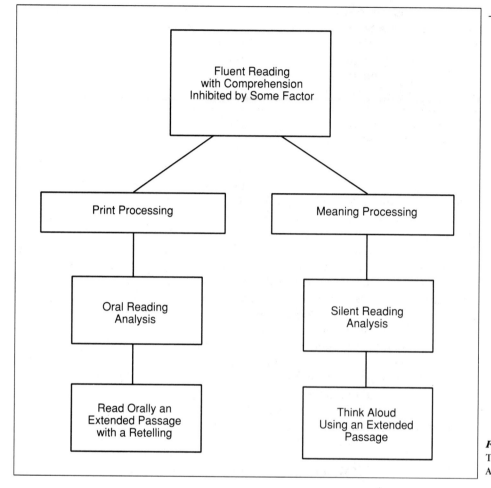

Figure 7–3
Types of Extended
Assessment

questions that require the student to understand the main idea or theme, identify supporting details or events, infer relationships within the information, and explain how the key words are used in the text.

If print processing is inhibiting fluent reading comprehension, the diagnostic teacher interprets oral reading behavior. She asks the student to read the selected text aloud while she records the errors or miscues (see "Scoring Criteria" in the Appendix). To cross-check oral reading behavior with comprehension, the oral reading is followed by an oral retelling. Then she asks the constructed comprehension questions that have not been answered. Finally, the student's reading errors or miscues are analyzed to identify the cueing system used to repair the reading error (see Goodman & Burke, 1980, for detailed procedures) and the pattern of reading behavior employed.

If meaning processing is the major concern, however, the teacher conducts a *think-aloud* assessment and prepares direct questions to measure comprehension. She divides the selected passage at strategic points. First, she asks the student to predict what the story is about and to read silently to strategic points in the story. Next she asks the student to summarize the information read. Using teacher-constructed questions, she then probes for a higher-level analysis of the text and key information omitted from the summary. When the student cannot answer the question, she knows that either reading understanding has broken down or that the question needs to be rephrased. When rephrasing the question does result in a response, the diagnostic teacher asks the student to find support for the answer in the text and read it out loud, which permits her to assess if word identification is interfering with comprehension (Cioffi & Carney, 1983). Then she asks the student to predict what will happen in the next segment of the story and why he thinks it will happen. She asks him to evaluate his previous prediction in light of the new information read and to decide if he wants to change the prediction, keep it, or discard it. When the student finishes reading the selected text, she asks any prepared questions that have not yet been answered. Each exchange during the think-aloud period is analyzed to identify patterns of reading behavior.

To assess the pattern of reading performance, the diagnostic teacher looks at the data collected when the student reads without assistance. When the student reads an extended passage that is moderately difficult, a pattern of trouble spots and correction strategies emerges. The diagnostic teacher analyzes the miscues and/or miscomprehensions to evaluate both the student's patterns when reading breaks down and the strategies he uses to fix mistakes while reading. Both oral reading analysis (of print processing) and silent reading analysis (of meaning processing) result in a more comprehensive understanding of the strategies that students use to interpret the text as they are reading. In the discussion that follows, the premises for each analytic process are laid out, together with the kinds of diagnostic data collected.

ORAL READING ANALYSIS

Premises

To interpret oral reading behavior, the diagnostic teacher evaluates how the reader miscalls words as he is reading. An error (or miscue) is an oral response that deviates from the printed text. The reader is viewed as an active interpreter of text. He creates an expectation, using his background knowledge. Then he confirms and/or revises this expectation as he reads and checks the text to see if his interpretation is making sense. A reader's miscues, therefore, are systematic attempts to derive meaning from text (Goodman, 1967).

Miscue analysis is a tool for evaluating the relative significance of miscues in the context of both the entire passage and the reader's experiences. Several frameworks for evaluating miscues have been developed; in this text, however, an adaptation of the procedures suggested by Goodman and Burke (1980) is used. This analysis is based on several theoretical assumptions:

1. Readers read to gain meaning.
2. Reading is not an exact process.
3. Some miscues or errors are more significant than others.
4. Miscues should be evaluated based on the degree to which they change meaning.
5. Readers use a consistent pattern of correction strategies that indicate their preferences for text processing.

In other words, miscues indicate the cue selected or the source of information the reader tends to use to gain meaning from the text. Miscues that change meaning and remain uncorrected are viewed as diagnostically significant. They indicate what happens when a reader cannot regain meaning as he is reading. Miscues that change meaning but are subsequently corrected reveal self-monitoring strategies and are viewed as efficient strategies. They offer information about how the reader regains meaning. Miscues that do not alter the meaning of the text are viewed as nonsignificant. Evaluating the nature of the information used to regain meaning reveals the student's approach to text interpretation.

The student may use various sources of information when he encounters an unknown word in his reading: (a) the context and his experience, (b) the way words sound in conversational speech, (c) graphic information, and (d) phonic information. Using the context and his own experience, he might try various words to see if they make sense in the context of the sentence and the story.

Sentence: The girl hit the baseball.
Reader: The girl bit the baseball. (*Oops that doesn't make sense. I'll try again.*) The girl hit the baseball.

Sometimes, he might check to see if how he is reading the sentence sounds like a real sentence.

Sentence: The girl hit the baseball.
Reader: The girl hitted the baseball. (*Oops that's not the way we talk. I'll try again.*) The girl hit the baseball.

At other times, he might check the graphic information by asking himself how the word begins and how long it is.

Sentence: The girl hit the baseball.
Reader: The boy hit the baseball. (*Oops the word is not* boy *because it starts with a* g *not a* b, *but it is the same length. It must be girl instead of* boy. *Yes, that looks right.*) The girl hit the baseball.

At still other times, he might check the phonic information to decipher unknown words by asking himself what sounds these letters make.

Sentence: The girl hit the baseball.
Reader: The girl hit the brassball. (*Oops, that doesn't sound right. Let's see* bbb-aaa--ss--bbb-all . . . *baseball. Yes, that sounds right.*) The girl hit the baseball.

Diagnostic Questions

Using these premises, diagnostic hypotheses can be developed. The diagnostic questions that follow are used to analyze oral reading behavior.

1. How close is the reader's interpretation (i.e., how much meaning change results from the miscue)?
2. Does the reader monitor oral reading (i.e., does he self-correct miscues that do not fit the context)?
3. Does the reader use top-down or bottom-up strategies to regain meaning?
4. How has previous instruction influenced the child's miscue pattern?
5. Do the words in the text influence the miscue pattern?

The pattern of strategies revealed by these questions indicates the student's application of reading skills in text. Each of the questions elicits data that contribute to a comprehensive analysis of the student's reading behavior.

1. How Close Is the Reader's Interpretation? Proficient readers' text interpretations maintain the basic intent of the author. Although they miscue and continue reading, their miscues are insignificant in terms of the context of the entire selection. However, problem readers make miscues that change the meaning. Instead of correcting themselves, they continue reading "as if they do not expect the text to make sense" (Smith, 1978, p. 34).

The diagnostic teacher evaluates each miscue as to the degree it changed the author's intended meaning. She uses this information to designate the significance of the miscue. As she continues her evaluation, she thinks about what the student did when the miscue changed the meaning. Those miscues that did not change meaning are not evaluated.

2. Does the Reader Monitor Oral Reading? Proficient readers typically correct those errors that change meaning but pay little attention to those oral reading errors that do not change the meaning (Clay, 1969). Inefficient readers, however, do not distinguish between the miscues that affect meaning and those that do not. There is little difference in the frequencies with which they correct either type of miscue. Therefore, inefficient readers do not *consistently* read for meaning and do not monitor their oral reading behavior. As a result, inefficient readers make more errors and correct them less often.

The diagnostic teacher summarizes the number of miscues that are corrected and those that are not corrected. She uses this information to decide which miscues to evaluate further. Miscues that change meaning and are corrected are closely evaluated to predict how the student combines sources of information when reading is efficient. The miscues that are left uncorrected and change meaning are evaluated to look for the student's attempts to trouble shoot when reading problems occur.

3. What Source of Information Does the Reader Use to Regain Meaning?

Proficient readers flexibly shift between sources of information when what they are reading does not make sense. They use what they already know (top-down approach) as well as what the text says (bottom-up approach) to check and revise their miscues. However, inefficient readers use only one source of information to correct problems when reading orally (Allington, 1984b). Whether they rely too much on what they already know or how the text looks, they invariably limit their remedial strategies to one source of information. This leads to one of three diagnostic hypotheses.

The first hypothesis is that when reading breaks down, the student makes his miscues fit *his* interpretation and background information rather than uses information from the text. For example, a student who consistently substitutes a word that does not resemble the text but retains the meaning reflects a processing preference for a top-down meaning search. He does not revise a miscue on the basis of the words in the text but relies solely on his background knowledge. If this is the pattern, the diagnostic teacher works with the student to encourage him to use how the words look as well as what he already knows. She chooses techniques that teach word identification as well as emphasize monitoring print processing.

The second hypothesis considered is that when reading breaks down, the student's miscues are similar to the graphic form of the text. For example, a student who depends on the graphic form for figuring out unknown words often produces a miscue that has the same initial letter and is approximately the same length as the word in the text and is a word that he has been taught. This reader is using what the text looks like but does not ask what the word would mean in this sentence. He needs to check not only the words he has been taught but also what word would fit in the meaning of the story. In this case, the diagnostic teacher chooses techniques that teach word identification using text cues as well as meaning cues.

The third hypothesis evaluated is that when reading breaks down, the student's miscues reflect an attempt to employ sound-symbol (phonic) associations. For example, a student who depends on graphophonic information produces miscues by sounding out a word one letter at a time, blending those sounds to form a nonword, and continuing to read. He sacrifices meaning for inaccurate decoding. This reader is said to be bound by the text and uses a bottom-up processing strategy. In this case, the diagnostic teacher decides if decoding is a proficient strategy. If it is, she uses techniques for word attack and incorporates strategy instruction in word identification into the remedial program. If decoding is an inefficient strategy for this reader, however, the diagnostic teacher looks for strategies that use overall meaning of the text rather than sounds of letters to decode unknown words.

The diagnostic teacher summarizes the data about the sources of information to look for a consistent pattern of print processing.

4. How Has Previous Instruction Influenced the Child's Miscue Pattern?

Young readers use the strategies that they have been taught. Therefore, readers differ in their strategies to regain meaning because of the instructional emphasis in their initial reading programs (Barr, 1974–1975). This emphasis affects a child's correction strategies through the third-grade reading level. Some reading programs emphasize using meaning and the initial letter of the word to remember words (meaning-emphasis programs). Other programs emphasize blending sounds together to remember words (phonics programs). Miscue patterns often reflect the type of initial reading instruction received.

Sometimes the child is using a system that he has been taught effectively. In a meaning-emphasis program, the student's attention is focused on the initial letter and word length along with context to figure out unknown words. As he reads for meaning, he develops fluent and appropriate phrasing while checking his guesses with the initial letter and word length. However, in a structured phonics program, the reader's attention is focused on the letter-sound relationships to identify words. Therefore, he sacrifices meaning for phonic decoding, reflecting less use of context and a higher tendency to focus on individual words to remedy reading errors (Dank, 1977).

The diagnostic teacher evaluates whether the student is using effectively the system he has been taught. If so, she plans a program to help him refine this system and integrate it with other cueing systems. In other words, if the student was taught phonics and is using it well, the diagnostic teacher continues to emphasize this cueing system while simultaneously asking the student to double-check his responses to see if they make sense.

At other times, however, the child may try to use a system that he has been taught but reverts to using sources of information more in line with his cognitive abilities. When there is a mismatch between the way a student has been taught to read and his cognitive abilities, often the student tries to use the cueing system that he has been taught but usually abandons this technique to rely on a source of information that seems more natural to him (Juel, 1984; Stanovich, 1981). For example, if a student has been taught to sound out words letter by letter but has no ability to synthesize sounds, he will *try* to sound out the word but abandon this strategy in favor of using meaning cues and the initial letter. Because he has been taught a system that he cannot use, he reverts to a strategy more in line with his cognitive abilities.

If the diagnostic teacher observes these phenomena, she can change her instruction to match the reader's strengths in word identification. She reinforces these strengths and plans for a more integrative use of cueing systems. For example, a reader who was taught phonics continually miscues by substituting a word that makes sense in the context without regard for the letters in the word. The teacher notes that he is overriding his instruction and using his preference. Therefore, she chooses techniques that develop word recognition using the overall meaning of the text. As the student becomes more accurate with this system, she calls attention to initial letter and word length.

5. *Do the Words in the Text Influence the Miscue Pattern?* The type of words in the text can affect the miscue pattern. A text that contains many decodable words is easier to read for the child who has had phonics instruction. However, if the text contains high-frequency words with a mixture of regular and irregular decodable words, the student who uses intial-letter and word-length cues has more success in reading the text (Juel, 1984). Consequently, before making final decisions about the student's correction strategies, the diagnostic teacher checks the text to see if it has caused an atypical error pattern.

In conclusion, oral reading patterns give insight into how the student is monitoring his reading behavior. The student's reading errors or miscues are analyzed to find the source of information used to remedy the reading error. The strategies that the student uses are affected by previous instruction, his cognitive abilities, and the text that is being read. The sensitive teacher considers all these influences when interpreting the student's oral reading behavior.

SILENT READING ANALYSIS

Premises

To analyze comprehension, the diagnostic teacher evaluates how the reader thinks through the comprehension of a passage. Using a *think-aloud* format of interrupted reading, the teacher observes how the student uses the text and what he knows to interpret the passage. A think-aloud analysis, therefore, is a tool for evaluating the reader's comprehension strategies in the context of the entire passage. Although several researchers have outlined think-aloud procedures, the approach discussed here has been drawn from the work of Olson, Duffy, and Mack (1984).

A think-aloud analysis is based on the three theoretical assumptions that follow.

1. Reading is an active process (i.e., a reader constructs a model of meaning as he reads).
2. To construct this model, the reader uses what he already knows (reader-based inferencing) and the information in the text (text-based inferencing).
3. Reading is a strategic process (i.e., the reader checks his model of meaning to see if it makes sense).

In other words, the reader is viewed as an active interpreter of text. He predicts what is going to happen. Then he confirms or revises this expectation using both what he already knows (reader-based inferencing) and the important information from the text (text-based inferencing). Finally, he checks his interpretations to see if they are making sense.

Asking the student to think aloud gives an indication of how the student is processing text. The think-aloud process shows the diagnostic teacher the strategies that the student uses to make sense of what he is reading. As with the oral reading analysis, interpretations that change the author's intended meaning and the reader does not revise are seen as diagnostically significant. They indicate what the reader does when he cannot interpret the text. Interpetations changing the author's intended meaning that the reader later revises are viewed as efficient strategies. They offer information about how the reader regains meaning. Interpretations that do not alter the author's intended meaning are viewed as nonsignificant. Evaluating the nature of the information used to regain meaning reveals the active comprehension strategies. Basically, the student uses various sources of information for text interpretation: (a) what he already knows, (b) facts stated in the text, and (c) a combination of both the text and what he already knows.

Diagnostic Questions

Based upon these premises, diagnostic hypotheses can be developed using the following questions.

1. How close is the reader's interpretation (i.e., how elaborate is the summary and are the important points covered)?
2. Does the reader monitor comprehension (i.e., how does he use new information to predict and revise his model of meaning)?
3. What sources of information (reader-based, text-based, or both) does the reader use?
4. How has previous instruction influenced the think-aloud process?
5. Does the text influence the think-aloud process?

The diagnostic teacher uses these questions to analyze silent reading behavior during the think-aloud experience. The pattern of strategies indicates the student's application of reading skills in text. When the student's interpretation changes the meaning, a careful analysis is needed to assess the strategies he uses to regain meaning. Each of these questions is designed to elicit the particular kinds of data necessary for a complete assessment of his silent reading behavior.

1. How Close Is the Reader's Interpretation? During the think-aloud assessment, the student summarizes out loud what he read silently. Summarizing, or retelling, forces the student to select information important in illustrating the message as he perceived it (Harste, Woodward, & Burke, 1984). For narrative text, a good summary includes the important elements of story grammar: setting (characters and place), problem, key events, and resolution. For expository text, a good summary contains the main idea and key details (Taylor, 1985). During the discussion, the diagnostic teacher evaluates how inclusive or narrow the summary is, the completeness of verbal responses, and the cohesiveness of the summary. After the student has finished his summary, the teacher uses questions to probe higher-level thinking, to focus on key ideas in the text, and to assess the student's knowledge of the meaning of the key words (Barr & Sadow, 1985).

The diagnostic teacher uses this information to designate the significance of the miscomprehension. As she continues her evaluation, she thinks about how the interpretation affects how the student constructs meaning. Summaries that do not change the overall interpretation of the story are considered the result of effective strategies. However, summaries where the student changes the meaning of the text are evaluated to form hypotheses about the reader's strategies.

2. *Does the Reader Monitor Comprehension?* The diagnostic teacher uses this question to evaluate how the student uses new information to predict and revise his model of meaning. At each interruption, the teacher asks him to predict what will happen next in the story and why he thinks so. She asks him to evaluate his previous prediction in light of the new information read, and then she gives him the option of changing the prediction, keeping it, or discarding it. As the student makes predictions and evaluates them, the teacher observes his strategies for monitoring comprehension. She observes the inclusiveness of the prediction and the amount of textual information used up to the point of interruption.

Basically, inefficient readers have been found to be less active than more efficient readers. They change their predictions less often than more proficient readers. Some students rely too heavily on their initial prediction and make the entire story fit it (Maria & MacGinitie, 1982). When they do revise their predictions, passive readers change only one part of their predictions. These readers do not use new textual information to revise predictions; rather they keep a prediction when it is no longer supported by the text (Baker & Brown, 1984). Less active readers hold onto previous predictions rather than become more tentative.

Active readers seem more comfortable keeping their models of meaning tentative. If there is no new information in the text, they delay making a prediction (Dybdahl, 1983). However, during a think-aloud experience, they change their predictions, adding and revising new information provided in the text and relating information throughout the procedure.

This phase provides diagnostic information about how the student is monitoring his reading comprehension. The teacher notes the point at which the reader realizes that his model of meaning does not fit the stated information in the text. Since the story has been presented in segments, the diagnostic teacher can easily observe strategies such as rereading previous segments to check the text, modifying predictions, or remaining tentative until more information has been read. She uses this information to decide which summaries and predictions to evaluate further. Those interpretations that changed meaning but were subsequently revised are closely evaluated to predict how the student combines sources of information when he encounters trouble spots in reading. The interpretations that were not revised and changed meaning are further analyzed to evaluate how the student attempts to make sense of what he is reading.

3. *What Sources of Information (Reader-Based, Text-Based, or Both) Does the Reader Use?* Beginning the think-aloud procedure by using the title of the text, the diagnostic teacher can assess the student's prior knowledge about the topic. Questioning the student about how he arrives at a prediction from just the title allows the diagnostic teacher to probe further background knowledge and begin to assess how the student uses this background knowledge as he reads the text (Watson, 1985). The teacher can observe the student as he constructs a rationale to support his prediction, and evaluate whether the support is text-based or reader-based. This process leads to one of three diagnostic hypotheses.

The first hypothesis is that when reading breaks down, the student's interpretation fits something he can understand instead of what the whole text says. Some readers ignore information that they do not understand. (They actually do not *know* that they do not understand.) When this happens, their responses are marked with an elaborate interpretation of the one or two events that they were able to comprehend. There is no line of reasoning that connects these students' responses to the story because they lack sufficient knowledge to interpret the text. If this pattern occurs, the diagnostic teacher needs to develop the necessary background knowledge for this particular student before he reads a story.

The second hypothesis suggests that when reading breaks down, the student's interpretations fit what he already knows and not what the text says. Some problem readers rely too heavily on their own knowledge and actually make their interpretations fit what they already know. For example, some students consistently answer questions with information that they know, using it to explain a line of reasoning for their answers rather than using information provided by the author. In these cases, the student understands what he reads but relies too heavily on his own experiences to develop reasons that are close to, but not exactly like what the author intended. When this pattern occurs, the diagnostic teacher uses techniques that show the student how to use what he knows in combination with what the text says.

The third hypothesis proposes that when reading breaks down, the student's interpretations fit what the text says without tying together information. Some problem readers rely too heavily on the text and fail to use their own knowledge to interpret the text (Spiro, 1979). They have too narrow an interpretation because they do not draw relationships between information in different parts of the text. If this pattern occurs, the diagnostic teacher uses techniques that first allow the student to discuss what the text says and then show him how to use what he knows to elaborate on it.

During the think-aloud process, the diagnostic teacher evaluates the source of information used to construct responses as well as the accuracy of the interpretation.

4. How Has Previous Instruction Influenced the Think-Aloud Procedure? The number and types of questions teachers ask students when discussing text affect children's comprehension. Guszak (1967) found that teachers ask predominately literal questions (70%) in classroom instruction and have an increasing tendency to ask more nonliteral questions at higher grade levels. Additionally, teachers discriminate between high-ability students and low-ability students. By sixth grade, half the questions asked the high-ability students are nonliteral, while only *30%* of the questions asked the low-ability students are nonliteral (Pearson,

1983). Furthermore, studies indicate that when teacher-generated questions are posed prior to reading, comprehension narrows because students read to answer those specific questions rather than to construct meaning (Singer & Donlan, 1982). Some students have learned to rely on the teacher's direction rather than to think independently. The diagnostic teacher analyzes the focus of previous instruction to find out how that focus has affected comprehension.

5. *Does the Text Influence the Think-Aloud Process?* Poor story construction affects the student's think-aloud process and the choice of interruption points. When story plots are engaging enough to motivate readers to find out what happens, then the teacher-reader interactions during the analysis period are elaborate; however, bland and boring texts give the students no reason to read (Olson, Duffy, & Mack, 1984). The diagnostic teacher needs to construct a story map of the selected story to determine if the story actually lends itself to a think-aloud process and is engaging enough to elicit an elaborate interaction. Some initial ambiguity of the story plot allows the diagnostic teacher to observe the child's approach to problem solving when reading. The type of text also affects the think-aloud analysis. Narrative text lends itself to prediction, revision, and monitoring, while expository text lends itself to summarizing, clarifying, and discussing the line of argument used by the author (Olson, Duffy, & Mack, 1984).

In conclusion, having the student think aloud as he reads allows the teacher to assess the strategies that he uses to construct meaning. This procedure provides diagnostic data to formulate instructional hypotheses and subsequently to select appropriate techniques for improving reading comprehension.

SUMMARY

The diagnostic teacher gathers data by asking questions that focus her evaluation of the strategies of the problem reader. First, she evaluates the student's performance across levels of text difficulty using the informal reading inventory. From this information, she designates a level that is moderately difficult for the student. She evaluates both oral and silent reading performance and determines the major presenting problem. After she decides whether print processing or meaning processing is inhibiting fluent reading with comprehension, she selects a story to continue her assessment. From the story, she constructs an on-level assessment that is either an oral reading or a think-aloud experience. This assessment gives her more data about the student's strategies when reading is difficult. The data about the reader's strategies consider influencing factors from the reading event, especially the text and past learning experiences. Then she conducts the assessment and analyzes the data to formulate her diagnostic hypotheses.

Formulating Diagnostic Hypotheses

To formulate the diagnostic hypotheses, the diagnostic teacher analyzes the information that he has gathered from assessment and instruction within the reading event (see Figure 8–1). He uses data from the informal reading inventory to assess the student's reading pattern in texts across a range of difficulty levels for both oral and silent reading. He performs an on-level reading analysis to assess the student's reading pattern when she reads a text that is moderately difficult either orally or silently. As he evaluates this information, he increases his specificity in selecting an instructional format that will result in improved reading performance. He reflects on the reading event and how it has influenced the data he has gathered. Then he reflects on the instruction and predicts which technique(s) will produce the desired reader change based on these data.

REFLECTING ON THE READING EVENT

After collecting the data, the diagnostic teacher reflects on the reading event. He returns to the model of the reading event discussed in Chapter 2 and uses it to evaluate the influence of the variables on the student's reading behavior. He remembers that the information he has collected is a result of the interactions that occurred in the reading event. He systematically evaluates the influence of the task, the text, the reader, and the context of the reading event on the data. He looks for key factors by asking, for example, "What task did the child do? Is this task an important consideration in establishing this student's instructional program?" He considers the relative strengths of the student's oral and silent reading in promoting fluent reading with comprehension. From this analysis, he formulates diagnostic hypotheses and selects teaching techniques to enhance reading growth.

How the diagnostic teacher uses the data from the initial assessments and relates them to the elements of the reading event is described in the pages that follow.

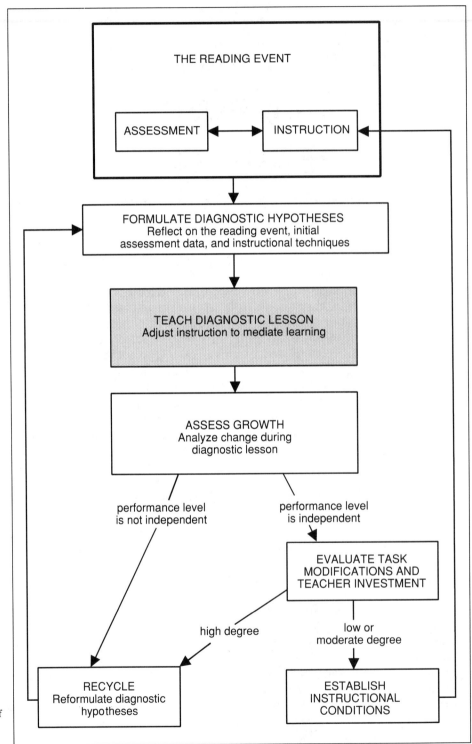

Figure 8–1
The Decision-
Making Cycle of
Diagnostic
Teaching

Included is the case study of a hypothetical third grader named Jenny, who is experiencing difficulty in fluent oral reading. As the teacher reflects on the reading event, he makes observations about the student's performance using the data he has collected. The *asterisk* (*) indicates key factors he has to consider when establishing this student's instructional program.

The Task

The diagnostic teacher analyzes the reading tasks that the student completes during the reading event. He carefully considers the range of possibilities related to the task and looks for key factors that might affect the student's reading behavior. During the informal reading assessment, he has already decided on the major presenting problem; now he uses this information to evaluate the effect that the question type is having on the reader's responses and to evaluate reasoning requirements. He compares the reader's performances on the informal reading inventory and the extended passage. From this comparison, he ascertains whether the task segment is affecting reading performance and whether production requirements are affecting reader response. The task analysis for Jenny is given in Table 8–1.

Table 8–1
Task Analysis for
Jenny

***Oral or silent reading:** Both oral and silent reading behavior were evaluated, with the student comprehending all passages where she could decode the words. Oral reading was the more difficult task. At the instructional level, silent reading comprehension was not a concern.

Task segment (words, sentences, paragraphs, stories, etc.): Short paragraphs were used for the evaluation.

Availability of text: The text was not available for referral when answering questions; however, student comprehension was elaborate.

Production requirements: Retelling was used to assess comprehension, followed by inferential questions. Comprehension was high on each task.

Question type: Literal and nonliteral responses were evaluated. She performed equally well in both cases.

***Purpose for the task:** Teacher-directed reading was used for evaluation. Informal conversation revealed that she liked to control her own learning.

Reasoning requirements of task: Factual recall and applicative reasoning was required. The student did well in both types of tasks.

Diagnostic hypothesis: The student reads with moderate difficulty at the second-grade level (1/11 oral accuracy and 75% comprehension) on an informal reading inventory. Oral reading presents the most difficulty for the student. Although she prefers silent reading, Jenny needs to read orally to improve fluency. Her informal comments ("I hate these stories") indicate that she prefers to control her own learning.

The Text

The type of text read during a reading evaluation can influence significantly the data to be analyzed. The diagnostic teacher routinely assesses the text and its influence on reading behavior to identify which characteristics are affecting the student's reading. Again he seeks the key factors about the text that affect this student's reading behavior. To do so, he looks at the information from the informal reading inventory, the extended passage, and the final question of the oral/silent reading analysis (does the text influence the results of this procedure). The text analysis for Jenny would contain the material covered in Table 8–2.

Table 8–2
Text Analysis for Jenny

Passage length: Short passages produced more oral reading miscues. The extended passage gave the student more opportunities to use overall context to self-correct errors.

*Passage type:** Both expository and narrative passages were read. The student made fewer miscues on expository text.

Type of content: The student read various subject content. It did not seem to affect her performance.

Background knowledge required of reader: Various levels of background knowledge were needed in the text, but the student knew about most topics.

*Grammatical complexity:** The more complex the sentence structure, the better the student read.

Word choices: Short words that fit the text were used. Elaborate word meanings were not required for comprehension.

Density of information: The high density of information did not affect comprehension, but this did affect the reader's miscue pattern. When too much information was presented, the student could not self-correct.

Elaboration or use of examples: Not enough examples of elaboration to establish a pattern.

Organizational structure: Not enough examples of organization to establish a pattern.

Coherence or unity of text: When the story structure did not reflect the title of the passage, the reader's miscues were affected because she tried to make the title fit the text.

Diagnostic hypothesis: Jenny needs a text that is coherently organized, and she appears to prefer expository text. Increasing the complexity of the sentence structure seems to have a positive effect on miscues (i.e., the longer the sentence, the more she is able to correct her miscues). Another possible influencing factor may be the word choices in the text. Since the student was taught with a synthetic phonic approach (see "Synthetic Phonics" in Chapter 6), words that are more decodable might improve performance.

The Reader

The reader is the major focus of traditional assessment. In diagnostic teaching, however, the reader is assessed in relation to herself as well as to the variables of the reading event. The teacher looks at the knowledge-based requirements of the tasks and how the student responds to them. From the informal reading inventory, the diagnostic teacher evaluates general skill proficiencies and deficiencies. Returning to the extended passages, the diagnostic teacher uses the answer to the first question ("how close is the reader's interpretation?") to assess general knowledge. He must judge whether the reader changes the meaning of the selection because she has no similar experience to use to evaluate the sense of the text. In addition, he uses data from the extended passage to evaluate the strategies the student employs as she reads. He specifically analyzes the data on self-corrections and revisions during oral and/or silent reading. Finally, he evaluates data on the sources of information used. Jenny's reader analysis is shown in Table 8–3.

Table 8–3
Reader Analysis for
Jenny

Knowledge-Based Differences

***Level of performance:** On the informal reading inventory, the student read at the borderline level (moderate difficulty) on the second-grade paragraph.

Skill proficiencies: Answering comprehension questions and retelling a story.

***Skill deficiencies:** Nonfluent oral reading; phonic knowledge is inappropriately applied.

Language proficiencies: The student used language well and often engaged in elaborate descriptions related to the story.

Language deficiencies: None observed.

Strategy-Based Differences

***Strategies used:** Context of the story was used to help identify unknown words. Many miscues were semantically based (i.e., she used reader-based inferencing more often than text-based knowledge).

***Strategies needed:** Self-correction during oral readings using *both* the semantic and graphic cueing systems.

***Source of information used** (text or background knowledge): During comprehension, the student used an integration of both textual knowledge and reader knowledge; however, during oral reading, she used either textual knowledge or reader knowledge but not both when she encountered difficulty.

Elaboration of response (one word or embellished): All responses were elaborate except when the student encountered frustration-level reading.

Level of response (literal or nonliteral): The student used both literal and nonliteral responses when answering questions.

Affective Needs

Need for structure: The student preferred to answer questions without help. She seems to have little need for structure.

***Type and need for feedback:** During comprehension, the student had little need for feedback, often supplying her own analysis of her answers. However, when reading orally, one miscue can trigger a series of errors due to the student's creating a new text that makes sense in light of the initial miscue; therefore, feedback is needed for monitoring print processing.

***Need for human sense:** The student exhibited disdain for the mundane stories at the first- and second-grade levels.

***Attribution for success or failure:** For print processing, the student attributed her failure to baby reading material, dumb stories, and bad luck rather than to the lack of appropriate strategies.

Diagnostic hypothesis: Jenny needs instruction in word identification and fluency. She needs to be shown the effective strategies that she uses (e.g., self-correction from background knowledge). She tries to use phonic knowledge but is consistently unsuccessful in her attempts. Jenny, therefore, relies too much on her background knowledge and general story meaning. When she does this, she reads a string of miscues that make sense. Her unsuccessful attempts at self-correction reflect the use of either meaning cues or phonic cues without the integration of both cueing systems. She appears to like to direct her own learning rather than have the teacher tell her what to do.

The Context

The diagnostic teacher evaluates the instructional context in which the assessment occurs and how much influence he is having on the reader's response. At the same time, he evaluates how previous instructional experiences might have affected the student's responses. He reevaluates the patterns of performance, thinking about how the student's previous instructional experiences have influenced her reading patterns. He double-checks his data, focusing on the context of the reading event. An analysis for the context of Jenny's reading behavior is shown in Table 8–4.

Table 8–4
Context Analysis for Jenny

> **Learning situation:** One-to-one assessment.
> **Previous learning situations:** One-to-one instruction in a resource room; placed during kindergarten.
> **Previous instructional emphasis:** Two-year program of intensive synthetic phonics (Orton-Gillingham-Stillman).
> **Teacher expectation:** High.
> **Composition of instructional group:** The student prefers group instruction where she can participate in the discussion using her background knowledge.
> *****Feedback or prompting:** Instruction needs to have minimal feedback from the teacher and maximal from the student. The teacher needs to prompt with this question: "What would make sense and start with a _____ ?"
> **Wait time:** Appropriate for the learner. She always had a response.
> **Time allowed on task:** Not evaluated.
> **Point of intervention during the lesson:** No lesson was conducted, but before this student reads, she needs to review new words to facilitate print processing.

Diagnostic hypotheses: Jenny's previous learning experiences affect both her perception of reading and her miscue pattern. When she miscues, she tries to sound out unknown words because that is the way she has been taught (two years of instruction in synthetic phonics). This strategy usually fails, however, and Jenny becomes discouraged. Having forgotten the meaning of the story, Jenny creates a string of miscues that make sense for the sentence but not for the entire story.

Conclusions

When cross-checking the elements of the reading event, the diagnostic teacher remembers that some of the factors may not be important in examining the particular reading event under scrutiny. Only the key factors affecting the student's reading performance are analyzed. For Jenny, the analysis resulted in the following key factors:

1. The type of text (expository) facilitates reading behavior and heightens interest.
2. The student has a negative attribution to reading (she states that she hates reading).
3. The student uses only one cueing system at a time when reading breaks down. (She tries to use phonics, but when this fails she uses sentence sense. She does not combine the sources.)
4. The more grammatically complex the sentence structure, the more the student can self-correct her errors.
5. The student would rather direct her own learning than have the teacher tell her what to do. (This may be a function of the extremely structured program that was used during her initial reading instruction.)
6. The student uses top-down sources to regain meaning when reading breaks down.
7. The student has a well-developed background of information that she uses when answering questions.

Having identified these key factors, the teacher is then able to select an appropriate diagnostic teaching technique.

REFLECTING ON INSTRUCTION

After the diagnostic teacher evaluates the student's reading level and formulates hypotheses about how the student reads, he plans the instructional lesson. Using the data collected, the diagnostic teacher identifies skills, strategies, or both (see Chapter 5) that are inhibiting reading performance. He reviews the skill development and the strategies employed by the reader. Then he selects an appropriate technique that will focus instruction on the targeted concern in order to improve the student's reading performance.

Skill Instruction

The diagnostic teacher looks for a skill that, if learned, will increase this student's reading. He reflects on the major skills of reading and evaluates their influence on this reader's performance. He looks at the level of performance that is at the borderline range and matches it with the targeted skills for that reading level. Then he checks previous instructional experiences to evaluate their influence on the targeted skill. Basically, he asks, "Has this student received instruction in this skill and is still not proficient?" If a skill needs to be taught, the diagnostic teacher uses Table 5–1, "Classifying Techniques by Reading Skills," to identify techniques that facilitate learning that skill. He remains tentative in his selection until he completes all the diagnostic questions.

Is there a skill that, if learned, would increase this student's reading?

_____ *Sight word vocabulary*
_____ *Word attack*
_____ *Fluency*
_____ *Meaning vocabulary*
_____ *Sentence comprehension*
_____ *Literal comprehension*
_____ *Nonliteral comprehension*
_____ *Study skills*

For Jenny, whose borderline range is around the middle of second grade, the teacher decides that instruction in phonics is not appropriate because of her attempts and subsequent failures in using this cueing system. Literal comprehension is well developed and thus not the best choice for instruction now. Only when she read text with just 1/7 words correct did she ever miss a question. Therefore, the teacher decides to work on reading fluency, a skill that is at the third-grade level (i.e., the next higher level).

Strategy Instruction

The diagnostic teacher then looks for a strategy that, if learned, will increase this student's reading. He reflects on the strategies that the effective reader uses and evaluates their influence on this reader's performance. He returns to the data he has collected and looks at the hypotheses he formed when he analyzed the reading event. He considers whether the context or the text is affecting the strategies employed by this reader. If a strategy needs to be taught, the diagnostic teacher uses Table 5–2, "Classifying Techniques by Reasoning Strategy," to identify techniques that facilitate learning the strategy. Again, he remains tentative in his selection until he completes all the diagnostic questions.

Is there a strategy that, if learned, will increase this student's reading?

_____ *Predict/select*
_____ *Monitor/revise*
_____ *Elaborate/integrate*

For Jenny, the diagnostic teacher decides that she needs instruction in monitoring print processing in order to check both what makes sense and what the word looks like. This strategy facilitates combining cueing systems when reading breaks down.

Instructional Framework

Next the teacher thinks about the framework of the diagnostic teaching session. He must decide how to orchestrate instruction during guided contextual reading. Therefore, he evaluates the underlying strengths and needs of the student and predicts at which points during the guided reading lesson she will profit most from mediated instruction. Augmenting instruction at critical points during the lesson enhances text interpretation. The selection of the technique depends not only on the child's abilities but also on the kind of text being read. These considerations are the focus of the question the diagnostic teacher asks himself, "At what point during the lesson framework will the student need assistance in order to interpret this type of text?" To answer the question, he returns to his analysis of the extended passage to look at monitoring and summarization strategies and to his evaluation of the data from the informal reading inventory. Using his interpretation, he refers to Tables 5–3 and 5–4 to select an appropriate technique for instructional intervention during the lesson.

What type of text am I using?

_____ *Narrative*
_____ *Expository*

At what point during the guided teaching lesson will the student need assistance?

_____ *Before*
_____ *During*
_____ *After*

During guided contextual reading, Jenny needs assistance in recognizing new vocabulary words prior to the instruction of the story. However, she does not need instruction during the story because she monitors comprehension. After instruction, the diagnostic teacher needs only to reinforce word recognition. The student also shows a preference for reading expository text.

Mode of Response

The diagnostic teacher thinks about the kind of responses that the student makes. He asks, "Will this student profit from discussing or writing about what she reads?" He realizes that both processes facilitate meaning construction. Writing provides a written record of thoughts so that the student can reflect on how she constructs meaning, while verbal discussion allows the reader to revise her ideas on the spot. The diagnostic teacher selects a technique that matches the learner's strengths and needs. He thinks about the mode of response that the techniques demand and refers to Table 5–5 to select one that will assist the reader.

Which mode of response will better assist this reader in analyzing her reading?

_____ *Discussion*
_____ *Writing*

For Jenny, whose language comprehension is elaborate and verbal abilities are strong, verbal discussion is most appropriate. During guided contextual reading, the diagnostic teacher allows ample time to discuss the stories that are read, thus using her strength. Furthermore, for skill and strategy instruction, the diagnostic teacher selects a technique that uses discussing fluency as well as practicing it.

Structure of Instruction

After the teacher has decided on the mode of response, he thinks about the student's reading performance and the information he has collected. He asks, "What kind of mediated instruction, implicit or explicit, will facilitate learning for this student?" In other words, does the student want direction on how to complete the tasks. Does she appear to need direct, explicit information before she attempts a reading task or does she want to control her own learning? The teacher theorizes about the kind of mediated instruction the student needs in order to change her reading behavior. The diagnostic teacher predicts whether implicit (student-discovered strategies) or explicit (teacher-directed learning) instruction will result in a greater change in reading performance. The teacher matches this prediction with an appropriate technique using Table 5–6.

In order to learn this skill or strategy, what kind of mediated instruction will be needed?

_____ *Implicit*
_____ *Explicit*

For Jenny, the decision is clear-cut. She prefers to control the decision making when she reads. During the retelling, for example, she stated, "I'm not saying this in order." She also made the self-evaluation about a statement that it "might not be right," which shows that she has control over her comprehension, although not over word recognition. Consequently, a more implicit technique to develop fluency is selected.

Cognitive Processing

Finally, the diagnostic teacher evaluates the sources of information used by the student to predict her strength of cognitive processing. He contemplates whether the student uses background knowledge more often than textual references (indicating a possible preference for simultaneous processing) or whether she stays relatively close to the text (indicating a possible preference for successive processing). The diagnostic teacher selects a technique that will use the child's processing strength to overcome the inhibiting behaviors. In other words, if fluency is an identified inhibiting behavior in the initial assessment, a technique that develops fluency would be chosen. Furthermore, if the child's cognitive processing appears to proceed from the overall meaning to the isolated parts (simultaneous understanding), a technique that develops fluency from a simultaneous perspective would be selected. The teacher looks at the data he collected and asks, "Does the reader use top-down (simultaneous) or bottom-up (successive) strategies to regain meaning?" Using Table 5–7, he then selects a technique that matches the student's processing style and will remedy the inhibiting reading behaviors.

What processing sequence does the student seem to prefer?

_____ *Simultaneous emphasis*
_____ *Successive emphasis*

Jenny appears to use simultaneous processing. She relates stories to what she already knows and often makes word substitutions that fit the overall meaning of the text. Although she has a successive strength in comprehension (excellent literal comprehension), she does not have these same successive strengths in word recognition. Her miscues often reflect letter and syllable reversals.

SUMMARY

Putting the Parts Together for Jenny

Reviewing Jenny's case, the teacher reaches the following conclusions. Jenny needs instruction in fluency (a skill) and self-correction (a strategy). She likes expository text and has a high need for stories to make sense. She also attributes her poor fluency to forces outside her control, thus increasing her negative attribution of reading failure. However, she prefers to control her own learning (implicit instruction) whenever she can. She also has a tendency to prefer material presented with the overall theme first (simultaneous), before learning the details.

When the diagnostic teacher looks at all the hypotheses, he selects a text that contains expository passages of interest to the student (predominately science stories) to use during guided contextual reading. Prior to instruction, he introduces key vocabulary words, which allows Jenny to elaborate her knowledge about the concepts and reinforce it by making her own word cards (implicit instruction). After the lesson, Jenny presents science facts to the class. She is allowed to use the assigned reading or her own research efforts.

To help Jenny attribute her success to effective strategies and to lead her to more flexible strategies when reading errors occur, a program of repeated readings (see "Repeated Readings" in Chapter 6) is used in skill and strategy instruction. After the first reading, an intervention to talk about efficient strategies is used. The teacher models the following self-statement consistent with implicit instruction: "What would make sense and start with a _____ ?" This procedure allows Jenny to assume increasing responsibility for her own oral reading fluency, while permitting her to use the overall meaning (simultaneous strength) of the selection to correct her miscues, thus respecting her natural preference for using prior experience and context to self-correct. Charting the repeated readings also helps Jenny attribute her increasing fluency to her own efforts and ability, reversing her negative attribution in word recognition.

Reviewing the Diagnostic Steps

The teacher's selection of a technique reflects the diagnostic hypotheses about a student's learning at that particular time and for that particular skill or strategy. To formulate the diagnostic hypotheses, the diagnostic teacher reflects on the reading event, considering each variable and its relationship to the reader's performance. He looks at the interactions among the task, the text, the reader, and the context to establish patterns of reading performance.

Then the diagnostic teacher systematically evaluates seven areas of instruction. He looks at both the skills and the strategies the reader has, as well as those she lacks. He considers the framework of the diagnostic lesson and the text he intends to use to establish a point of intervention. He reflects on the mode of response as well as the kind of structure he will use. Finally, he matches the reader's preference for cognitive processing with the appropriate emphasis. Based on this lengthy evaluation, he selects a technique.

To verify the hypotheses that have led to this selection, the teacher conducts a diagnostic lesson. The guidelines for conducting this lesson are found in Chapter 9, "Assessment Using Diagnostic Lessons."

Assessment Using Diagnostic Lessons

9

After the diagnostic teacher formulates her hypotheses, she teaches a lesson using techniques based on the hypotheses (see Figure 9–1). Diagnostic lessons provide a tool to assess the amount of growth that actually occurs as a result of the instructional adjustments. To begin, the teacher chooses a reading passage that is moderately difficult and divides it into three sections. The diagnostic teacher uses the first section to assess reading performance without assistance. It is read *at sight* (without any period of familiarization) and without assistance to establish baseline data. The middle section of the passage is taught using the selected technique (see Chapters 5 and 6). This is the actual implementation of the hypotheses and requires keen observation of the changes that improve text interpretation. To assess the degree of change in reading due to instruction, the third section is also read at sight and without assistance. As a result of the mediated instruction, changes in reading performance should be apparent. If the instruction has been appropriate, the student should now be able to read the third section of the text at the independent reading level and exhibit patterns of performance that reflect a more integrated use of reader-based and text-based processing. Using the information from the diagnostic teaching lesson, the diagnostic teacher establishes the conditions that result in the optimal learning for the student. The following discussion delineates the purpose for each of the three sections of the diagnostic lesson.

ESTABLISHING BASELINE DATA

Having the student read the first section at sight and without assistance serves two functions: (a) to add information to the diagnostic hypotheses (see Chapter 8) and (b) to establish baseline behaviors so that the effectiveness of instruction can be evaluated. This section is about 250 words long and may be read either orally to evaluate print processing or silently to evaluate meaning processing (see Chapter

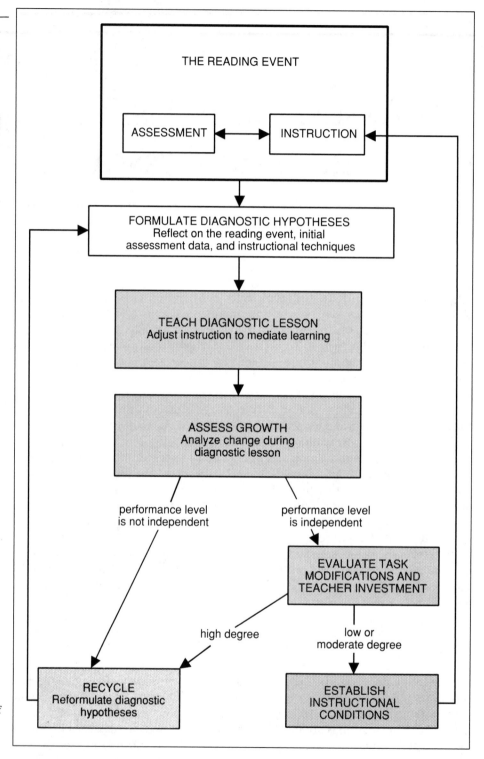

THE READING EVENT

ASSESSMENT ◄──► INSTRUCTION

FORMULATE DIAGNOSTIC HYPOTHESES
Reflect on the reading event, initial
assessment data, and instructional techniques

TEACH DIAGNOSTIC LESSON
Adjust instruction to mediate learning

ASSESS GROWTH
Analyze change during
diagnostic lesson

performance level
is not independent

performance level
is independent

EVALUATE TASK
MODIFICATIONS AND
TEACHER INVESTMENT

high degree

low or
moderate degree

RECYCLE
Reformulate diagnostic
hypotheses

ESTABLISH
INSTRUCTIONAL
CONDITIONS

Figure 9–1
The Decision-
Making Cycle of
Diagnostic
Teaching

7). The data are analyzed by computing the percentage of comprehension and/or error rate as well as evaluating the patterns of the reading performance.

The diagnostic teacher reviews the data to expand her diagnostic hypotheses. However, her primary purpose for collecting baseline data is to measure growth due to instruction. Baseline data reflects the student's reading performance without aid and before adjusted instruction. During the instructional lesson, the teacher establishes the instructional conditions that mediate learning. To assess growth, the diagnostic teacher compares the student's performance without aid and his performance after specified instruction. This baseline data is used to evaluate reading growth due to instruction during the third section of the diagnostic lesson.

ESTABLISHING THE CONDITIONS OF LEARNING

After the baseline data has been established, the teacher designs a diagnostic lesson based on her hypotheses about the student's reading performance. She selects a technique that matches the reader's profile. However, the purpose of the second section is to establish the optimal conditions for learning new reading strategies. As she teaches the lesson, her modifications are summarized and become part of the diagnostic data collection. Unlike the first section, where the teacher constructs diagnostic hypotheses based on a relatively static assessment of reading perform-ance, during the instructional lesson, the teacher's assessments are dynamic. Modi-fications of these hypotheses occur often as the teacher responds to the student's needs during instruction (Cioffi & Carney, 1983).

When using repeated readings with Ted, a second grader, for instance, the diagnostic teacher found that simply discussing the miscues did not result in de-creased errors, so she modeled her own self-correction process by saying, "Oops, that doesn't make sense; let's see what would make sense and start with a *g*. Oh, *girl* starts with a *g*. *The girl hit the homerun.* Yes, that makes sense and sounds like it looks." Then Ted read the passage again, and the teacher recorded the er-rors and evaluated the amount and kind of change evidenced in the reading per-formance. Since there was a decrease in the number of errors and an increase in fluent reading, the teacher recommended the procedure with the modifications tried during the diagnostic lesson.

On another occasion, a fourth-grade student named John needed assistance in active comprehension. The diagnostic teacher formulated her hypotheses while she conducted a think-aloud assessment during the first section. During the sec-ond section, the teacher used a directed-reading-thinking activity. During the lesson, John could not answer an inferential question, so the diagnostic teacher rephrased the question to include some factual information to facilitate his answer-ing the question. John still had no clue about how to arrive at an answer, so she asked him to find the part of the story that told about the factual information and to read it aloud. The ability of the student to perform this action indicates whether or not he understands the sequence of the story, as well as his ability to read the words without difficulty. He easily found the part of the text that contained the answer and read it without difficulty.

Again, the teacher began the line of questioning; however, this time she began with a factual question. Then she asked John to relate relevant personal experiences to the facts. After this discussion, the original inferential question was rephrased to see if instruction did result in an inferential understanding of the story based on factual information. Since this instructional sequence facilitated comprehension, the teacher hypothesized that John comprehends better if the instructional sequence begins with the facts and then develops an inferential understanding of the story.

During the diagnostic lesson, records of the instructional modifications are kept so that the amount and kinds of teacher intervention can be assessed. When conducting a diagnostic lesson, however, the teacher's primary goal is to teach the student. Her second goal is to assess those instructional modifications that are producing increased reading performance. In effect, the diagnostic teacher establishes the instructional conditions necessary to increase the reading performance.

EVALUATING GROWTH

To evaluate the effect the instructional adjustments have on the student's reading performance, the diagnostic teacher conducts a final assessment using the third section of the passage. She uses the same format as for the first section, either recording oral reading responses or a think-aloud experience. The final assessment, conducted at sight and without assistance, provides a systematic method for assessing the effects of instructional intervention on the student's reading. The teacher assesses reading growth during the lesson as well as the amount of task modification and teacher investment needed to produce that growth. These measures not only determine placement but also establish optimal instructional conditions.

Reading Growth Due to Instruction

First, the diagnostic teacher must establish the amount of change that has occurred as a result of instruction. If the instruction was appropriate, the resulting scores should indicate an independent reading level (98% word identification and 90% comprehension). Since the student received instruction in precisely those strategies that were inhibiting performance, there should be an increase in the number of questions answered correctly and a decrease in word identification errors. Reading growth should be evident.

Reading growth indicates a decrease in word recognition errors and an increase in the number of questions answered correctly.

Next, the diagnostic teacher compares the patterns of reading behavior assessed on the first section with those assessed on the third section. Oral reading should reflect more semantically and syntactically appropriate miscues and an increase in self-corrections. This pattern indicates that the student is using his knowledge of the story theme to figure out unknown words. The think-aloud experience should reflect a more integrated use of textual and nontextual information as well as more elaborate responses to questions. Spontaneous self-monitoring and the student's awareness of the sources of information he uses to construct responses should also be increasingly evident.

Reading growth is also indicated by an increasing use of both *reader-based processing and text-based processing and by more self-monitoring for understanding.*

Figure 9–1 highlights the final steps involved in assessing reading growth using diagnostic lessons. When the diagnostic teacher analyzes growth in this last phase of the decision-making cycle, two conclusions can result. There can be a positive change in reading behavior (independent level obtained) or there can be no change in reading behavior (independent level not obtained). These two outcomes necessitate different responses from the diagnostic teacher. If mediated instruction produces an independent reading level, the diagnostic teacher carefully evaluates the task modifications and teacher investment, or assistance, to establish the instructional modifications that produced the change. If mediated instruction does not produce reading growth, the diagnostic teacher eliminates those techniques and modifications that were used. She returns to her diagnostic hypotheses, adds any new information collected during the diagnostic lesson, and reformulates her hypotheses. Then she selects a new technique and conducts another diagnostic lesson.

Determining the Amount of Task Modification

Prior to instruction, the diagnostic teacher selects a technique to implement during the diagnostic lesson. She determines how she is going to present the reading task. She decides if the reading task will be silent or oral and whether the story will be read as a whole or in segments. She decides if she will introduce new vocabulary words and how to do it. As she teaches the lesson, the teacher modifies these original tasks so that the student can read fluently with comprehension. It is these modifications that the teacher records and evaluates.

For example, the diagnostic teacher decided to use self-directed questioning (see "Self-Questioning" in Chapter 6) with Luis, a third-grade student who was relatively passive when reading. He did not guess about the story or revise the few predictions he did make. The teacher began instruction by modeling the steps of self-directed questioning. As she silently read the text, she thought aloud when important information was presented. Next, she asked Luis to read silently and then to think aloud about the text. Luis readily began to talk about his interpretations. The teacher and student continued this process by alternately thinking aloud about the text. Luis began to make guesses and then to revise his thinking about the text.

In this example, the teacher needed to make relatively few task modifications. The student learned the new task and readily applied it. The teacher concluded that the passive reading behavior was due to a lack of experience with the task. It was evident that Luis had not transferred his active stance in other problem-solving situations to silent reading behavior before the instruction.

When evaluating Terry, another passive reader, the diagnostic teacher decided to use self-directed questioning again. As with the other student, the diagnostic teacher modeled the steps of self-directed questioning by thinking aloud about the text. Then she asked Terry to read silently and think aloud about the text when important information was presented. Terry read a long segment silently, then stopped and looked at the teacher for questions. However, he could not talk about the text. The teacher asked him to read the segment aloud and think out loud about the text. Again he read the words without stopping to think about their meaning. Therefore, the teacher modeled the same segment of the text, emphasizing how she thought about the text as she read out loud. Terry followed the teacher's model. However, he mainly recounted exactly what was stated in the text. He did not tie together events to make predictions or revise any previous thoughts.

The teacher modeled the next segment of the text. Terry was asked to follow the model, but he again read the words without thinking. The teacher, therefore, modified the task by segmenting the section into sentences. Reading sentence by sentence, she modeled her thinking about each sentence. Finally, Terry began to think aloud about the sentences and draw relationships among the sentences in the paragraph. During this segment, the teacher modified the procedures by asking questions like these: "What makes you say that? Was this character important? How do you know?"

To help this passive reader learn more active strategies for achieving reading comprehension, the diagnostic teacher needed to make modifications in a number of instructional areas. She changed the task from silent to oral reading when Terry could not talk about what he had read silently. She segmented the passage into sentences when he could not follow the modeled paragraphs. Moreover, she shifted from modeling only to modeling with inquiry questions to help him see relationships among the ideas in the text.

The diagnostic teacher evaluates the amount of modification necessary to create a change in the student's reading performance. One student may require no task modification for the original task and learn the task readily. Another student, however, may require substantial modification by the introduction of new steps into the original procedure. The degree of task modification becomes a key factor in determining future task assignments. If there is a high degree of task modification, a less difficult text or a different technique should be selected. If there is a low degree of task modification, however, a more difficult text or task can be employed.

The degree of task modification is considered in establishing the conditions necessary to produce reading growth.

Determining the Amount of Teacher Investment

During assessment, the diagnostic teacher becomes a powerful determiner of reading performance. She thinks about how she set up instruction according to the procedures of the technique. Were these procedures sufficient for improving text interpretation? Or did she have to change the procedures, draw out of the student his own knowledge, and then show him how to relate this information to what he was reading? She evaluates how many times she had to rephrase questions and how many clues she needed to provide for the student.

Sometimes relatively little teacher investment, or assistance, is needed. For instance, Bobby could not recognize the word *skated* in this sentence: "The girl skated around the rink." The teacher told him to read to the end of the sentence. Bobby did so, thought for a minute about the word, and then read, "The girl skated around the rink." In this case, very little teacher investment was needed to encourage self-correction. With the simple prompt "read to the end of the sentence," the student was able to figure out the word.

Another student had the same difficulty with word recognition, but he needed more teacher investment. With the same prompt, Fred read to the end of the sentence but could not recognize the word *rink* either. In this case, the teacher had to probe further. She asked Fred to think about the story and what the girl might be doing. Still there was no response. The teacher then said, "In the picture there is an ice rink. Now, what do you think the girl is doing?" "Skating" was his reply. The teacher instructed him to read the sentence again. Fred now read: "The girl . . . skated around the . . . rink."

The diagnostic teacher assesses these modifications in terms of the amount of teacher investment necessary to create a change in the student's reading performance. Bobby required relatively little assistance, so there was minimal teacher investment. However, Fred required a great deal of assistance, so there was a higher degree of teacher investment.

The amount and kind of teacher investment are evaluated to identify the conditions that produce reading growth.

Conclusion

The diagnostic teacher assesses reading growth due to instruction by selecting a reading passage that is moderately difficult. She follows the procedures for the diagnostic lesson: establishing baseline data on the first section through the student's reading at sight, instruction during the second section, and establishing post-instruction data on the third section through more reading at sight. She evaluates whether or not the third section was read at an independent level. When the third section does not produce reader change, she reformulates her hypotheses and conducts another lesson. When the student reads the final section at an independent level, the diagnostic teacher assesses the amount of task modification and teacher investment that produced that growth. This assessment determines under what conditions subsequent instruction will be conducted.

1. If there was little task modification and teacher investment used to produce the desired change, the diagnostic teacher considers using a more difficult text for instruction.
2. If there was a moderate amount of task modification and teacher investment, the diagnostic teacher continues to use those adjustments in the same level of text.
3. If there was a great deal of task modification and teacher investment, the diagnostic teacher reformulates her hypotheses and selects either another technique or an easier text.

SPECIAL CONSIDERATIONS

The procedures outlined are used when considering only one technique or instructional modification for the student. In many instances, however, the diagnostic teacher needs to consider several options before establishing the optimal instructional conditions. Therefore, she compares growth under different techniques, uses several adapted lessons for the beginning reader, and combines techniques to increase her effectiveness.

Comparing Reading Growth Under Different Techniques

At times the diagnostic teacher will conduct a series of diagnostic lessons so that she can identify the most efficient instructional procedure. After the final assessment with each technique, the diagnostic teacher compares the performances under the different instructional conditions and evaluates the effectiveness of each technique. For example, Jason, a third-grade reader, was identified as having an oral reading fluency problem. In working with the child, the diagnostic teacher first formulated her hypotheses. From the data collected, the teacher designed a program of repeated readings (see "Repeated Readings" in Chapter 6), including a discussion of the errors after the first reading. She selected a text and conducted a reading-at-sight evaluation to establish baseline data. For the second section of the passage, she instructed Jason using a repeated readings format and discussed his errors with him. On the last section of the selected text, she conducted another reading at sight but without assistance. Jason decreased his error rate from 1/10 on the first section to 1/15 on the last section.

Since this technique resulted in only minimal change in reading performance, the diagnostic teacher designed another lesson. She decided to use the talking books technique (see "Talking Books" in Chapter 6) during the instructional phase of the diagnostic lesson. She followed the same procedure: first establishing baseline data through unaided reading at sight, next instruction, and finally establishing postinstructional data through more unaided reading at sight. This time Jason decreased his error rate from 1/10 on the first section to 1/50 on the last section.

The diagnostic teacher compared the resulting changes from the two sets of readings to decide which technique was most effective. The talking books technique produced the most change; moreover, it required less teacher investment since the tape recording provided the words that would have needed the teacher's prompting under the repeated readings approach. As a result, the teacher used taped stories in the diagnostic teaching program. Whenever the diagnostic teacher can conduct a series of diagnostic lessons to compare the effectiveness of several techniques, she increases her ability to confirm the diagnostic hypotheses and select the best possible instructional approach for the reader.

Special Cases: The Beginning Reader

The beginning reader requires a modification in the procedures of the diagnostic lesson since he cannot read enough text for a standard initial assessment. Consequently, the diagnostic teacher begins by teaching a lesson and *then* conducting an oral reading analysis of the student's reading. If the technique was effective, the passage should be read at the independent level even after a delayed period of time. These procedures are similar to the learning-methods tests developed by Mills (1956) and Ray (1970). After the lessons, the diagnostic teacher compares reading growth under several different techniques as recommended above.

A diagnostic teacher was working with Neil, a second grader who was a nonreader (he knew only five words by sight). The diagnostic teacher began her diagnostic assessment with a language experience lesson (see "Language Experience" in Chapter 6). She created an experience, Neil dictated a story, and they read the story together numerous times. The story was chunked onto cards and the cards flashed in story order. Then Neil read the story on his own and performed at the independent level (error rate 1/50). Later during the day, he read the story with an error rate of 1/10. This technique could be used for Neil in future instruction, but it required a high degree of teacher investment to achieve the recorded growth, and he seemed to memorize the story without looking at the words. Neil could, however, correct many of his mistakes when the teacher repeated the preceding part of the sentence (moderate teacher investment). Therefore, the teacher wanted to explore another approach.

For this diagnostic lesson, the teacher used the predictable language approach (see "Predictable Language Approach" in Chapter 6). Neil and the teacher were supposed to read the story simultaneously; however, he did not look at the text. Neil did, however, begin to read the text as the teacher omitted words in the language pattern. As she omitted more words, Neil paid more attention to the words on the page and reread the text with an error rate of 1/50. He also corrected many of his miscues by rereading sentences on his own. Later in the day, Neil still read the story with only 1 error every 50 words. The diagnostic teacher concluded that this technique was more effective than the language experience lesson because he was able to use the language pattern to self-correct his errors.

To see if there was a technique that required less teacher time but had similar results, the teacher conducted another diagnostic lesson. This time she used the talking books technique (see "Talking Books" in Chapter 6). Neil listened to a short story on a tape recorder until he had the story memorized. Then he read the story to the teacher, producing an error rate of 1/15 and losing his place many times. Listening to the book repeated, Neil had memorized the words but not associated them with the printed words. Later that day, he read the book with an error rate of 1/10. In this case, the diagnostic teacher continued using the predictable language technique and placed Neil in a small group where he was still able to maintain a high rate of success.

Using a series of modified diagnostic teaching lessons, the diagnostic teacher selects the most appropriate technique to teach the beginning reader. These lessons use two readings of the text—one immediately after instruction and another after several hours' delay—to establish a learning rate for that particular instructional technique. For the beginning reader, the diagnostic teacher pays special attention to the teacher investment and task modification needed to ensure fluent reading.

Special Cases: Using More Than One Technique at the Same Time

Sometimes the diagnostic teacher needs to combine several techniques to produce the desired change. In these cases, the combined techniques are more effective than using either one of them alone. The decision-making process that results in combining techniques is illustrated in the case of Charles, a fourth-grade reader with a comprehension problem. Initially, the diagnostic teacher designed a program using self-directed questioning (see "Self-Questioning" in Chapter 6). She selected a story, divided it into three sections, and conducted a think-aloud assessment that was unaided. She recorded her data. Next, she instructed the lesson using self-directed questioning. She modeled the process using the concepts missed during the first section. Charles had a great deal of difficulty remembering the steps in self-directed questioning, even after the diagnostic teacher had written them down (task modification). Charles was never able to do the task independently (high degree of teacher investment). The final section of the story was read like the first, as an unaided think-aloud assessment. There was only minimal change (from 55% to 65% improvement in comprehension).

The diagnostic teacher decided to try the reciprocal teaching technique (see "Reciprocal Teaching" in Chapter 6), which is similar to self-directed questioning but is more structured. She again conducted an unaided think-aloud assessment on the first section of the selected text. Next she instructed the lesson using reciprocal teaching, returning to concepts missed during the first section of the text to model the process and to clear up misconceptions about the story. Charles was to follow her model and summarize, ask a good question, clarify difficult parts, and predict what the next segment would say. However, he had a great deal of difficulty learning this task, so the teacher used a high degree of modeling on each segment. Charles was not able to do the task independently. The final section of the story was read like the first, as an unaided think-aloud assessment. When this technique resulted in only minimal change in reading performance (from 55% to 75% improvement in comprehension) despite a high degree of teacher modeling, the diagnostic teacher decided to add another technique to her procedure.

The teacher selected another story and followed the same procedure: having the student read at sight to establish baseline data, instruction, and having the student read at sight again to establish postinstructional data. During the instructional phase of the diagnostic lesson, the diagnostic teacher introduced a story map (see "Story Map" in Chapter 6) along with reciprocal teaching. First, she modeled the combined sequence: add new information to the story map, summarize using the story map, use the story map to ask a good question, clarify any difficult parts that do not fit on the map, and finally, use the components of the story map to predict what will happen next.

Following instruction in this combined approach, Charles began to take over the teaching. He began to teach the lesson independently. For him, using the story map was more concrete than either self-directed questioning or reciprocal teaching alone. During the final third of the lesson, the diagnostic teacher conducted a think-aloud assessment, which revealed a change in his monitoring of understanding. Charles had begun to revise his predictions as he encountered new information. This resulted in a growth from 55% to 90% in reading comprehension. As in this case, the diagnostic teacher may combine reading techniques to evaluate if the new combination results in greater reading growth. If it does, she uses the combined, or piggy-back, approach rather than either technique alone.

SUMMARY

The job of the diagnostic teacher is to identify appropriate techniques for instruction. By teaching a lesson using selected materials and techniques, the diagnostic teacher assesses the student's learning as she teaches and reading growth due to her instruction. She also measures the task modification and teacher investment needed to ensure this growth. Then she establishes the most appropriate instructional conditions for the student. Once these conditions are in place, the diagnostic teacher introduces more difficult tasks or texts and observes the student as he learns the task or reads the text. The diagnostic teacher becomes a teacher and an evaluator. Her purpose during the diagnostic lesson is to record changes in reading behaviors and the instructional adjustments that produced them. She focuses on teaching rather than testing to reveal those instructional adjustments that produce optimal reading growth for a particular student.

Epilogue

This text has included the means that effective teachers have used to adapt instruction to individual student needs. Intuitively, teachers have always changed their instruction as they encountered problems in teaching. Diagnostic teaching recognizes this decision-making power and places assessment in the hands of effective teachers.

SOME POINTS FOR ASSESSMENT

Although different from the traditional forms of assessment, diagnostic teaching produces practical, efficient, and valid information about the learner.

1. It is practical because suggestions for instruction can be incorporated immediately into the instructional program.
2. It is efficient because reading instruction and learning do not stop in order to test; instead they become an integral part of assessment.
3. It is valid because diagnostic teaching assesses reading in the same kind of instructional situation that is used throughout the student's educational plan.

SOME FINAL POINTS ON INSTRUCTION

1. Selecting techniques from the tables should be considered tentative and subject to confirmation through teaching.
2. The student's response to instructional techniques changes as she learns.
3. The student's response to instruction is an interaction among instructional variables in the reading event. Every event has a different set of interactions.

4. Instructional placement is based not only on how the student performs with aided instruction (mediated level) but also on the degree of task modification and teacher investment. The basic premise for placement is this: "If I can find a way to teach easily what the student needs to know, I can place the student at a higher reading level."

Appendix: Administering an Informal Reading Assessment

1. Select texts that sample a range of reading levels, or use a published informal reading inventory.
2. Establish the readability of the text, if necessary.

Table A–1
Scoreable Errors (to be used in computing error rate)

Substitutions or mispronunciations (the replacement of one word for another): Mark the mispronounced word by drawing a line through it and writing the substitution above the word.

"The man ~~went~~ *want* to the store," said Ann.

Omissions (leaving out words): Circle the word omitted.

"The man went to (the) store," said Ann.

Insertions (adding extra words): Draw a caret and write the inserted word above it.

"The man went *away* ∧ to the store," said Ann.

Transpositions (changing the word order): Mark with a ⌐‾‾‾⌐ .

"The man went to the store," said Ann.

Prompted words (words that have to be prompted or supplied by the teacher): Write the letter *P* above these words.

"The man went to the *P* store," said Ann.

3. Prepare questions that focus on important information, coherent textual structure, and key concepts. If you use a published informal reading inventory, be sure to check the questions for coherence and importance.
4. Establish rapport quickly and begin assessment.
5. If necessary, use a word recognition list to establish a beginning level for assessment.
6. Start with a passage that you think will be at the independent level of difficulty.
7. Have the student read the passage orally.
8. Using the coding system in Table A–1 and Table A–2, record the student's performance as he reads. Both scoreable errors (Table A–1) and recordable errors (Table A–2) are coded. Scoreable errors determine whether a passage was read at the independent, instructional, or frustration level. Recordable errors are additional errors used to evaluate a reader's strategies but are not computed in the error rate.
9. Assess comprehension by asking the prepared questions.
10. Find the oral accuracy score by calculating the error rate (Table A–3) or the percentage of oral accuracy (Table A–4).

Table A–2
Recordable Errors (these are not computed in the error rate for an IRI)

Repetitions (words or phrases that are repeated more than once): Draw a line over the word and write the letter *R* over the line.

R
"The man went to the store," said Ann.

Repeated repetitions (words or phrases that are repeated several times): Draw a line over the word or phrase and mark it with a *2R* over the line.

2 R
"The man went to the store," said Ann.

Self-correction: If the child corrects an error, a line is drawn through the previously marked error and the letter *C* is written at the end of the line.

went C
"The man went to the store," said Ann.

Pauses: Long pauses that are used to gain meaning are marked with slashes.

"The man / went to the store," said Ann.

Punctuation errors (ignoring punctuation symbols): Draw a circle around the omitted punctuation mark.

"The man went to the store," said Ann. "Then he went home."

1. Determine the number of scoreable errors per passage read.

   Example: Brian made 4 scoreable errors.

2. Estimate the total number of words in the passage read.

   Example: Brian read 86 words.

3. Divide the total number of words by the number of scoreable errors. Round off the quotient to the nearest whole number.

   Example:
   $$\frac{21\ r\ 2}{4\,\overline{)\,86}} = 21$$

4. The quotient determined in Step 3 becomes the denominator in the error rate and the number 1 becomes the numerator.

   Example: Brian read the passage with 1 error every 21 running words; the error rate is 1/21.

Table A–3
Calculating Error Rate

---

1. Estimate the number of words read.

   Example: Brian read 80 words.

2. Count the number of scoreable errors.

   Example: Brian made 4 errors.

3. Subtract the number of scoreable errors from the number of words read.

   Example: 80 words – 4 errors = 76 words

4. Divide the number of words read correctly by the number of words read.

   Example:
   $$80\,\overline{)\,76.00}\quad .95$$

5. Multiply the resulting decimal number by 100 to find the percentage of oral accuracy.

   .95 × 100 = 95%

Table A–4
Calculating Percentage of Oral Accuracy

---

11. Compute the comprehension percentage score for the passage by (a) dividing the number of questions answered correctly by the total number of questions asked and (b) multiplying the resulting decimal number by 100. Example: Brian answered 8 of 10 questions correctly.
    (a)
    $$10\,\overline{)\,8.00}\quad .80$$
    (b) .80 × 100 = 80%

12. Administer another passage on the same level. Have the student read the paragraph silently.

13. Assess comprehension by an oral retelling followed by direct questioning.

14. Decide the level of performance for each passage the student read. Use either Powell's criteria (1978) from Table A–5 or Betts' criteria (1946) from Table A–6.

Table A–5

Scoring Criteria by Performance Grade Level Suggested by W. R. Powell (1978)

Reading Level	Word Recognition Error Rate	Comprehension Percentage
Independent		
1–2	1/17 +	80 +
3–5	1/27 +	85 +
6 +	1/35 +	90 +
Instructional		
1–2	1/8–1/16	55–80
3–5	1/13–1/26	60–84
6 +	1/18–1/35	65–90
Frustration		
1–2	1/7 –	55 –
3–5	1/12 –	60 –
6 +	1/17 –	65 –

Note. From *The Finger Count System for Monitoring Reading Behavior* (pp. 7–11) by W. R. Powell, 1981, unpublished paper. Adapted by permission.

15. Using the information from Step 14, decide how to continue the assessment.
    a. If the student is reading at an independent level, move him up to the next level.
    b. If the student is reading at an instructional level, move him down to the next level to establish independent reading.
    c. If the student is reading at a frustrational level, consider moving him down two levels to establish independent and then instructional reading experiences.
16. Continue using this procedure, alternating between oral and silent reading at each level until a passage is read at the frustration reading level for both oral and silent reading.
17. Summarize the results using the Informal Reading Inventory (IRI) Summary Sheet reproduced in Table A–7.

Table A–6

Scoring Criteria Suggested by Betts (1946)

Reading Level	Word Recognition	Comprehension
Independent	99% +	90% +
Instructional	95%	75%
Frustration	90% –	50% –

Student's Name _____ Age _____ Grade _____

Examiner _____ Date _____

IRI Used _____ Form _____

Levels of Performance   Oral   Silent

Independent Level   _____   _____
Instructional Level   _____   _____
Frustration Level   _____   _____

Level	Scoreable Errors (Error Rate)	Percentage of Comprehension Oral	Silent
pp			
p			
1			
2			
3			
4			
5			
6			
7			
8			
9			
10			
11			
12			

Bibliography

Adams, A., Carnine, D., & Gersten, R. (1982). Instructional strategies for studying content area texts in the intermediate grades. *Reading Research Quarterly, 18,* 27–55.

Allington, R. L. (1977). If they don't read much how they ever gonna get good? *Journal of Reading, 21,* 57–61.

Allington, R. L. (1980). Teacher interruption behaviors during primary grade oral reading. *Journal of Educational Psychology, 72,* 371–377.

Allington, R. L. (1983). Fluency: The neglected reading goal. *Reading Teacher, 36,* 556–561.

Allington, R. L. (1984a). Content coverage and contextual reading in reading groups. *Journal of Reading Behavior, 16*(2), 85–96.

Allington, R. L. (1984b). Oral reading. In P. D. Pearson (Ed.), *Handbook of reading research* (pp. 829–864). New York: Longman.

Anders, P., Bos, C., & Filip, D. (1984). The effects of semantic feature analysis on the reading comprehension of learning disabled students. In J. Niles & L. Harris (Eds.), *Changing perspectives on research in reading/language processing and instruction* (pp. 162–166). Rochester, NY: National Reading Conference.

Anderson, R. C., Hiebert, E. H., Scott, J. A., & Wilkinson, I. A. G. (1985). *Becoming a nation of readers: The report of the commission on reading.* Washington, DC: National Institute of Education.

Andre, M., & Anderson, T. H. (1978–1979). The development and evaluation of a self-questioning study technique. *Reading Research Quarterly, 14,* 605–623.

Andrews, N. (1977). Six case studies in learning to read. (Doctoral dissertation, Indiana University, 1976). *Dissertation Abstracts International, 37,* 4838A.

Au, K. (1979). Using the experience-text-relationship method with minority children. *Reading Teacher, 32,* 677–679.

August, D., Flavell, J., & Clift, R. (1984). Comparison of comprehension monitoring of skilled and less skilled readers. *Reading Research Quarterly, 20,* 39–54.

Aukerman, R. C. (1984). *Approaches to beginning reading* (2nd ed.). New York: John Wiley & Sons.

Aulls, M. (1982). *Developing readers in today's elementary school.* Boston: Allyn and Bacon.

Baker, L., & Brown, A. (1984). Metacognitive skills and reading. In P. D. Pearson (Ed.), *Handbook of reading re-*

search (pp. 353–394). New York: Longman.

Barr, R. (1972). The influence of instructional conditions on word recognition errors. *Reading Research Quarterly, 7,* 509–579.

Barr, R. (1974–1975). The effect of instruction on pupil reading strategies. *Reading Research Quarterly, 10,* 555–582.

Barr, R., & Sadow, M. (1985). *Reading diagnosis for teachers.* White Plains, NY: Longman.

Beck, I. L., & McKeown, M. G. (1981). Developing questions that promote comprehension: The story map. *Language Arts, 58,* 913–918.

Beck, I. L., Omanson, R. C., & McKeown, M. G. (1982). An instructional redesign of reading lessons: Effects on comprehension. *Reading Research Quarterly 17,* 462–481.

Beck, I. L., McKeown, M. G., Omanson, R. C., & Pople, M. T. (1984). Improving the comprehensibility of stories: The effects of revisions that improve coherence. *Reading Research Quarterly, 19,* 263–277.

Bereiter, C., & Englemann, S. (1966). *Teaching disadvantaged children in the preschool.* Englewood Cliffs, NJ: Prentice-Hall.

Bereiter, C., & Englemann, S. (1970). *The Distar reading program.* Chicago: Science Research Associates.

Berglund, R. L., & Johns, J. L. (1983). A primer on uninterrupted sustained silent reading. *Reading Teacher, 36,* 534–539.

Berliner, D. C. (1981). Academic learning time and reading achievement. In J. T. Guthrie (Ed.), *Comprehension and teaching: Research reviews* (pp. 203–226). Newark, DE: International Reading Association.

Betts, E. A. (1946). *Foundations of reading instruction.* New York: American Book.

Bloome, D., & Green, J. (1984). Directions in the sociolinguistic study of reading. In P. D. Pearson (Ed.), *Handbook of reading research* (pp. 395–421). New York: Longman.

Bloomfield, L., & Barnhart, C. (1961). *Let's read: A linguistic approach.* Detroit: Wayne State Press.

Bond, G. L., & Dykstra, R. (1967). The cooperative research program in first-grade reading instruction. *Reading Research Quarterly, 2,* 1–142.

Brennan, A. D., Bridge, C. A., & Winograd, P. N. (1986). The effects of structural variation on children's recall of basal reader stories. *Reading Research Quarterly, 21,* 91–104.

Bridge, C. (1979). Predictable materials for beginning readers. *Language Arts, 50,* 503–507.

Bristow, P. S. (1985). Are poor readers passive readers? Some evidence, possible explanations, and potential solutions. *Reading Teacher, 39,* 318–329.

Brophy, J. (1984). The teacher as thinker: Implementing instruction. In G. Duffy, L. Roehler, & J. Mason (Eds.), *Comprehension instruction: Perspectives and suggestions* (pp. 71–92). New York: Longman.

Brown, A. L., & Campione, J. C. (1986). Psychological theory and the study of learning disabilities. *American Psychologist, 41,* 1059–1068.

Carbo, M. (1978). Teaching reading with talking books. *Reading Teacher, 32,* 267–273.

Cazden, C. B. (1981). Social context of learning to read. In J. T. Guthrie (Ed.), *Comprehension and teaching: Research reviews* (pp. 118–139). Newark, DE: International Reading Association.

Chall, J. (1985). Afterward. In R. C. Anderson, E. H. Hiebert, J. A. Scott, & I. A. G. Wilkinson, *Becoming a nation of readers: The report of the commission on reading* (pp. 123–125). Washington, DC: National Institute of Education.

Chomsky, C. (1978). When you still can't read in third grade: After decoding what? In J. Samuels (Ed.), *What research has to say about reading in-*

struction (pp. 13–30). Newark, DE: International Reading Association.

Cioffi, G., & Carney, J. J. (1983). Dynamic assessment of reading disabilities. *Reading Teacher, 36,* 764–768.

Clay, M. M. (1969). Reading errors and self-correction behavior. *British Journal of Educational Psychology, 39,* 47–56.

Clay, M. M. (1979). *The early detection of reading difficulties: A diagnostic survey with recovery procedures* (2nd ed.). Exeter, NH: Heinemann Educational Books.

Cohen, R. (1983). Self-generated questions as an aid to reading comprehension. *Reading Teacher, 36,* 770–775.

Collins, A., Brown, F. S., & Larkin, K. M. (1980). Inference in text understanding. In R. F. Spiro, B. C. Bruce, & N. F. Brewer (Eds.), *Theoretical issues in reading comprehension* (pp. 385–410). Hillsdale, NJ: Lawrence Erlbaum Associates.

Collins, A., & Smith, E. (1980). *Teaching the process of reading comprehension.* (Technical Report No. 182). Urbana, IL: University of Illinois, Center for the Study of Reading. (ERIC Document Reproduction Service No. ED 193 616)

Combs, W. (1980). Sentence-combining practice aids in reading comprehension. In D. Sawyer (Ed.), *Disabled readers—Insight, assessment, instruction* (pp. 104–112). Newark, DE: International Reading Association.

Dale, E. (1969). *Audiovisual methods in teaching* (3rd ed.). New York: Holt, Rinehart & Winston.

Dank, M. (1977). What effect do reading programs have on the oral reading behavior of children? *Reading Improvement, 14,* 66–99.

Das, J. P., Kirby, J. R., & Jarman, R. F. (1979). *Simultaneous and successive cognitive processes.* New York: Academic Press.

Deford, D. E. (1985). Validating the construct of theoretical orientation in reading instruction. *Reading Research Quarterly, 20,* 351–367.

Delain, M. T., Pearson, P. D., & Anderson, R. C. (1985). Reading comprehension and creativity in black language use: You stand to gain by playing the sounding game! *American Educational Research Journal, 22,* 155–173.

Duffy, G. G., & Roehler, L. R. (1986). *Improving classroom reading instruction.* New York: Random House.

Duffy, G. G., & Roehler, L. R. (1987). Teaching reading skills as strategies. *Reading Teacher, 40,* 414–418.

Durkin, D. (1978–1979). What classroom observations reveal about reading comprehension instruction. *Reading Research Quarterly, 14,* 481–533.

Dybdahl, C. S. (1983, October). *Comprehension strategies and practices.* Paper presented at the Annual Conference of the College Reading Association, Atlanta, GA.

Dybdahl, C. S., & Walker, B. J. (1986). *Predictions strategies and comprehension instruction.* Unpublished paper, Eastern Montana College, Billings, MT.

Ekwall, E. E., & Shanker, J. L. (1983). *Diagnosis and remediation of the disabled reader* (2nd ed.). Boston: Allyn and Bacon.

Elkind, D. (1983). Stress and learning disabilities. In D. Carnine, D. Elkind, A. D. Hendrickson, D. Meichenbaum, R. Sieben, & F. Smith (Eds.), *Interdisciplinary voices in learning disabilities and remedial education* (pp. 67–80). Austin, TX: Pro-ed.

Faas, L. A. (1980). *Children with learning problems: A handbook for teachers.* Boston: Houghton Mifflin.

Fernald, G. (1943). *Remedial techniques in basic school subjects.* New York: McGraw-Hill.

Feuerstein, R. (1979). *The dynamic assessment of retarded performers: The learning potential assessment device, theory, instruments, and techniques.* Baltimore: University Park Press.

Finn, P. J. (1985). *Helping children learn to read.* New York: Random House.

Fowler, G. L., & Davis, M. (1985). The story frame approach: A tool for improving reading comprehension of EMR children. *Teaching Exceptional Children, 17,* 296–298.

Galda, L. (1982). Playing about a story: Its impact on comprehension. *Reading Teacher, 36,* 52–58.

Gambrell, L. B. (1985). Dialogue journals: Reading-writing interaction. *Reading Teacher, 38,* 512–515.

Gambrell, L. B., & Bales, R. J. (1986). Mental imagery and the comprehension-monitoring performance of fourth and fifth grade poor readers. *Reading Research Quarterly, 21,* 454–465.

Gambrell, L. B., Wilson, R. M., & Gantt, W. N. (1981). Classroom observations of task-attending behaviors of good and poor readers. *Journal of Educational Research, 74,* 376–381.

Garner, R., Alexander, P., Slater, W., Hare, V. C., Smith, T., & Reis, R. (1986). Children's knowledge of structural properties of expository text. *Journal of Educational Psychology, 78,* 411–416.

Gentile, L. M. (1983). Lance M. Gentile's comments. In D. Carnine, D. Elkind, A. D. Hendrickson, D. Meichenbaum, R. Sieben, & F. Smith (Eds.), *Interdisciplinary voices in learning disabilities and remedial education* (pp. 81–85). Austin, TX: Pro-ed.

Gillet, J. W., & Temple, C. (1986). *Understanding reading problems* (2nd ed.). Boston: Little, Brown.

Giordano, G. (1982). Outlining techniques that help disabled readers. *Academic Therapy, 17,* 517–522.

Gipe, J. P. (1978–1979). Investigating techniques for teaching word meanings. *Reading Research Quarterly, 14,* 624–644.

Glass, G. (1973). *Teaching decoding as separate from reading.* Garden City, NY: Adelphi University Press.

Glass, G., & Burton, E. (1973). How do they decode: Verbalization and observed behaviors of successful decoders. *Education, 94,* 58–63.

Glazer, S. M. (1984). Liberating students to write. *Early Years, 15*(1), 67–69.

Goodman, K. S. (1967). Reading: A psycholinguistic guessing game. *Journal of the Reading Specialist, 6,* 126–135.

Goodman, Y. M., & Burke, C. (1980). *Reading strategies: Focus on comprehension.* New York: Holt, Rinehart & Winston.

Graves, M. (1986, January). *Prereading, reading, and postreading activities to foster comprehension and enjoyment of difficult selections.* Paper presented at Seventh Rocky Mountain Regional Conference of the International Reading Association, Colorado Springs, CO.

Guszak, F. J. (1967). Teacher questioning and reading. *Reading Teacher, 21,* 227–234.

Guszak, F. J. (1985). *Diagnostic reading instruction in the elementary school.* New York: Harper & Row.

Hare, V. C., & Borchardt, K. M. (1984). Direct instruction of summarization skills. *Reading Research Quarterly, 20,* 62–78.

Harris, A. J. (1977). Ten years of progress in remedial reading. *Reading Teacher, 31,* 29–35.

Harris, A. J. (1984). The diagnosis of reading disabilities. In A. Harris & E. Sipay (Eds.), *Readings on reading instruction* (pp. 416–426). New York: Longman.

Harris, A. J., & Sipay, E. R. (1985). *How to increase reading ability.* New York: Longman.

Harste, J., Burke, C., & Woodward, V. (1982). Children's language and world: Initial encounters with print. In J. Langer & M. Smith-Burke (Eds.), *Reader meets author/bridging the gap: A psycholinguistic and socialinguistic perspective* (pp. 105–132). Newark, DE: International Reading Association.

Harste, J., Woodward, V., & Burke, C. (1984). *Language stories and literacy lessons.* Portsmouth, NH: Heinemann Educational Books.

Haussler, M. M. (1985). A young child's developing concepts of print. In A. Jaggar & M. T. Smith-Burke (Eds.), *Observing the language learner* (pp. 73–81). New York: International Reading Association & National Council of Teachers of English.

Heckelman, R. G. (1969). A neurological-impress method of remedial reading instruction. *Academic Therapy, 4,* 277–282.

Heimlich, J. E., & Pittleman, S. D. (1986). *Semantic mapping: Classroom applications.* Newark, DE: International Reading Association.

Helfeldt, J. P., & Lalik, R. (1979). Reciprocal student-teacher questioning. In C. Pennock (Ed.), *Reading comprehension at four linguistic levels* (pp. 74–80). Newark, DE: International Reading Association.

Herber, H. L. (1978). *Teaching reading in content areas* (2nd ed.). Englewood Cliffs, NJ: Prentice-Hall.

Johns, J. L. (1981). *Basic reading inventory* (2nd ed.). Dubuque, Iowa: Kendall/Hunt Publishing Company.

Johnson, D. D. (1982). *Three sound strategies for vocabulary development* (Ginn Occasional Papers, No. 3). Lexington, MA: Silver Burdett & Ginn.

Johnson, D. D., & Pearson, P. D. (1984). *Teaching reading vocabulary* (2nd ed.). New York: Holt, Rinehart & Winston.

Johnston, P. H. (1983). *Reading comprehension assessment: A cognitive basis.* Newark, DE: International Reading Association.

Johnston, P. H. (1984). Assessment in reading. In. P. D. Pearson (Ed.), *Handbook of reading research* (pp. 147–182). New York: Longman.

Johnston, P. H., & Pearson, P. D. (1982). Assessment: Response to exposition. In A. Berger & H. A. Robinson (Eds.), *Secondary school reading—What research reveals for classroom practice* (pp. 127–142). Urbana IL: ERIC Clearinghouse on Reading and Communication Skills and National Conference on Research in English.

Johnston, P. H., & Winograd, P. N. (1985). Passive failure in reading. *Journal of Reading Behavior, 16,* 279–302.

Jongsma, E. A. (1980). *Cloze instruction research: A second look.* Newark, DE: International Reading Association.

Juel, C. (1984). An evolving model of reading acquisition. In J. Niles (Ed.), *Changing perspectives on research in reading/language processing and instruction* (pp. 294–297). Rochester, NY: National Reading Conference.

Kann, R. (1983). The method of repeated readings: Expanding the neurological impress method for use with disabled readers. *Journal of Learning Disabilities, 16,* 90–92.

Kaufman, A. S., & Kaufman, N. L. (1983). *K∗ABC Kaufman assessment battery for children: Interpretive manual.* Circle Pines, MN: American Guidance Services.

King, J. R., Biggs, S., & Lipsky, S. (1984). Students' self-questioning and summarizing as reading study strategies. *Journal of Reading Behavior, 16,* 205–218.

Kogan, N. (1971). Educational implications of cognitive styles. In G. S. Lesser (Ed.), *Psychology and educational practice* (pp. 242–292). Glenview, IL: Scott, Foresman.

Labov, W. (1972). *Language in the inner city.* Philadelphia: University of Pennsylvania Press.

Langer, J. A. (1982). The reading processes. In A. Berger & H. A. Robinson (Eds.), *Secondary school reading* (pp. 39–52). Urbana, IL: ERIC Clearinghouse on Reading and Communication Skills and the National Conference on Research in English.

Leu, D. J., DeGroff, L. C., & Simons, H. D. (1986). Predictable texts and inter-active-compensatory hypotheses: Evaluating individual differences in reading ability, context use, and comprehension. *Journal of Educational Psychology, 78,* 347–352.

Luria, A. R. (1973). *The working brain.* London: Penguin.

Manzo, A. V. (1969). The request procedure. *Journal of Reading, 2,* 123–126.

Maria, K., & MacGinitie, W. H. (1982). Reading comprehension disabilities: Knowledge structures and non-accommodating text processing strategies. *Annals of Dyslexia, 32,* 33–59.

Mason, J. M., & Au, K. H. (1986). *Reading instruction for today.* Glenview, IL: Scott, Foresman.

May, F. (1986). *Reading as communication: An interactive approach* (2nd ed.). Columbus, OH: Merrill.

McClure, A. A. (1985). Predictable books: Another way to teach reading to learning disabled children. *Teaching Exceptional Children, 17,* 267–273.

McKeown, M. (1985). The acquisition of word meaning from context by children of high and low ability. *Reading Research Quarterly, 20,* 482–496.

McNeil, J. D. (1987). *Reading comprehension: New directions for classroom practice* (2nd ed.). Glenview, IL: Scott, Foresman.

Meichenbaum, D. (1977). *Cognitive-behavior modification: An integrative approach.* New York: Plenum Press.

Meichenbaum, D. (1983). Teaching thinking: A cognitive-behavioral approach. In D. Carnine, D. Elkind, A. D. Hendrickson, D. Meichenbaum, R. Sieben, & F. Smith (Eds.), *Interdisciplinary voices in learning disabilities and remedial education* (pp. 127–142). Austin, TX: Pro-ed.

Memory, D. M. (1981). The impress method: A status report of a new remedial reading technique. *Journal of Research and Development in Education, 14,* 102–114.

Miller, G. M., & Mason, G. E. (1983). Dramatic improvisation: Risk-free role playing for improving reading performance. *Reading Teacher, 37,* 128–131.

Mills, R. E. (1956). An evaluation of techniques for teaching word recognition. *Elementary School Journal, 56,* 221–225.

Moore, D., & Cunningham, J. (1984). Task clarity and sixth-grade students' main idea statements. In J. Niles (Ed.), *Changing perspectives on research in reading language processing and instruction* (pp. 90–94). Rochester, NY: The National Reading Conference.

Moyer, S. B. (1982). Repeated reading. *Journal of Learning Disabilities, 15,* 619–623.

O'Hare, F. (1973). *Sentence-combining* (NCTE Report No. 15). Urbana, IL: National Council of Teachers of English.

Olson, G. M., Duffy, S. A., & Mack, R. L. (1984). Thinking-out-loud as a method for studying real-time comprehension processes. In D. E. Kieras & M. A. Just (Eds.), *New methods in reading comprehension research* (pp. 253–285). Hillsdale, NJ: Lawrence Erlbaum Associates.

Orton, J. (1966). The Orton-Gillingham approach. In J. Money (Ed.), *The disabled reader* (pp. 119–146). Baltimore: Johns Hopkins University Press.

Palincsar, A. S., & Brown, A. L. (1984). Reciprocal teaching of comprehension-fostering and comprehension-monitoring activities. *Cognition and Instruction, 1,* 117–175.

Paris, S. G., & Myers, M. (1981). Comprehension monitoring, memory, and study strategies of good and poor readers. *Journal of Reading Behavior, 13,* 5–22.

Park, B. (1982). The big book trend—A discussion with Don Holdaway. *Language Arts, 59,* 815–821.

Pauk, W. (1974). *How to study in college* (2nd ed.). Boston: Houghton, Mifflin.

Pearson, P. D. (1982). *Asking questions about stories* (Ginn Occasional Papers No. 15). Lexington, MA: Silver Burdett & Ginn.

Pearson, P. D. (1983). A critique of F. J. Guszak's study: Teacher questioning and reading. In L. Gentile, M. Kamil, & J. Blanchard (Eds.), *Reading research revisited* (pp. 271–281). Columbus, OH: Merrill.

Pearson, P. D. (1985a). Changing the face of reading comprehension instruction. *Reading Teacher, 38*, 724–738.

Pearson, P. D. (1985b, July). *The triple read method for expository text*. Seminar presentation, Eastern Montana College, Billings, MT.

Pearson, P. D., Hansen, J., & Gordon, C. (1979). The effect of background knowledge on young children's comprehension of explicit and implicit information. *Journal of Reading Behavior, 11*, 201–209.

Pearson, P. D., & Johnson, D. D. (1978). *Teaching reading comprehension*. New York: Holt, Rinehart & Winston.

Pearson, P. D., & Raphael, T. E. (1985). Increasing student's awareness of sources of information for answering questions. *American Educational Research Journal, 22*, 217–235.

Pearson, P. D., & Spiro, R. J. (1980). Toward a theory of reading comprehension instruction. *Topics in Language Disorders, 1*, 71–88.

Pellegrini, A. D., & Galda, L. (1982). The effects of thematic fantasy play training on the development of children's story comprehension. *American Educational Research Journal, 19*, 443–452.

Peters, E., & Levin, J. R. (1986). Effects of a mnemonic imagery strategy on good and poor readers' prose recall. *Reading Research Quarterly, 21*, 179–192.

Pichert, J. W. (1979). *Sensitivity to what is important in prose*. (Technical Report No. 149). Champaign, IL: University of Illinois, Center for the Study of Reading. (Eric Document Reproduction Service No. ED 179 946)

Powell, W. R. (1973). Acquisition of a reading repertoire. *Library Trends, 21*, 177–195.

Powell, W. R. (1978, May). *Measuring reading informally*. Paper presented at the International Reading Association, Houston, TX.

Powell, W. R. (1984). Mediated (emergent) reading levels: A construct. In J. Niles (Ed.), *Changing perspectives on research in reading language processing and instruction* (pp. 247–251). Rochester, NY: The National Reading Conference.

Powell, W. R. (1986, December). *Emergent (mediated) reading levels: A new construct for placement from a Vygotskian view*. Paper presented at the National Reading Conference, Austin, TX.

Raphael, T. E. (1982). Question-answering strategies for children. *Reading Teacher, 36*, 186–190.

Ray, D. D. (1970). *Ray reading methods test* (Experimental ed.). Stillwater, OK: RRMT Publications.

Ray, D. D. (1971). Specificity in remediation. In B. Batemen (Ed.), *Learning disorders* (pp. 180–191). Seattle, WA: Special Child Publications.

Readence, J. E., Baldwin, R. S., & Rickelman, R. J. (1983). Instructional insights into metaphors and similes. *Journal of Reading, 27*, 109–112.

Reynolds, R. D. (1980). The effect of attention on the learning and recall of important text elements (Doctoral dissertation, University of Illinois, 1979). *Dissertation Abstracts International, 40*, 5380A.

Robinson, F. P. (1946). *Effective study*. New York: Harper and Bros.

Rowe, M. B. (1973). *Teaching science as continuous inquiry*. New York: McGraw-Hill.

Rupley, W. H., & Blair, T. R. (1978). Characteristics of effective reading instruction. *Educational Leadership, 36*, 171–173.

Samuels, S. J. (1979). The method of repeated readings. *Reading Teacher, 32*, 403–408.

Samuels, S. J. (1980). The age-old controversy between holistic and subskill approaches to beginning reading instruction revisited. In C. McCullough (Ed.), *Persistent problems in reading education* (pp. 202–221). Newark, DE: International Reading Association.

Santa, C., Danner, M., Nelson, M., Havens, L., Scalf, J., & Scalf, L. (1986). *Content reading in secondary school: Learning across the curriculum*. Unpublished manuscript, Kalispell School District No. 5, Kalispell, MT.

Schneider, E. J. (1979). Researchers discover formula for success in student learning. *Educational Research and Development Report, 2*, 1–6.

Sinatra, R. C., Berg, D., & Dunn, R. (1985). Semantic mapping improves reading comprehension of learning disabled students. *Teaching Exceptional Children, 17*, 310–314.

Singer, H., & Donlan, D. (1982). Active comprehension: Problem-solving schema with question generation for comprehension of complex short stories. *Reading Research Quarterly, 17*, 166–185.

Slater, W. H. (1986, December). *Expository text features which influence comprehensibility*. Paper presented at the National Reading Conference, Austin, TX.

Sloyer, S. (1982). *Readers theatre: Story dramatization in the classroom*. Urbana, IL: National Council of Teachers of English.

Smith, F. (1978). *Reading without nonsense*. New York: Teachers College Press.

Smith-Burke, M. T. (1982). Extending concepts through language activities. In J. Langer & M. T. Smith-Burke (Eds.), *Reader meets author/bridging the gap: A psycholinguistic and sociolinguistic perspective* (pp. 163–180). Newark, DE: International Reading Association.

Spiro, R. J., (1979). *Etiology of reading comprehension style*. (Tech. Rep. No. 124). Champaign, IL: University of Illinois, Center for the Study of Reading.

Spiro, R. J., & Myers, A. (1984). Individual differences and underlying cognitive process. In P. D. Pearson (Ed.), *Hand-book of reading research* (pp. 471–504). New York: Longman.

Stanovich, K. E. (1980). Toward an interactive-compensatory model of individual differences in the development of reading fluency. *Reading Research Quarterly, 16*, 32–71.

Stanovich, K. E. (1981). Attentional and automatic context effects in reading. In A. M. Lesgold & C. A. Perfetti (Eds.), *Interactive processes in reading* (pp. 241–262). Hillsdale, NJ: Lawrence Erlbaum Associates.

Stauffer, R. (1970). *The language experience approach to the teaching of reading*. New York: Harper & Row.

Stauffer, R. (1975). *Directing the reading-thinking process*. New York: Harper & Row.

Stein, N. L., & Trabasso, T. (1982). What's in a story: An approach to comprehension and instruction. In R. Glaser (Ed.), *Advances in instructional psychology* (Vol. 2, pp. 213–254). Hillsdale, NJ: Erlbaum.

Strange, M. (1980). Instructional implications of a conceptual theory of reading comprehension. *Reading Teacher, 33*, 391–397.

Straw, S. B., & Schreiner, R. (1982). The effect of sentence manipulation on subsequent measures of reading and listening comprehension. *Reading Research Quarterly, 17*, 339–352.

Taylor, B. (1985). Toward an understanding of factors contributing to children's difficulty summarizing textbook material. In J. A. Niles & R. V. Lalik (Eds.), *Issues in literacy: A research perspective* (pp. 125–132). Thirty-fourth Yearbook of the National Reading Conference. Rochester, NY: National Reading Conference.

Tiedt, I. M., Bruemmer, S. S., Lane, S., Stelwagon, P., Watanabe, K. O., & Williams, M. Y. (1983). *Teaching writing in K–8 classrooms*. Englewood Cliffs, NJ: Prentice-Hall.

Tierney, R. J. (1982). Learning from text. In A. Berger & H. A. Robinson (Eds.), *Secondary school reading—What research reveals for classroom practice*. Urbana, IL: National Conference on Research in English and ERIC Clearinghouse on Reading and Communication Skills.

Tierney, R. J., & Cunningham, J. (1984). Research on teaching reading comprehension. In P. D. Pearson (Ed.), *Handbook of reading research* (pp. 609–656). New York: Longman.

Tierney, R. J., & Pearson, P. D. (1983). Toward a composing model of reading. *Language Arts, 60,* 568–580.

Tierney, R. J., Readence, J. E., & Dishner, E. K. (1985). *Reading strategies and practices: A compendium* (2nd ed.). Boston: Allyn and Bacon.

Trelease, J. (1985). *The read-aloud handbook*. New York: Penguin Books.

Vaca, R., & Vaca, J. (1986). *Content area reading* (2nd ed.). Boston: Little, Brown.

Vygotsky, L. S. (1978). *Mind in society.* Cambridge, MA: Harvard University Press.

Walker, B. J. (1982). A new approach to language experience. *Journal of Language Experience, 5,* 25–30.

Walker, B. J. (1985a). Right-brained strategies for teaching comprehension. *Academic Therapy, 21,* 133–141.

Walker, B. J. (1985b). *Using guided fantasy to teach reading.* Paper presented at the Second Rupertsland Regional Reading Conference of the International Reading Association, Regina, Saskatchewan, Canada. (ERIC Document Reproduction Service No. ED 253 850)

Walker, B. J., & Mohr, T. (1985). *The effects of self-questioning on reading comprehension.* Paper presented at the Washington Organization for Reading Development—Research Conference, Seattle, WA. (ERIC Document Reproduction Service No. ED 262 392)

Watson, D. (1985). Watching and listening to children read. In A. Jaggar & M. T. Smith-Burke (Eds.), *Observing the language learner* (pp. 115–129). Newark, DE: International Reading Association and National Council of Teachers of English.

Weaver, G. C. (1979). Using the cloze procedure as a teaching technique. *Reading Teacher, 32,* 632–636.

Wertheimer, A. (1974). Story dramatization in the reading center. *English Journal, 64,* 85–87.

Wilson, R. M., & Cleland, C. J. (1985). *Diagnostic and remedial reading for classroom and clinic* (5th ed.). Columbus, OH: Merrill.

Witkin, H. A., Moore, C. A., Goodenough, D. R., & Cox, P. W. (1977). Field-dependent and field-independent cognitive styles and their educational implications. *Review of Educational Research, 47*(1), 1–64.

Index

The Author

Barbara J. Walker is associate professor and co-ordinator of the Reading Clinic at Eastern Montana College. She holds a joint appointment between the Division of Elementary and Secondary Education and the Institute of Habilitative Services. Dr. Walker was the 1987 recipient of the Eastern Montana College Faculty Achievement Award for scholarship and creativity. She received her Ed.D from Oklahoma State University in Curriculum and Instruction specializing in reading disabilities. Her research interests focus on individual assessment, learning styles, and imagery instruction. Before entering college teaching, Dr. Walker was a reading specialist in the elementary schools of Stillwater, Oklahoma; organized and taught in the college reading program at Vernon Regional Junior College in Vernon, Texas; and coordinated the educational program at the Hogar Paul Harris in Cochabamba, Bolivia.

Dr. Walker is a frequent presenter at state, regional, and national reading conferences, where she speaks on individual differences in the acquisition of literacy. She is active in various professional organizations, including the Montana State Reading Council (where she is editor of the *Montana Reading Journal*) and the International Reading Association.